CRISIS
EXPERIENCE
IN MODERN LIFE

CRISIS EXPERIENCE

IN MODERN LIFE

Theory and Theology for Pastoral Care

Charles V. Gerkin

ABINGDON PRESS
Nashville

CRISIS EXPERIENCE IN MODERN LIFE

Library of Congress Cataloging in Publicatin Data

GERKIN, CHARLES V 1922-
  Crisis experience in modern life.
  Bibliography: p. 340.
  Includes index.
  1. Pastoral counseling. I. Title.
  BV4012.2.G47   253.5   79-892

ISBN 0-687-09906-4

MANUFACTURED BY THE PARTHENON PRESS AT
NASHVILLE, TENNESSEE, UNITED STATES OF AMERICA

Acknowledgments

I am profoundly indebted to a number of persons and at least one institution for ideas, encouragement, critical comments, and general support as I struggled to write what follows in these pages. To Emory University and its administrative officers both for the sabbatical year that was provided and, even more, for the confidence placed in one whose path toward academia has been a rather roundabout and maverick one, I shall always be grateful. To my close colleagues, Rodney Hunter, James Laney, and William Mallard, for their labor in reading the manuscript in one or another of its several redactions, and for their helpful comments and suggestions, I am happy to express both my deep gratitude and my personal esteem and affection. To the many others who across the years have helped shape the ideas and intentions in the writing: colleagues in teaching and in clinical pastoral education, students in both academic and clinical contexts, and pastors for the enrichment of whose ministry the book is intended, I hereby express my thanks and acknowledge my debt. Most of all, I express my appreciation to the considerable number of persons who have, by sharing their deepest concerns with me, enriched my ministry and stimulated my desire to look again and more deeply at the human condition.

There were others who did very practical and invaluable things. Helen Banks typed an early version of the first few chapters and shared her support and wisdom in making a beginning of the task. Bobbie Norvell transcribed hours of tapes of lectures. Two work-study students at Candler School of Theology, Gay Thorson and Jeanne Boland, typed and cheered. Helen Patton put the final secretarial touches to the completed manuscript. To all these friends I express my appreciation and best wishes.

Contents

Introduction

This is a book for pastors about life crisis as it is experienced most commonly by contemporary persons. It is written at a time when the pastoral ministry itself is in a state some would describe as a state of crisis. The intention behind the writing is therefore pastoral in a double sense of concern for persons who undergo those times of acute and critical stress and for persons who attempt faithful ministry in situations of crisis.

The book is not a how-to-do-it manual for crisis ministry, though I would hope that one of the results of its study would be that the reader will have found some fresh perspectives on how to approach ministry in crisis. There are already available several books that present themselves as methods manuals for crisis ministry.[1] Pastors who are primarily interested in learning some relatively simple methods of performing what has come to be called in the mental health professions "crisis intervention" will want to read them and may find them more concretely helpful than what follows in this book. I must, however, admit to having two misgivings about such straightforward efforts to transpose the methods of crisis intervention from the secular mental health professions into ministry theory. They tend, in my view, both to narrow the focus of the pastor's attention to some fairly simplistic delimitations of the problem at hand and, in part because of that narrow focus, to lack theological depth.

The point of view that lies back of what follows here is that the strength of ministry vis-a-vis the other helping professions lies in a certain capacity to see particular human problems with both great breadth and profound depth of perspective. Ministry must attempt to see problems wholly, fully in their most profound dimension as evidences of the human condition. To narrow the focus of attention to a single perspective on a problem or to reduce ministry to a simple methodology risks losing touch with this fundamental approach to understanding the way things are with us. It risks reductionism not simply in terms of reducing a human problem to simple, answerable questions, but also in terms of reducing the range of vision so that the problem in its most profound dimensions is missed altogether.

Seen from this stance, pastoral care ministry may be understood as growing fundamentally out of the ability to understand what is going on in a given human situation with the greatest breadth and richness of perception possible and the accompanying ability to relate these perceptions to a coherent and comprehensive theological framework. Thus ministry involves a peculiar way of perceiving and reflecting on what is presented in the human situation at hand. The methodology of ministry consists in the behavior and language of reflection that emerges as response to what has been perceived and understood when those perceptions and understandings have been considered in the light of, though not necessarily expressed directly in the language of, a theological framework.

The argument for breadth of perceptive vision in considering human problems from the standpoint of ministry sets one agenda for the chapters that follow. Pastoral care theory has in the modern period drawn very heavily on its relationship to psychology, psychoanalysis and related individual and interpersonal disciplines of inquiry into the human condition. That relationship will be very much apparent in these pages. The benefits to pastoral care of persons coming from the dialogue with individual and interpersonal psychology have been enormous. But if ministry is to emerge from breadth of perceptual vision, limiting our interdisciplinary relationships to psychology may be itself too narrow and constricting. Particularly in a time such as ours, marked by the coming to full flower of the impact of secularization, rapid social change, and pluralism, pastoral care ministry must widen the angle of its perceptive lens. Attention must now be given to the dynamic role these societal forces play in shaping the lives and, most particularly, the crisis experiences of persons. One important task this book attempts is that of exploring what comes into view that may enrich our perceptive capacities when wide-angle perceptive tools are utilized to bring these social forces into our consideration of individual and family crisis experiences.

Readers interested in the social sciences will no doubt be looking for evidence of a basic theoretical approach to understanding the crisis experience data when viewed from that general perspective. They will find by and large that the specific cases of crisis experience are first approached heuristically from a phenomenological standpoint rather than an empirical one in any strict sense. The cases are allowed simply to speak for themselves as they presented themselves in the clinical pastoral situations in which they were encountered. Interpretations of the data are frequently made within the general framework of psychoanalytic ego psychology. Identity theory as formulated most particularly by Erik Erikson will provide an approach to integrating the various historical, sociocultural, and psychological data. Erikson's theory of identity is most useful because of its integration of social-contextual and individual-existential interpretations.

The pastoral theological purpose of the book is to attempt an in-depth exploration of the meaning of a number of profound human experiences that seem to become most visible in crisis: experiences which together make up the human experience of finitude and vulnerability. It is at this level that Christian ministry must take place. Christian ministry in its effort to attain the broadest and deepest insight into the human condition is obligated to make full use of whatever tools are provided by the secular psychological and social scientific disciplines. It may at times make use of the therapeutic methodologies those disciplines develop. But Christian ministry must be prepared to engage the issues of human crisis experience at that other level where the ambiguities of our common humanity issue in the spoken or unspoken questions of ultimate meaning and value, the questions of faith.

If there is a crisis in pastoral ministry today, it may be said to be a reflection of a crisis of faith. In what we perhaps nostalgically are inclined to think of as less difficult days when to be faithful meant to believe rightly and to conduct one's life in obedience to commonly held notions of what was godly and good, the pastor knew well what was called for in times of crisis. In word and example the pastor was the reminder of that other transcendent order over which God ruled and within which all the uncertainties and threats to human hopes were contained and made finally secure. That reminder carried with it the expectation of a believing, obedient response that could carry the person through whatever might come in life without loss of faith. The faithful community of believers that surrounded the Christian could be expected to support both the faithful belief and the obedient conduct. The right words to evoke this response in the believer were well known and held enough in common that to a great extent the response was predictable. Though there were differences in shadings of doctrinal belief, exposure to radical plural-ism had not yet eroded and made relative both the affirmation of God's providential care and the commonly held views of right conduct.

In this world shaped by otherworldly Christian vision a common faithful response to crisis was not simply an

14

individual matter of faith or doubt. Rather this corre-spondence between belief and life was both commonly understood and socially enforced. Once admitted to that fellowship of Christ's followers, one could be certain that, come what may, God's redemption was sure, and neither crises of life nor crises of death could separate persons and God. The metaphysical order assured, at least for the common folk, an orderly and safe outcome to any crisis humans could experience in the chaos of earthly existence. Ministry simply meant the faithful and loving reminder of that overriding and undergirding affirmation.

This faithful and metaphysically ordered context for ministry in crisis still exists in some communities and with some individuals. But, whether the pastor wishes it or not, this world view that contains and explains whatever may come within a traditional Christian view of belief and conduct is for many people no longer fully viable. The language in which what is experienced in crisis is expressed, and traditional, particularly biblical, language of faith are no longer for most people synonymous. The traditional word can no longer be expected to elicit the obedient response. The reminder of God's transcendent providential will is met with the honest doubt of question and uncertainty. Even the faithful under the threat of crisis may use the language of faith more in plea for reassurance than in affirmation of certain faith.[2]

Presented with this changed situation, the Christian pastor is often wracked with doubt and uncertainty about his or her ministry. Faced with persons suffering the double crisis of chaotic experience and muddled faith, the pastor may well be tempted in two opposite directions both leading toward pastoral identity crisis. Speaking the right words that no longer evoke the expected response becomes a vacuous exercise that leads to the despair of having been rendered impotent. On the other hand, there is the temptation so to identify with the bewilder-ment and confusion of the doubting victim of crisis that the pastor becomes a victim of that doubt that renders ministry an apology. Somewhere between these two extremes of verbally faithful ministry that fails to communicate, and debilitating doubt that forsakes the pastoral task, the Christian pastor must find his or her integrity.

A few paragraphs earlier it was proposed that Christian pastoral ministry should be marked by both a certain breadth of vision in considering any human situation and depth of theological insight. The latter dimension of ministry sets a second major agenda for the writing that is to follow. Breadth of vision that makes use of as many avenues of approach to understanding what is going on with contemporary persons as possible is important if the pastor's perception of the situation encountered is not to be narrow and restrictive. But breadth of vision and a variety of standpoints from which to look are not in themselves enough. Breadth must be conjoined with in-depth theological reflection that seeks to uncover the theological problem at the core of the experience being examined. Once identified, the theological problem then becomes the central concern which gives ministry coherence and undergirding purpose. Without concern for a theological problem as the organizing center for pastoral practice, ministry in the modern world runs the risk of either traditional proclamation that ignores the present context of ministry, on the one hand, or fragmented purpose shaped more by secular views of reality than by Christian faith, on the other.

In proposing a theological problem as the organizing concern around which ministry to persons is to be shaped, it is recognized that present-day pastors are themselves caught in the contemporary cultural situation marked by doubt, pluralism, and the threatened loss of power of traditional theological language. Pastors will, of course, vary considerably in their identification with that present human condition. Be that as it may, it is the basic theological questions that must provide coherence to ministry in the modern world. Theological answers to contemporary ways of experiencing these questions can only be heard as they emerge from genuine engagement of the questions in the form in which they are presented by present-day persons.

The primary theological problem at the heart of much of crisis experience in contemporary life is, in the argument of this writing, the question of God's providential participation in what happens to persons when crisis comes. In contrast to that sturdy faith in divine providence that assured the ultimately meaningful outcome of any crisis because God was in his heaven and his will would in the end prevail, we now live in a time when the future has itself become problematic. The meaning of divine providence when crisis strikes has become nebulous. For Christian ministry this means that the task is one of search for viable ways of restoring to modern persons a more potently functional sense of God's promise to participate in and ultimately assure the outcome of human life in the crises of the present and the uncertainty of the future. With this task as the primary theological problem of the book we will turn our pastoral attention to an exploration of the possible appositeness of theologies of hope and the future. This is not to suggest that any one theological perspective can be expected to provide the final answer to our problem. To do that would itself violate one of the cardinal principles of the theologies of hope. But it is to suggest a possible direction the pastor may take in searching for ground upon which a renewal of the power of divine providence in times of human crisis can be restored. While the alternative being taken by many moderns of a frankly humanistic response to the contemporary crisis of faith will be acknowledged, the argument will be made that even heroic humanism places more weight of expectation on human shoulders than they can bear.

What follows then is intended as an exploration, a

search that will likely conclude with suggestive notions, clues, intimations, rather than a set of prescriptions for crisis intervention ministry. Some techniques may emerge. Some broader and deeper ways of organizing pastoral perceptions of what goes on with persons in crisis will be explicated. Our primary purpose will, however, be to uncover human vulnerability as it appears in the throes of the crises that most characteristically come to us in our present life and to reflect on the implications of what we then see for pastoral ministry. Our pastoral claim to participation in the search for more viable frameworks to support the care of one human for another is simply that we are here, called to this work of ministry, descendants of that long line of men and women who have cared for the sick and the distressed in the style of their time. Our claim rests upon the faith that we have been called to participate in a mystery—the mystery of God's grace appearing in human existence.

CHAPTER I

Crisis: The Experience of Finitude and Vulnerability

Images
Every human effort to understand something emerges from some vision of the whole of reality, some image that, wittingly or unwittingly, provides the key to unlocking what the subject under consideration is all about. Furthermore, the images we have developed for understanding one set of circumstances, one piece of reality, tend to provide models for understanding other situations, other aspects of reality. Human beings are organizers of bits and pieces of knowledge, perceptions of the way things are, fragments of truth, be they fragments of fact or value, into images of the whole of things. We order our experience in our images.[1]

One of the important ideas that have emerged from recent efforts to understand the sociology of knowledge is the notion that in any age, in a given culture, there tends to be a broad-gauge image that becomes the organizing structure or principle for understanding all aspects of the world and the place of humans in it. In ancient biblical times that image was the three-storied universe. God was in heaven; the Evil One was below. Humans lived somewhere in the middle, pulled both ways by the good and evil spirits. Nineteenth-century Western culture was dominated by the image of the machine, an image provided by the industrial revolution.

Infinite Aspirations and Finite Possibilities
This book about crisis experience in contemporary late-twentieth-century society is built around an image

that seems to me best to describe the contemporary consciousness in much of Western society. It is the image of life as caught between infinite aspirations, on the one hand, and the boundaries of finitude, on the other. It is the image of humankind coming of age, captured by the vision of human potential for mastery of one after another of the contingencies that impinge on the length and quality of human life, yet having to come to terms with our finitude and the vulnerability that finitude entails.

Technological achievement, that gigantic enterprise that has so drastically altered the quality and style of human life while nurturing human aspirations, runs head-on into ecological limitations, pollution, and the strident demand for acceptance of limits to human achievement. On the one hand, human hopes for a long and prosperous life (perhaps even extended beyond our present expectancy of three score and ten, if we are to believe newspaper accounts of advances in microbiology and genetic engineering) are tied to the expectation that there are no limits to what scientific, technical man can achieve. On the other hand, there is the growing realization that there is an end to what is humanly possible both in the future and in the frustrations of present reality.

The pastor who is at all reflective about what he or she observes in ordinary twentieth-century folk will hear echoes of these larger polarities, particularized images of expectation and limitation, in the struggles of people, young and old, to find integrity and purpose for their lives. He or she will see young people unable to commit themselves to a life vocation or a marriage because it might not be just the right one to fulfill the potential of a life that seems somehow to have become more burden than promise. He or she will see midstream crisis manifested by divorce, sudden job change, or that creepingly debilitating awareness that a life that was once so full of high prospects for the future has become a drudge.

Since this image of infinite aspirations and finite possibilities will be reappearing again and again in the course of our exploration of crisis experience, it may be useful to dramatize the image by reflecting on the impact of space exploration on the modern consciousness. When Neil Armstrong first put his foot upon the moon's surface he characterized the act as "one small step for a man, one giant step for mankind." In the flush of that victory over space and distance, many Americans felt a surge of excitement over the possibility that humankind was indeed entering the space age. The planet Earth was no longer to provide the physical boundaries for human life. President Nixon, in what now seems to have been a considerably exaggerated mood of expansiveness, characterized the event as "the greatest since creation!" Science fiction writers had long had the vision of man with the ability to explore the vast reaches of the universe with the triumphs of human technology. Now that age was dawning. But another somewhat disturbing symbol emerged from that same moon journey. It was the picture of Earth taken from outside its familiar orbit, revealing our world as—by comparison with the vast distances of space and the barren, airless landscape of the moon—a tiny blue-green ball floating in an enormous, trackless emptiness. The mental image of the planet Earth as a tiny space ship became the visual image around which urgent new concerns for Earth's ecology began to cluster. Here we are in our earthly space ship existence, utterly dependent upon very fragile and vulnerable life support systems.

My thesis is that these two symbols somehow characterize the paradoxical nature of the twentieth-century consciousness—the open-ended promise of space travel and the tiny, fragile, enclosed atmosphere of earthly existence. The irony of that contradiction is both obvious and pervasive. Are we to be the conquerors of the limits of our life, or are we fated to live our limited days on our space-bound planet ship and disappear into the emptiness of space-time? That imagery has filtered its way into every nook and cranny of modern life. Possibilities and boundaries, potentialities and actualities, aspirations and limitations, enticements and obstacles, wishes and confining circumstances, hopes and fears—these are the polarities around which many if not most people struggle with their lives. On the one hand, we have been convinced that we are persons "come of age" and thus able to take charge of our existence and make of it what we desire and have the potential to achieve. On the other hand, we have become preoccupied with life's limitations, the boundaries that hem us in and make it impossible for us to become what we have the potential to become. We have become preoccupied with those elements in the human situation over which we do not yet have control: where and when we are to be born and where and when we are to die, the forces within ourselves over which we seem to have little control—forces that make for violence, alienation, and despair. Each individual's experience of this consciousness is particularized by his or her own situation and individual self-consciousness, but the commonality of aspirations and limitations seems pervasive.

To say that these symbols are the archetypal symbols of our age is not, of course, to say that they point to an exclusively twentieth-century sensibility. Human beings have always, since the dawn of self-consciousness, been aware of their finitude in some fashion. Humans have always wished for an enlarged and lengthened existence. The apocryphal hope for immortality, for infinite life, has been central to the religious consciousness in every age. It has often been affirmed to the extent of being almost taken for granted. Rather the suggestion is that in the epigenesis of human development the coming of age of the human community is marked by a surfacing or heightening of concern with finite boundaries.

If one is psychologically minded and familiar with the notion of epigenesis and a developmental process in the formation of selfhood such as that developed by Erik Erikson and others,[2] then one is tempted to posit an analogy between the development of human consciousness as a whole and the development of the individual through the various stages in the life cycle. From the perspective of that analogy, the tension in contemporary consciousness between possibilities and limitations may be understood as comparable to the concern with boundaries that characterizes the emergence of the person from adolescent and young adult strivings into the full awareness of adult responsibility.

If we allow ourselves to press the developmental analogy, it suggests to us the possibility that in earlier periods of human development, as man (use of the masculine seems appropriate here) explored and to some degree mastered his finite world, the collective experience of persons in Western culture was more childlike both in the sense of growing mastery of the world and in taking for granted the boundaries of life as natural or even providential. It was God the Father who set the boundaries of human life, and he could be trusted as the good parent to sustain and maintain not only the order of existence, but the promise of life unlimited by lack of knowledge or power of his children. Man was becoming more powerful, and he could bank on some day being powerful enough to take his fate in his own hands. Meanwhile we could trust the good parent God.

The Question of God's Providence

It is just at this point that the symbols of possibilities and limits begin to have meaning of the most profound religious significance. As was suggested in the introduction, one can observe at all levels of modern life that people (including many pastors) are no longer certain in the same sense as was prescientific man that the Father

God does indeed assure the ultimately good and meaningful outcome of the human individual or collective pilgrimage. To the extent that this is the case, life has become more contingent in the ultimate sense, more fraught with limitations. Persons are thrown back upon their own powers without that sure sense of God's authority and power over life and death. Nor is scientific, achieving humankind any longer content to accept our lot in life as fixed. Like the young adult, we are pressed to take our situation into our own hands and shape our own destiny, set our own boundaries.

An example from current culture is perhaps illustrative. Anyone who has observed the number and variety of biographical books, movies, and television films that have emerged in recent years that develop themes related to death and coming to terms with death cannot help being struck by the common theme of heroic effort to "take charge of one's own death" and live life to its fullest right up until the final boundary of death itself. The film *Love Story* is a good example of the genre. Here is a young couple full of the promise and uncertainty of moving into adult vocational and marital commitments, portrayed as people full of life and brimming with potential for joy and fulfillment, who suddenly are confronted with the stark reality of death of the young wife by cancer. The harshest of boundaries closes in on what had before seemed boundless and promising. As the story unfolds it is one of heroism, of human pressing back the boundaries as far and for as long as possible. No transcendent note is introduced save that which the two persons are able to muster for themselves. The boundary must be accepted; yet it is to be resisted and thereby transcended temporarily by human effort and the power of human relationship for as long as possible. Religious themes, insofar as they are present, are highly personal, muted and marked by absence of a supporting religious community or commonly held belief system.

A similar theme is struck by a number of biographical

or autobiographical books that have come forth in the recent surge of literature about death and dying. Most of these often moving documents are accounts of courageous bouts with terminal illness faced squarely for what it is or equally heroic reports of a tragic loss followed by a long and tortuous recovery and restoration to involvement with life. One of the more moving of these stories of heroism is Lael Tucker Wertenbaker's *Death of a Man*.[3] Both Ms. Wertenbaker and her husband are writers, talented and trained in the humanities. They represent the best of the breed of mid-twentieth-century liberal, humanistic tradition. Wert, the husband, develops terminal cancer. The book tells the story of their mutual decision that he will die with dignity and at a time chosen by him rather than submit to the dehumanizing process of medical delaying tactics. It is a tender, sensitive, and moving story that reveals the motif of living life to its fullest possibilities in the privacy of intimate relationships. Death's limit is heroically accepted. The impact of the account is made the more convincing simply because the hero is a person who in the very best sense is prototypical of the humanism that has emerged in American culture. "Don't you let me let myself down!" Wert demands of his wife as he is facing the stark reality of his situation. Later, as the time to decide to die approaches, Wert declares his faith: "The earth was enough, life as it was and you dealt with it was enough, and a good man was worth trying to be for the sake of being one."

The common theme that emerges from accounts of crisis experience such as that of the Wertenbakers is clearly the lonely and heroic effort to come to terms with boundaries, contingencies, inevitables in the midst of a consciousness of aspirations that can never be fully realized.

Absent is any undergirding, firm assurance of God's providence, at least as that providence can be particularized to give any surety to the ultimately happy and good

25

outcome of an individual's life and death. Rather the coping with both present and future is experienced as an individual project to be carried through with as much courage and integrity as possible, supported only by whatever close relationships of care are available from family, friends, and professional caretakers. Thus there is a reliance on a certain active stoicism in the midst of great awareness of vulnerability. One must muster one's courage to come to terms with one's fate as best one can, living as near as possible up to the potential one has for as long as humanly possible.

Pastoral experience with persons from all walks of life, the rich and poor, white and black, overtly religious and silently secular, suggests to me that this privatized and heroic style of coping with the vulnerability of crisis experience has become more and more characteristic particularly of American middle-class culture. Even among urban church folk who verbally may speak of trust in God's providence, the deeply felt, almost taken-for-granted confidence in God's providence that one occasionally glimpses in the simple religious faith of rural or poor black people has eroded and in its place is left only the acute awareness of vulnerability in an uncertain, contingent life with which one must somehow cope.

Historically, of course, we can identify a similar theme. The questions of freedom and destiny, the givenness of existence and humankind's responsibility for their own life pervades the history of human religious experience. Likewise, we can identify the theme of ambivalence about whether God is to be experienced primarily from outside or inside the boundaries of human existence. Is God the transcendent one who sets the boundaries of our habitation and breaks into our existence providentially to set aside the order of creation? If so, when and under what circumstances can his transcendent breaking in on our behalf be expected? Or is God to be experienced primarily as immanent within our existence ordering the contingent events of our life so as to assure some happy outcome of human history, individual and corporate? How can life be both contingent and continuous with God's purpose? These have been questions of both theology in the formal sense and of individual religious faith and practice throughout history. The double tragedy of much of contemporary consciousness is that both the image of God as the transcendent one who sets and maintains the natural order of things with its boundaries between finite and infinite and the image of the God who is with us in our contingent life, shielding us from its vulnerability, have become so dimmed to modern folk as to have lost their power when crisis strikes.

Reflection on traditional modes of experiencing God's providence as shielding persons from ultimate tragedy and therefore ultimate vulnerability to the contingency of life reveals that this confidence in God's providence has to do with his assurance of continuity, of sameness, of the "foreverness" of human hopes, relationships, and purposes. "God will take care of you" has come to mean to ordinary folk that God will see to it that in the end all continuities that are humanly valuable will be restored and assured as continuous. The "hope of everlasting life" in common beliefs about death and the life hereafter contains that expectation that relationships begun in this life now broken by death will be restored. However, it is precisely these expectations of God's providential assurance of continuity that have been shattered for those who have been grasped by the modern consciousness.

This contemporary consciousness is best described as characterized by a loss of the power of the image of God's providence in its ability to sustain life in its continuity and a consequent throwing back upon the individual of both questions about the ultimate meaning of things and the sustaining of courage to cope with life's contingent events.

For pastoral theology the problem then becomes one of both pastoral practice and constructive contribution to

27

ongoing theological search. A basis must be found for restoration of that sure sense of the viability of talk about God's providence in a world where the old images of God's immutable will have for many been shattered. How is ministry in God's name to be carried through in a world in which the vision of God's power and control of events has grown dim? Can our openness to that situation, our vulnerability in the concrete experiences of crisis ministry offer any possibility of opening up new avenues for theological inquiry into the meaning of God's consolation and providential care?

A Theological Basis
for Exploration of Crisis Experience

These are questions to which we will be returning again and again in the course of our exploration of various paradigms of crisis experience. Because this book is based upon the presupposition that theological truth can only be expected to emerge in a very provisional way from the full and open entering into the process of experiencing and reasoned reflection upon experience, rather than having been given to us in some *a priori* sense as once and for all revealed truth, we cannot fully lay out in the beginning what our theological answer will be to the problem of contemporary consciousness. Neither can we state in a prescriptive fashion what theologically viable pastoral practice will entail. Hopefully some provisional and tentative answers to our questions will emerge as the exploration proceeds, but we will leave until the end of this particular exploration the task of pulling all the threads of our inquiry together and the formulation of a tentative prolegomenon to a theology of crisis ministry.

I do owe it to the reader, however, to disclose the tentative basis upon which the theological aspects of our exploration are to proceed, because that basis will set the style for our search and to that extent predetermine our findings. Our beginning point is provided by the realization that much of the pastoral care literature that still forms the basis for the greatest proportion of pastoral care practice has been based upon an implicit, if not explicit, theological stance heavily influenced by nineteenth-century pietism. That literature thus tends to assume the continuing viability of the image of God's providential care that we have described as traditional. Our present effort will be based upon the judgment that of all the theological options now on the horizon, the most promising basis for a ministry that seeks to restore a sense of God's providence in response to human vulnerability is to be found in the so-called theologies of hope and the future.[4]

The basis for this setting of a tentative direction for our theological exploration has directly to do with the image of contemporary consciousness set forth earlier. Our image of contemporary persons as caught between infinite aspirations and finite possibilities points to our awareness of human caughtness in time and the historical process. Old things are passing away, and it is paradoxically both up to the human individual to create his or her own future and highly uncertain as to what the contingencies of time and the historical process will force upon us. Vulnerability and the anxiety of the unknown future that changes and relativizes everything heretofore experienced and believed about self, life, and the meaning of things go hand in hand for contemporary people. The traditional consciousness of God's providence, as we have already suggested, had to do with continuity, with the undergirding and overarching will of God that could be counted on to continue and not change. God's care and the ongoing continuity of our human purposes were somehow linked together. Images of solidarity, dependability, unchangingness, certainty, and stability were all facets of the image of God's providence in the mind of common folk. God's providence and the orderliness of his creation were symbolically conjoined. The turn of the seasons, the certainty of the sun's rising, the changeless pattern of God's rain on the just and the unjust—all these were part and parcel of the image of divine providence.

With the coming of technological-scientific understanding of the natural processes of creation, particularly with the growing awareness of the seeming randomness of evolutionary processes, this sense of God's providential purpose in all things has been broken open. Likewise, the coming of common awareness of cultural pluralism and the processes of socio-historical change has brought about in the minds of many persons a loss of the sense of continuity of the future with the past. We are no longer sure that "it will all work out for the best." Continuity as a basis for confidence in God's providence has thus been harshly, if subtly eroded.

In response to this situation the theologians of hope and the future have offered as an alternative basis for confidence in God's providence a fresh interpretation of a theology of the kingdom of God as coming toward our present existence out of the very contingency and change of the future. God's transcendence, and thereby his providence, is not to be thought of as some transcendent, unchanging order "out there" somewhere to which God can be expected by his power to bring the world of existence into conformity. God's transcendence is not static but dynamic, in process. God's kingdom, his rule, is in process of coming into being; it belongs to the future. Pannenberg goes so far as to say that "in a restricted but important sense, God does not yet exist. Since his rule and his being are inseparable, God's being is still in the process of coming to be."[5]

Placed alongside the image of God's providence as expressed in continuity and preservation of human relationships and purposes, we are at first confronted in the theologies of hope with what appears as a contradiction. God's rule, the assurance of God's providential power, is seen in the very openness and contingency of the future which in the traditional image was seen as the threat to our security in God. The image is of future emergence of God's power, not past preservation of God's unchangeable will and purpose. Pannenberg links openness to the future and human capacity for freedom. To be free is to be open to God's power coming toward us out of the unknown future of his kingdom. It is in the power to transform the present made possible by the coming of the kingdom of God that persons are to find their security in God's purpose. All efforts to find security, to grasp for God's providence in the preservation of what has been, are in the end both futile and sinful. Likewise, it is in the openness toward what is to be that persons can find their full power to transcend the limitations and suffering of the past and present.[6]

The theologies of hope are, of course, not simply concerned with the futurity of the kingdom of God; they are also very strongly rooted in the Christian tradition we receive from the past, most particularly the christological tradition flowing from the life, death, and resurrection of Jesus. For Pannenberg, for example, God's arriving future does not render the past obsolete or reject it, but takes it up in renewed and transformed ways into itself. The past is creatively fulfilled through its transformation. However, in terms of the need we have for continuity with the past, these theologies find their confidence in the continuity of God's promises as yet to be fulfilled in the largest sense. God's relationship with the children of Israel was from the beginning marked by God's promises that were to be fulfilled in the ongoing process of history. Thus the sense of continuity and purpose was built upon expectation of fulfillment of those promises, often in ways that were surprising and unexpected, rather than God's sustaining of human life as it had been. For these theologians, hope and expectation, promise and waiting for fulfillment are therefore the predominant themes of Israel's religious life. It is on this tradition of hope and futurity that the theologians of hope are seeking to build a renewed confidence in God's providential relationship to his people.

From this all too brief summary of the direction taken by the theologies of hope and the future we see offered a possible avenue of pastoral response to persons whose grasp of the power of God's providence to meet human vulnerability has been lost. Much more work of testing and translating of this futuristic image of God's providence remains ahead of us in relation to the specifics of crisis experience, but a possible direction for our response to contemporary consciousness has been charted. A theological option and question has been put to us. Can modern persons be helped toward a renewed faith in God's providence as participant in the crises of finite life while at the same time (and the second is dependent on the first!) they are enabled to open themselves to the changes and possibilities thrust upon them by the radical experience of human vulnerability in times of crisis and transition?

A Theological Definition of Crisis

All that has been said up to this point has been leading us toward a statement of definition of crisis experience for modern people. Testing this definition and exploring the implications for crisis ministry that flow from it will provide the predominant theme for all that is to follow. Stated succinctly, our beginning thesis is this: A crisis situation is, for modern persons, an extreme or boundary situation in which the fundamental contradiction between human aspirations and finite possibilities becomes visible in such a way as to demand attention. In the situation of crisis we are confronted with our human vulnerability, our finitude, the utter impossibility of our deepest hopes and wishes. In that situation a most elemental choice is forced upon persons that is at its core a religious or "faith" choice. Either persons must defend themselves against the contradiction with whatever human defense is possible, be that denial or heroic courage, or they must open themselves to the vulnerability of the unknown future, trusting in the power and care of God coming out of the change and contingency of the unknown.

The Purpose of Crisis Ministry

Many powerful forces, personal, cultural, and situational, come together to shape the direction of human choice in the time of crisis. To understand what occurs in that nexus of forces as they come together will require considerable analysis and reflection utilizing the perspectives of a number of disciplines. But the core of crisis experience is awareness of contradiction, finitude, and vulnerability; and the elemental choice presented the person is one of faith. To facilitate a grasp of faith in God's providence coming toward the person out of the very openness and contingency of the crisis situation is the fundamental purpose of crisis ministry. All techniques appropriated from the human sciences designed to strengthen the self's reliance on itself, helpful as they may be, must for the pastor be tempered with an awareness of final human vulnerability. To minister to persons in crisis is to open oneself to that vulnerability with the hope of glimpsing God's providential care coming toward both the minister and the one to whom ministry is given. The consolation of pastoral ministry in crisis is thus the consolation of openness to what is to appear, not certainty as to what has been, is expectancy, not reassurance, save the reassurance of God's promises to meet us in the ever open-ended future.

The question as to what the pastor is to represent as he or she stands with the person in the situation of crisis is perhaps further clarified by recognizing that the pastor is in the position of both seeking with the other for glimpses of God's providential care and representative of that tradition that calls persons into relationship with God. As representative the pastor is called upon to represent both sides of our traditional understanding of God's relationship to human life, both his immanence and his transcendence. In the contemporary situation, this means that often the central question confronted by our representative stance is the question of God's presence or absence. For the pastor this means both representing the reality of existential boundaries and human limitations on the one hand and searching authentically with the other for intimations, signals, symbols of God's presence within existence—his coming toward us. Though the pastor will receive pleas for God's rescue from finite existence from persons whose consciousness remains within a two- or three-storied universe, ministry to modern people in crisis will more often involve acceptance of the fact that for many moderns the transcendent God who saves or rescues persons from this life into another heavenly kingdom is largely experienced as absent. The plea will more often be for human strength to endure or to conquer the limits that have become visible in the crisis. The God who sets the boundaries may even be perceived as the enemy, or at the very least the absent one who is indifferent to our finite fate. It is the present, incarnate God who must become real if God is to be real to the person in extremity. Thus the theological theme of our exploration of the dimensions of crisis ministry may be seen as the theme of ministry as incarnation, as that symbol can be made to speak to modern persons in the throes of crisis experience.

Stated in somewhat more psychological terms, the problem of pastoral ministry to persons in crisis in our time is one of facilitating trust in the person who has experienced something which, in its impact on the person's structuring of his or her life, has undermined the very basis of trust. Trust for modern folk is largely rooted in two immediate aspects of their life, their competence to cope with life's problems and contingencies, and their valued human relationships. For many the avenues toward deeper (in the sense of more nearly ultimate) levels of trust in that reality that upholds the final and fundamental meaning of things, which traditionally we have called God, have fallen into disuse or have lost their power to evoke trust. In their place have developed personal and social avenues of security through controls and safeguards—relationships to job, place, technological experts and close human relationships. Crisis experience occurs when these sources of security are threatened or prove utterly inadequate for coping with the threat, as, for example, in the case of life-threatening illness or acute awareness of aging and death.[7]

Ministry to persons in crisis must therefore not only be directed toward enabling persons to make the fullest use possible of the security systems that have been useful to them in the past, utilizing as appropriate the techniques of crisis intervention that have been developed by the secular helping disciplines, but, more importantly, must be directed toward opening up avenues of eschatological trust. Eschatological trust is here conceived as trust in the larger, final sense of trust in the ultimate outcome of things that can only be secured in the mystery of God's purpose for creation yet to be fulfilled.

"Yet the infinite God cannot become the object of my trust if it does not appear in a comprehensible, finite form."[8] Precisely in this sense, trust in the infinite God has become incomprehensible for many modern people. The Christian symbols of God's epiphany, his becoming incarnate in the finite form of the man Jesus, have become so obscured, so clouded by modern scientific, empirical ways of thinking that simply pointing to that set of traditional symbols for trust in God cannot be expected always to evoke the response of trust and faith. Yet to restore trust in God's providence, we must break through or move beyond the humanly constructed security systems to reunite the need of the person for trust with that infinite context in which trust in the ultimate sense is possible. In short, trust in the incarnation—God with us—must be restored. How is this to be accomplished?

Methodological Strands
in the Pastoral Care Tradition

In the pastoral care tradition there has been a number of different strands of methodological approaches to this problem. Though our purpose here is not to explicate in the fullest sense this history of the pastoral traditions, three broad groupings of pastoral methodologies may for our purpose be designated:

a. Proclamation. Here the person in crisis is simply reminded—by prayer and sacrament, by use of the biblical language of faith in God's promises, and, most explicitly, by a call to faith in God's incarnation in Jesus Christ—that the infinite God is present and active in behalf of the person in whatever situation of crisis may exist. Pastoral care becomes in this tradition quite analogous to the proclamation of the gospel in the context of pulpit ministry. The tacit assumption is that the biblical language of the Christian tradition is a kind of universal language which, when spoken with care and concern, will speak with a kind of universal applicability. The most often quoted and contested contemporary exponent of the proclamation stance in pastoral care is Edward Thurneyson.[9] For Thurneyson, pastoral care is distinguished by its explicit use of traditional biblical and Christian language, and any care that does not make use of this language falls within simply human concern for another.[10]

b. Ministry as relationship conceived as analogous to the incarnation in Jesus. Here the pastor seeks, more often implicitly than explicitly, to represent the thrust of the gospel message in the pastoral relationship. Thus the pastoral relationship is seen as analogous to the relationship of Jesus as the Word Incarnate in finite human existence. In the words of Luther, the pastor seeks to be a "little Christ" to another. Much of the recent pastoral "therapeutic" tradition is based on this methodology insofar as it embraces a pastoral theological methodology.[11]

c. A more recent strand of pastoral methodology might be designated the engendering of an incarnational style of tending to present life experience. God's incarnation is here seen as his appearance within human, finite existence in the ongoing process of human history. God may be perceived as he appears, his clearest and most definitive appearance having been that in the life and death of Jesus, the Christ. Pastoral care is then seen as that relationship to the other person which seeks to open both pastor and parishioner to glimpses, signals, signs of God's presence, to engender the quality of expectancy of God's disclosure.[12]

There will be echoes of all three of these approaches to pastoral methodology in what is to follow because in some sense each represents an important facet of an understanding of the pastoral office. The central thrust of our work, however, will be to explore the potential for crisis ministry of a methodology growing primarily out of the third less well developed methodological tradition. The intention here is not to explicate this method as something new for pastoral care designed to replace other avenues of approach. Rather our purpose expresses our theological intention: namely, the recovery for modern persons of a powerful sense of God's providential care in times of crisis and vulnerability to the awareness of finitude. The method of pastoral care ministry must be adapted to meet that need.

We shall return to the image of contemporary consciousness as caught between infinite aspirations and finite possibilities, with the accompanying question of God's participation in that existential situation, at a number of points later on in our discussion of particular paradigms of crisis experience. At this point, however, we need to turn from explicit theological reflection to a more detailed analysis of the factors that enter into the formation of crisis experience, utilizing the resources of the social and behavioral sciences. The depth and complexity of crisis experience formation will become apparent as we consider the problem from a number of perspectives, each shedding its own light on some facet of the many factors that go to shape crisis experience for a particular individual, family, or community.

CHAPTER II

The Shaping of Crisis Experience

In the commonsense view, crisis is most often associated with some event or happening that interrupts the normal or everyday course of events. Events such as death, divorce, illness, or job loss are precipitants of crisis for everyone who experiences them. But common sense also tells us that all deaths are not alike, nor are all divorces experienced in the same way. Multiple factors and shadings of difference in experience go together to shape or form a crisis experience, no matter what the event itself might be. Here the methods of the social sciences become quite useful to us. The several approaches of the social sciences can, taken together, provide a kind of schema or skeleton for sorting out pertinent data so that crisis experience of similar order can be elucidated. In doing this we are not in an empirical sense looking for causation as if to say that crisis events can be understood as being determined or "caused" by any one factor or set of factors. Rather we will be exploring crisis as a multidimensional experience in which a complex network of factors comes together to shape a particular crisis experience. Here we adopt a modified field theory approach which views human experience as taking place within a field of forces or life space. In the language of the preceding chapter, we are attempting to examine more in detail the pressures and processes that take place within the finite boundaries of a given personal, family, or community existence.

Differentiation of Crisis Event and Crisis Experience

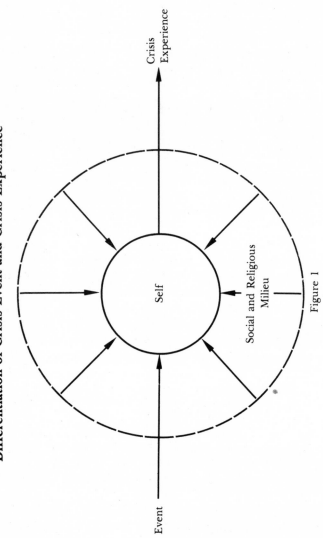

Figure 1

Crisis Event and Crisis Experience

Schematically, we thus begin with a relatively simple drawing (see Fig. 1) that illustrates the necessity of differentiating between crisis event and crisis experience. By "crisis event" we mean almost any occurrence in the course of human life that triggers or initiates a set of dynamic forces and processes within and around an individual, family, or community that, taken together, make for crisis. Ordinarily the crisis event is one or another of the common occurrences that take place within finite life which is associated with crisis. This is not necessarily the case, however, since an event that might be identified as ordinary or routine for most individuals may be experienced as an extreme or crisis event by a given individual, family, or community because of the peculiar meaning of the event for the person or group in question. In using the term "crisis experience" I am referring to that nexus of meanings, ideas, and feelings, conscious and unconscious processes, and relationships which taken together form a gestalt. Since crisis experience is shaped by these multiple factors taken together, it is of course highly individual and can only be fully understood by utilizing a highly individualized approach. Members of communities of persons will share certain common perceptions and expectations of particular events. Families may share an even more common and particular set of perceptions and expectations. Individuals within families will evidence a very highly particularized response shaped not only by cultural and familial factors, but also by unique private meanings and emotions. Thus the pastor who wishes to understand his or her parishioner's crisis experience at a deeper level than the superficial, commonsense response to crisis event must utilize psychological, sociological, and even historical perspectives in an effort to break open the circle of meanings and dynamic factors that shape the experience for a given person. The converging arrows in Fig. 1 are intended to indicate that crisis experience is shaped not simply by the event, but by the self, family, and community in the center of convergence of a complex field of forces, meanings, and dynamic influences.

Dimensions of Crisis Experience

We can begin sorting out these multiple factors that enter into the shaping of crisis experience by utilizing a set of broad categories under one or another of which most of the dynamics of crisis experience may be classified for the purpose of analysis. These may be thought of as the broad dimensions of which crisis experience is the function or outcome.

1. The dimension of social and cultural history.

Our modern historical consciousness has made us significantly aware of the way in which all human experience, including crisis experience, is shaped by the course of human events we call history. Written large, of course, this points to the great movements of history that have produced styles of existence—customs, patterns of perception of the realities of life, moral and colloquial standards of conduct, and religious ritual and ideologies. While the history of cultures like our own has made us much more aware of the relativity of such time and place pictures of reality, it has not enabled us to escape being men and women of our own time and place. Backing off far enough to get a glimpse of the roots of our present time-place orientation can be a useful and liberating exercise. For our purpose here, however, consideration needs to be given to the way in which ordinary people in any time-place context tend to perceive that orientation as "reality"—the way things are.[1]

Of perhaps more immediate concern for the pastor is the consideration of how the ordinary middle-class or lower-class parishioner experiences what Alvin Toffler has called "future shock."[2] Reality experienced as rapid, inevitable, and shocking change (often referred to in

common conversation as "one damn thing after another") with all the connotations of temporariness and
contingency that entails, certainly makes for a quite
different shaping of crisis experience than did, for
example, the more cyclically ordered existence of rural
life in nineteenth- and early twentieth-century America.
In the context of such perceptions of human circumstances, life can be experienced as one continuous crisis
with brief respites from change that will inevitably come
again.

On the other hand, in what may on the surface appear
to be a contradictory tendency, as I trace the course of my
circuit rider grandfather's life in Illinois by reading the
carefully kept record of marriages, births, and deaths in
the family Bible, I recognize that with the loss of two wives
by death, the first in childbirth, and the loss of several of
his eleven children through diseases of childhood, his
experience of the crisis of birth or death must surely have
been radically different from such experiences by
persons in the 1970s with all the technology of modern
medicine. We can speculate that the very common
occurrence of death in childbirth created for my
grandfather a level of awareness of the fragility of life
from which twentieth-century persons are much of the
time protected. This very protection can heighten the
experience of vulnerability when events that confront us
with life's frangibility occur. That this awareness of the
fragile and vulnerable nature of life was matched by a
strong and invulnerable faith in the overarching omnipotence of the transcendent God made for a consciousness
concerning the crisis of death that stands in stark contrast
to the twentieth-century consciousness. For twentieth-
century people, death may be experienced as something
that should not happen, what with all the life-saving
technologies that modern science possesses. Death or the
threat of death may then be experienced as failure—failure of the self or of those who are supposed to protect one
against the threats of terminality. This trend in contem-

porary consciousness, as we have already suggested, cannot be assuaged by faith in the transcendent God's "promise of everlasting life."

It is important to keep in mind that these historical elements that enter into the formation of crisis experience are not usually named by the victim of crisis. They rather appear as aspects of the automatic, largely unconscious and unreflective responses to crisis events. In that regard they appear as "givens" or as if they were objective realities not subject to refutation, argument, or change of mind. The intellectually sophisticated pastor, not recognizing these historical elements as inherent in the setting of the experience, may fall into the trap of treating them as mistaken ideas that are open to alteration by intellectual discussion. To the extent that these are automatic or unconscious responses embedded in the way of constructing reality characteristic of a given historical period, they are not subject to alteration by argument or persuasion, at least not within the situation of crisis.

The pastor should keep in mind that particular communities or individuals within communities may live in widely varying historical time frames. In much of the rural South, for example, one can still find whole communities of persons whose orientation to reality is much more like that of my grandfather than it is like what we have pointed to as characteristic of the twentieth-century consciousness. I am reminded here of a grave decoration that can be seen in a number of North Georgia mountain cemeteries. On a large rectangle of plastic styrofoam are mounted some plastic flowers and a toy plastic telephone. The caption reads simply, "Jesus called." Here we see a peculiar mixture of thoroughly twentieth-century materials and a nineteenth-century religious consciousness!

It is suggestive to consider the crisis of abortion as a current example of a crisis which is undergoing drastic reshaping in the experience of people because of a rapid and radical change that is taking place in Western society relative to sexuality, marriage, and family life. Within a relatively short period of time, American society has moved a considerable distance away from an ethos that required a woman pregnant out of wedlock not only to bear her child but to do so in secrecy, often away from her home environment in an anonymous institution for unmarried mothers. In some segments of middle-class American society this is indeed still the norm. But the cultural movement has been sharply in the direction of taking for granted that the young girl or woman who "makes a mistake" (by getting pregnant, not by having sex out of wedlock) will, with as little interruption as possible in her daily life, get an abortion. Pastoral counseling experience would seem to indicate that for many young women this creates a quite differently shaped crisis relative to out-of-wedlock pregnancy.

Jane R., age 29, comes to see her pastor after having made and broken several appointments. She begins the conversation by saying that she does not really know why she came because she ought to be able to "handle her own problems herself." With no visible indications of guilt or self-condemnation she reports that she has just returned to work after having had an abortion arranged through an abortion clinic, the pregnancy having occurred as a result of intercourse she has been having regularly with a young man to whom she has been "sort of engaged." Subsequent conversations reveal that this is her third abortion, each of the others having taken place under similar circumstances but with different men. In each case she was at the point of being "sort of engaged" when the pregnancy and abortion took place. In each case this has precipitated the ending of the relationship. Now she is wondering if she is not having a problem about making a commitment to marriage. The more she has thought about it, the more frightened and disturbed about herself she has become. She finally has very reluctantly made the decision to talk to her pastor about it.

Ruth E., age 40, is a highly qualified secretary who has never married. For the first thirty years of her life she remained a virgin, but has been sexually active with several men during the last ten years, always involved in a single affair at any given time. Some, but not all, of her affairs have been with married men. Twice she has had an abortion, the first time illegally at the insistence of her sexual partner. She recalls the considerable stress she experienced at that time. More recently she has had a legal abortion arranged through her physician. She has recently become preoccupied with the feeling that she really wants to have a child. She feels resentful that society permits her to engage in sexuality freely, but denies her the right of parenthood as a single woman. She comes to talk with her pastor to get his views about what she experiences as mounting crisis of middle life as a single woman.

Though numerous factors are undoubtedly involved in shaping what each of these women is experiencing as a crisis in her life, the rapid and massive changes in the ways that a society constructs its reality and sets its values has had enormous influence in shaping what is experienced as crisis by both women. That these factors have themselves been shaped by the course of history, with its interaction between ideas and values on the one hand and the situational problems of a society's history on the other, could undoubtedly be traced by careful historical study. For our purpose here, the important considera-tion is that the changed perceptions of reality and value are more or less accepted as givens by the individual involved in crisis. This is perhaps more true for Ruth than it is for Jane simply because of the difference in their ages. In a time of rapid social and historical change, eleven years' difference in age can make a truly prodigious difference in the extent to which a given individual will be identified with the changes taking place. In both cases, however, we can identify what amounts to a virtual reversal in the influence of sexual values in shaping crisis experience from what would conceivably have been the case as little as twenty-five years ago. In both cases the question of out-of-wedlock sex seems not to be of grave enough concern to produce conscious guilt. Vestiges of former values may linger in the form of unconscious guilt. Rather than the question of sex outside of marriage, the question now seems for one that of commitment in marriage, and for the other the rights and responsibilities of single women.

At this point the automatic, unconscious attitudes and feelings of the pastor become exceedingly important. To be both an effective and faithful pastor in ministering to persons such as Ruth and Jane, it is of utmost importance that the minister involved have sorted out his or her views with regard to a Christian conception of existence from those automatic responses as a participant in his or her generation's historical consciousness. This is to say that the careful pastor will not confuse Christian criteria with whatever social norms may have characterized his or her own upbringing or, on the other hand, the latest avant-garde views of what is proper or "liberated" behavior. It may not be possible for the pastor to keep Christian norms and social norms utterly separated. Indeed, historical-critical studies seem to indicate the impossibility of that! It does seem both possible and important that the pastor work at being aware of the difference between the two.

2. Personal and Family History.

Crisis experience is not only shaped by the broad sweep of social and cultural history, it is in many respects a function of individual, personal, and family history. It would probably be fair to say that it was the burgeoning and ubiquitous rise of interest in psychodynamic factors related to early family experience subsequent to Freud's seminal work that, as much as anything else, brought about the modern revival of pastoral care as a disciplined function of ministry. The commonly accepted understanding that present identity and behavior are to a great extent influenced by what Seward Hiltner referred to in one of his early pastoral care works as "dated emotions" has become an important tool for the pastor in understanding what is going on with parishioners.[3]

Clinical pastoral education has made extensive use of personal and family history approaches to both the problem of analysis of pastoral care case studies and the personal preparation of the pastor for the work of ministry. To be sure, some recent developments in the pastoral care field influenced by the rise of phenomenological and self-actualization approaches to personality theory, have emphasized more strongly here-and-now experience and immediate relationships. These efforts, while significant, do not seriously detract from the importance of an examination of biographical data in comprehending the depth dimensions of current crisis experience in individuals and families. Thus the pastor who seeks to relate helpfully to Jane or Ruth will find data such as the following of vital importance in coming to understand the crisis of abortion each is experiencing:

Jane described her mother as rather cold and ungiving, though not totally rejecting of her. She recalls that her mother was in her view somewhat too dependent on Jane's father during the years that Jane was growing up. She remembers her father, a professional man, as much more warm and even sensuous in his fathering toward his daughter. Her parents were divorced when she was fifteen and the father subsequently died when Jane was twenty-three. She thus felt very much on her own after her parents divorced, although she and her mother now have a pleasant if somewhat distant relationship. Jane has had a struggle with vocational choice. She tried being a secretary, a buyer for a department store, but then considered the ministry or a medical career. What she is doing now she considers temporary.

Ruth describes her mother as possessive and domineering, so much so that Ruth had difficulty making the decision to leave home. What she says of her father is vague and unclear. Essentially he comes across as a weak and ineffectual person who was "just around" as Ruth was growing up. Ruth still struggles at times with her ambivalence between pleasing her mother and doing the things she wants to do herself. She remembers much petty quarreling between her parents during her teen-age years and recalls that her desire to get away from home was in part a desire to get away from the unhappy marriage between her parents. She now wonders if she made a mistake by not marrying earlier in her life, but feels that it is "too late" for that. She admires the current man in her life because she perceives him as strong and decisive, yet she wonders at times if she is not allowing him to dominate her too much. On one occasion this concern slipped out as "maybe mother had the right idea about men."

Such an approach would certainly suggest that the crises that Jane and Ruth are experiencing have been in part shaped by their experience growing up in particular homes with particular parents. Jane has had difficulty working out her self-understanding as a woman in part because of her strained and distant relationship with her mother. To become a wife and mother risks therefore the necessity of working through to a more firm acceptance of herself as in some sense like her mother with whom she has never been close. Close relationships with men are, on the other hand, compatible with her close relationship with her father. But to marry risks becoming dependent on a man even as her mother was. These themes of identity struggle undoubtedly play a large role in shaping the way Jane is experiencing the crisis, the outward manifestations of which have to do with becoming intimately related to a man, becoming pregnant, aborting the pregnancy, and breaking off the relationships only to be left feeling unfulfilled and temporary in her commitments.

So, too, with Ruth. Here the complications of identity formation and maintenance in a person whose childhood and adolescence has been filled with conflict with a dominant and possessive mother become evident. Likewise, the image of men as weak and ineffectual gained from childhood years relating to such a father interferes with Ruth's efforts as an adult to work out her relationships with men. The quarreling of her childhood home leaves deep scars that discourage Ruth from taking the risk of marriage and bring about postponement of the decision until it seems to her too late. Possibly we catch glimpses of Ruth's dominant mother in Ruth's wishes to resist society's restrictions on unwed motherhood.

Although such personal history information as this does not necessarily "explain" the current behavior and thus fully expose the "cause" of the crisis these two persons are experiencing, it is suggestive of the wealth of personal and family depth experience that enters into the shaping of crisis experience for Ruth and Jane. Recent studies in what has come to be called the family therapy movement have seemed to demonstrate that family myths about all aspects of family life, from sexual roles to styles of relating and expressing emotion, persist in families over several generations. As these myths encounter other images from the family of the spouse, new and highly complex patterns of both continuity and change within family traditions emerge.

In order to make competent use of family history data in formulating the appropriate pastoral response in a situation of crisis, the pastor needs to have appropriated thoroughly one of the psychodynamic and/or structural models of personality theory so that the connections made between personal history and present problems are more than simply commonsense hunches. Some combination of ego psychology built upon psychoanalytic theory and family structural theory offers perhaps the most cogent and useful approach which lends itself to integration with a theological perspective.

Further elaboration in detail of the significance of personal and family history factors important to understanding crisis experience is necessary. However, this may better be delayed until we come to the discussion of particular categories of crisis experience in which these factors are in some specific sense important.

3. Time and Aging.

Already implicit in what has been said up to this point is the underlying notion, almost taken for granted, that crisis experience is a function of time. Indeed, time and its passage provide the existential structure, that most inevitable of all givens, that makes crisis experience not only common but universal for humans. It is the boundary from which no finite human escapes. We say we "possess" it, yet it "escapes" us. We speak of "killing time," yet we know that in the end time kills us. We speak of "allotting time" to a project or undertaking, yet we "never have enough time" and "there aren't enough hours in the day." "Time heals everything," we say, yet time brings death, the grim reaper.

Simply to reflect deeply upon the contradictions involved in these common sayings concerning time can create in our awareness a sense of crisis not unlike the feeling of panic. It is as if time-related panic hovers in the background of our awareness awaiting an event that will trigger its flooding in upon us. Thus time and human awareness of our finite state seem so intertwined as to be almost identical. But the human experience of time itself is multidimensional, and our understanding of crisis experience can be greatly illuminated by reflecting upon these several dimensions.

(a) *Time and the Developmental Process.* Many of life's crises come to us simply because time and one's own aging process will not stand still. Growth brings new tasks, new dilemmas, new expectations and inclinations. It is an interesting and useful exercise to consider each stage of the human life cycle beginning with birth and ending with senility and death and list all the things that can happen to people simply because they are growing older. Certain crises tend to cluster around periods of transition from one age level to another. Our list would begin, I suppose, with all the things that can go wrong in a maternity hospital ward: birth anomalies, the stillborn fetus, the unwanted or ambivalently wanted baby, multiple births in a family with limited financial and/or emotional resources.

51

At the other end of the spectrum cluster all the potential crises of old age:

Ralph W. was a surgeon, and a good one. At age 63 he was a highly respected senior surgeon in a large hospital, well known in both his professional and social communities. Having lunch with him one day I noticed a weary slackness in his posture and a quiet tiredness in his voice. "You know, I got to thinking while I was doing that abdominal cancer this morning, Reverend. It was a long operation, one of those tedious, grubby ones. After about three hours I got a crick in my shoulder. I looked around at all those young bucks assisting me and it suddenly hit me that any one of them could probably do that operation as well as I can or better and not get near as tired. I'm either going to have to go down to the 'Y' and get in shape or get out of this business." Six months later Dr. W. had a coronary, not a severe one, but severe enough that, given his age, he was away from his work for about two months. One day some months after that I met him on the street walking toward the hospital. There was a slight incline and as I fell in beside him, assuming my usual gait, he said in a tone that was tinged just slightly with pleading, "You'll have to go a little slow with me. Since that heart attack I've been trying to take it a little easy." Six months later Dr. W. was dead. In our conversations during all those months after that first luncheon the subject of time was nearly always included in one way or another.

The crisis in Dr. W.'s life was a common crisis of transition from one period of lifetime to another. From a time of full and fruitful life he was entering upon a period of declining productivity and physical capacity for his chosen work. But much more was happening than simply a decline in physical stamina. His whole-person response to the boundary of lifetime led him almost inexorably into the crisis that ended ultimately in his death. Though many factors were involved, at the existential center his crisis experience clustered around the issue of growing older and the limits of finite existence that age made visible.

The pastor who would prepare for ministry to persons

involved in one of the transitional or developmental life crises will find his or her ministry enriched by careful study of the psychological literature in this field. The most notable as well as perhaps the most lucid and readily understood contributor to an in-depth understanding of the psychology of the life cycle is perhaps Erik Erikson. Building upon and modifying Freud's understanding of psychosexual development, Erikson formulates an epigenetic approach to explicating the stages or levels of development within the human life cycle. His approach is essentially dialectical in that he identifies a two-sided dilemma which seems to characterize each of the eight stages or "ages" in the course of human life. For the tiny infant the dilemma is between trust and mistrust. Is the world into which I have been born a friendly and trustworthy one, or is it a frightening and insecure place of danger and hurt? Each succeeding stage has its own predominant dilemma within which an identity stance must be taken for good or ill. The final stage presses the issue of integrity versus despair. Dr. W.'s situation described above takes on meaning of the most profound religious depth when this concept is applied to the data of the pastoral encounters I had with him over the months preceeding his death.[4] In the language of the preceeding chapter, Dr. W. was experiencing the closing in of the boundaries of his finite existence as time inexorably moved him toward death. His high aspirations for his personal and professional life were being contradicted by the very finite physical self and its diminishing powers. One could even suggest that his trust for the future was too tightly wrapped up in his competence to do his work. Thus the passage of time pressed him toward more and more profound crisis.

The importance of transition points in the life cycle for understanding crisis experience will become more clearly evident later as we seek to develop a typology of models or paradigms of crisis. For now we simply wish to establish the significance of the human time sense,

The Self and Time as Present, Past, and Future

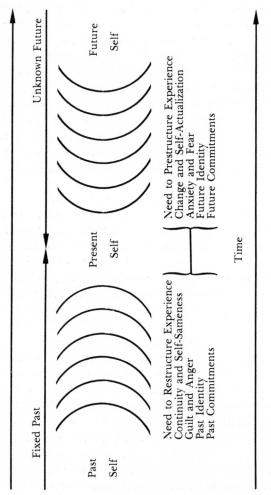

Time

Fixed Past

Unknown Future

Past
Self

Present
Self

Future
Self

Need to Restructure Experience
Continuity and Self-Sameness
Guilt and Anger
Past Identity
Past Commitments

Need to Prestructure Experience
Change and Self-Actualization
Anxiety and Fear
Future Identity
Future Commitments

Time

Figure 2

constructed as lifetime, as a determining element in the formation of crisis experience.

(b) Time as Present, Past, and Future. As our earlier theological reflection suggested, time is not only experienced as the boundary of lifetime. More immediately, time sets boundaries in that it must be experienced moment by moment. Science fiction expresses the human wish in its fantasies about time machines that can take us backward or forward in time, but in the literal sense the most immediate human existential boundary is that we must live moment by moment. But the human capacity in memory and imagination to transcend these momentary boundaries creates for us a sense of the present self as being suspended between a fixed past and an unknown future. As Thomas C. Oden has made clear, the structure of awareness concerning past, present, and future presents to humans the necessity of coming to terms with our past choices, actions, and relationships while yet coping with the open-ended future that keeps moving toward us.[5]

Figure 2 presents schematically the way in which the boundaries of time as past, present, and future shape the experience of time and self in the present. In relation to past experience, persons are, within the frustrating and confining actual boundary of the present, continuously re-imaging and therefore restructuring their past experience. This process of re-imaging fulfills the human need for continuity and self-sameness while yet accommodating to the changes of perception of the past that increasing distance and new experience bring about. But, as Thomas Oden's analysis demonstrates, this restructuring process brings with it the realization of value negations of the past, of fresh perceptions on old relationships that reveal their ambivalences and conflict. Thus re-imaging the past forces a coming to grips with guilt and anger, disappointment and envy, as memories are sorted over and personal history is revised. Likewise, there is a continuous process of re-imaging the self-concept, a revision of self-identity going on all the time, combined with a restructuring of commitments, past and present. In a very general sense one can say that this past self, actually fixed because of the flow of time but constantly re-imaged because of the human capacity for self-transcendence, is constantly exerting its influence upon present experience. Observation of persons in crisis seems to indicate that the influence of the past self upon the present self-identity is greatly heightened in times of crisis.

But the self-transcendence of the present self is not only continuously re-imaging its past, but is also continuously presented with the necessity of pre-imaging and pre-structuring its future self and experience. Our biographies of the future are also being continuously rewritten. The unknown quality of the future opens the possibility of change and self-actualization which must then be held in tension with the need for continuity and self-sameness brought into the present moment from the past. The affective experience concerning the future is most often anxiety of a greater or lesser degree. Whereas guilt and commitment have to do with the fixed quality of the past, anxiety is related to the open-endedness of the future. The possibility of change, forced or voluntary, presents to the present self the open-endedness of future time filled with both mysterious threat and the possibility of greater exercise of freedom. Just as crisis events open up the self to flooding of present awareness by past self-understanding, so also memories of events can flood the self with questions and fears about the future.

The importance of this structure of awareness of the self in time as past, present, and future (as adapted from Oden for crisis ministry) will become more apparent particularly when we deal with the paradigms of bereavement as loss and the generation gap as alienation. In general, however, it may be said that any crisis event seems to trigger the heightening of the human capacity for self-transcendence such that the present moment is flooded with confused perceptions and emotions from both past and future orientations. Much of the confused behavior, confused expression in word and feeling, and sense of being overpowered exhibited by persons in acute crisis can be understood as the result of this flooding.

(c) Periodic or Episodic Time. The words of the Preacher in Ecclesiastes, "For everything there is a season . . . ," points to one of the styles of structuring time that seems to have characterized the ancient Hebrew life-style. To the extent that this model of time experiencing has influenced Western society, this is true for contemporary Western Christian and secular life-styles.[6] In simple terms it may be said that time is structured by Western humans as if it were a story or complex intertwining of stories of persons in time. Structured in this fashion, our time boundary is experienced as having a beginning or beginnings, a middle or development, as of a plot, and an end. Thus we speak of beginning a new job or new relationships, fulfilling a task or purpose, undertaking a project, and ending an episode or era. Upon reflection we may even view our particular life cycle as an episode in the ongoingness of time.[7]

This human structuring of time into episodes, periods, and plots (or stories) matches, of course, much that is given in the natural world of finite life. The change of seasons, the cycle of life and death in plants and animals, the sense of process and fulfillment all about us, all provide a "naturalness" of expectation by which we construct our own intentions, anticipations, and segmentations of lapsed time into episodes and periods.[8]

The importance of episodic or periodic time for our exploration of crisis experience comes primarily at two levels. First, the episodic or storied structuring of time involves a quality of intentionality. We think of ourselves as the authors of our life story. This intentionality does not ordinarily take into account the interruption or diversion of the intended plot by contingencies not accounted for in the loosely structured, but often quite definite, pre-imaging of the future as fulfillment of a story. Crisis experience is, therefore, most often experienced as interruption or the intrusion of the unexpected. Death of a loved one, for instance, is frequently spoken of as coming "just when we thought we had things worked out," or "just when we thought we were about to reap the reward of our hard work," or "just when I needed him the most since the children left home," and so on.

This experience of time as episode, and crisis as interruption, makes for a psychology of crisis that presses for a quick return to whatever was normal or anticipated. It makes for greatly heightened confusion about intentions, directions, hopes, and expectations. Even at the expense of denial of the profound impact of the crisis event on the individual at every level of his or her existence, there is often overwhelming need to get back to the way things were before the crisis event occurred. If that is not possible, there is the alternative pressure to make new plans, put together a new story, a revised plot. Frequently the pressure to "adjust" is so great that insufficient time and attention is given to ending or concluding the episode that has been catastrophically interrupted. Thus crisis ministry may at times involve not only helping people rewrite a life story that has been tragically interrupted, but also helping them to pause long enough to assimilate all that can be learned from reflecting on the meaning of what has occurred.

Time experienced as the story of the self presents the possibility of opening awareness to linkages between the self's story and the larger stories of the human pilgrimage and of God's promise and intention with human history. Questions concerning what God is now doing or how God is speaking to the person or the community in times of crisis point to this linkage. The direction taken in the theological work of the last chapter suggests that these questions emerging out of the image of human life and God's activity as story should not be dealt with too quickly or with too easy reassurance. Such moments of acute awareness of abrupt change in life story offer the opportunity, when met with profound seriousness, of opening the person as well as the pastor to fresh insights and new signs of God's activity and intention. If God in his activity in history comes toward us out of the open-endedness of the future, as the theologians of hope have suggested, it may be just at such times of abrupt interruption of the self's life story that a fresh vision of God's intention for the person's life may be grasped.

This last observation about crisis ministry suggests a second, often useful and salutary level at which episodic time functions in crisis experience. It affirms the necessity of undergoing the period of crisis in the fullest sense possible. The pre-imaging that "this too will pass" or "I can live through this" can support the person in crisis in the necessity of experiencing the self in the crisis time as fully as that self is capable of experiencing. We shall see that the psychological perspective on crisis experience affirms the value of just such experiencing or "working through" of the crisis time if the person is to be able to move on to a new episode in his or her life unhampered by repressed and suppressed conflicted feelings and relationships from the past. To the extent that the person experiences the "plot" or "story" of his or her life as happening *to* him or her without the person having any part in working out his or her own story, the person will be crippled in efforts to work through the episode of crisis and begin a new life story. This will need to be kept firmly in mind by the pastor in any discussion of God's historical activity in relation to the person's life story.

4. The Climate of the Community
Within Which Crisis Takes Place.

Crisis experience is not only relative to the flow of time and history, it is also strongly influenced by the more immediate social situation within which it takes place. If the crisis affects an individual, how it is experienced will depend upon whether or not there is a network of relationships surrounding that individual that gives support, understanding, and encouragement. The same may be said for a family or a community. The financial crisis in New York City a few years ago suggests that even large, complex communities are dependent upon a support system that is friendly to their needs when crisis comes.

In a sense modern pastoral care has for a long time been cognizant of the importance of these environmental factors. To the extent that pastoral care has emerged from a psychodynamic view of human motivation, relationships, and behavior, family and other environmental influences have been considered. But because modern pastoral care has been so heavily individualized in its approach, it has not given significant attention to the corporate dimensions both of care and of crisis dynamics. The fact is, of course, that individual or family crisis is not contained within the skin of the individual or the household of the family. The social milieu of the surrounding community acts both to define the crisis and provide or withhold those supporting relationships that make coping with crisis possible or impossible.

Eric Bermann in his carefully documented case study *Scapegoat*[9] presents a devastating critique of the typical white middle-class community which at all levels fails a family experiencing a complex family crisis triggered by the threat of death to the father from heart disease. The book begins as a case study of a young boy, Roscoe, who is having behavior problems at school. Home visits for observation of the family milieu reveal that the father's illness and potential death is a taboo subject in the home. The middle-class neighborhood in which the family lives not only is an environment in which death or the threat of death must be denied but also an environment in which the appearance of success and family solidarity must be upheld at all costs. Caught quite unawares in this impossible conflict, the family sets about transforming the threat of evil from the threat of death to the father into the threat of evil of bad behavior in Roscoe. Roscoe thus becomes the scapegoat who enables the family to remain in solidarity with its community.

The moral of the story of Roscoe is plain. Pastoral care of families like Roscoe's must include significant attention to the care and nurture of communities in which families may face their crises with openness and honesty, assured of the support of their neighbors. In short the pastoral and the prophetic dimensions of ministry must be conjoined in some fashion if we are to engage the environmental dimensions of crisis experience.

One problem encountered by the pastor who seriously seeks tools for engagement of community care issues is that as one looks to the social sciences for assistance, one encounters a very confused state of affairs. The currents of controversy run in many directions among social psychology theorists of recent years. On the one hand, there are the Freudian revisionists such as Erich Fromm and Karen Horney who extend Freudian theory into the social and economic realms.[10] Fromm is particularly helpful in his analysis of the interplay of the value structure of Western capitalism and individual bondage. His utopian vision of the society that supports individual freedom and love of neighbor and stranger provides a grasp on the ideal community of support and care that is needed to combat the depersonalization of much of modern urban life.

One can look in quite the opposite direction toward either the resurgence of behaviorist approaches to social psychological theory as represented most potently by B. F. Skinner[11] and his disciples or to the developing body of theory of what has come to be called social psychiatry.[12] Both of these schools view the human animal as essentially a reactor to social and environmental influences. The focus of concern moves in either case toward the manipulation of the environment in order to "condition" behavior of persons in a given socially prescribed direction.

At the very practical, operational level, the pastor has long felt the tension between conceptualizing his or her work in terms of ministry to individuals, on the one hand, and ministry to congregations of people, on the other. Caught in the conflict between the person in need who comes seeking a one-to-one relationship, with all the time that involves, and the congregational group demands for leadership, many pastors have found themselves unwittingly caught in an inconsistency. In the private, one-to-one relationships of pastoral care, they have found themselves responding more often with support, encouragement, and sympathy rather than with confrontation. What is more, they may have found themselves communicating that they "understand" even though the community may not. These relationships tend to become "soft" and accepting. In relation to the larger congregational community, on the other hand, pastors may find themselves responding more often in a prophetic, confronting style which may on occasion degenerate into wrist-slapping and moralistic scolding.

Even the pastor who avoids this kind of blatant inconsistency between pastor-to-person and pastor-to-congregation relationship may very often realize upon reflection that these two levels of relationships are being carried on out of two quite different frames of reference. When confronted with a situation of bereavement, for example, the pastor may do his or her work with a focus primarily upon the individual one-to-one relationship between pastor and parishioner. In doing this the pastor may be disregarding the potential for healthy, growth-producing grief work that can be done by the individual when surrounded by a community of persons who with some consistency support the grief-stricken person in the work of grief and subsequently of return to the ongoing life of the community.

Here we are confronted anew with the need for a unitary frame of reference for ministry that will facilitate coherence in what the pastor does with individuals and in relation to the larger community of faith and life. Such a unitary approach needs to take cognizance of both good theologizing about the human situation and of the continuous process of development of theory in the social sciences. The pastoral perspective needs, therefore, to be both interdisciplinary and normative in the sense of application of theological norms to methodological choices.

5. The Unique Individual Self.

From the standpoint of a Christian world view, we cannot speak of the formation of crisis experience without including the unique dimension of the self as the center of life and of crisis experience. In doing this we are affirming a central core of freedom on the part of the individual self to structure its own reality in its own idiosyncratic way, making use of the options provided by history, the flow of time and the social milieu in which the self finds itself.

In affirming the self as prime shaper of crisis experience, we recognize that we are involved in ambiguity. The self that structures its experience, directs its intentions, and forms its own life and history is also structured, formed, and developed by others, by the structures of the corporate life of humans generally, and by the boundaries of existence itself.[13]

One useful way of elucidating this ambiguity of the self as primary shaper and object of shaping forces in crisis experience is found in a systems or field theory approach that focuses upon the interaction between the self and a set of surrounding systems or levels of interacting space.

Figure 3 presents schematically such a systems or field theory of crisis experience. Here we see the self as the center of a series of concentric circles designed to represent the larger world of influences that shape the experience of the individual's life space. As we move from the centered self toward the outer perimeters of the concentric circles, we become both psychologically and existentially more distant from the experiencing self.

Self-World Vectors of Relationship

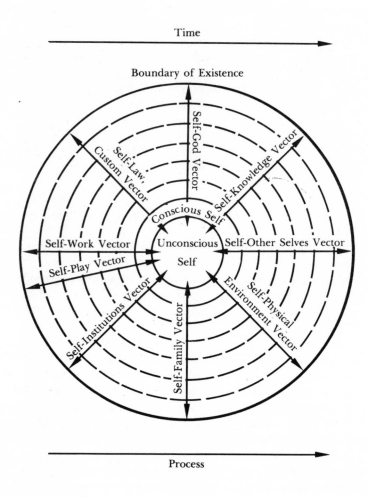

Figure 3

Influences that come from the outer circles tend to be experienced by the self as more remote, more objective, and less responsive to the self's initiative. Likewise, the closer we move in the concentric circles toward the self, the more the influences represented are experienced as personal, as subject to influence and change by the self, and as subject-subject rather than subject-object in mode. Our effort is to represent an open system in which there is constant transaction, interaction and exchange of influence between the self and the larger world.

Figure 3 also suggests that one of the modes of structuring the self-world relationship in a highly complex and constantly changing human situation is by means of various avenues of communication between self and the surrounding systemic environment. These avenues are referred to as "vectors" of interaction in the schema of Figure 3. As we have already considered at length, the entire interacting network of self and world is under the influence of inevitable movement through time.

Within this schema may be visualized our most fundamental understanding of crisis experience, namely, that crisis experience is shaped by a complex network of interacting dynamic influences in process centered in the self. Crisis can thus be seen as the result of both emergence and intrusion. As initiator and prime shaper of its own experience, the self is constantly emerging into its world and thus initiating what may become crisis experience. This aspect is often referred to in crisis intervention literature as developmental crisis. At this point all that we learn from the study of intrapsychic experience in the framework of psychoanalytic thought and developmental or life cycle psychology is of paramount importance. But crisis experience is also evoked by intrusion of both remote and immediate influences external to the self. Even developmental crises are encountered by intrusive forces from systems within which the self is incorporated. Likewise, one avenue of experience may intrude upon another and thus set up a dynamic process that becomes pervasive, affecting all avenues of communication between the self and its world.

An example of family crisis experience may serve to illustrate the usefulness of the schema of Figure 3.

John Brown, age 43, worked for General Motors, an employment relationship which he had maintained during most of his working life. Having been orphaned as a small boy and reared in first one and then another home of various relatives, he grew into manhood with more than the ordinary amount of insecurity and need for esteem from others. Early on in his work as a car salesman he learned that his gift for making himself at home with strangers paid off in both the number of sales he could make and in the praise and promotions he received from his employers. By virtue of hard work and absolute loyalty he had by the time he was forty worked his way up the ladder to assistant district sales manager. One price he had up to now been willing to pay for this success-oriented self-image bestowed by his company was his willingness to pick up his household and move, often long distances, whenever the opportunity for a promotion came along.

John was married to a very strong and self-reliant woman we will call Mary. Her self-reliance emerged from a long and difficult struggle to free herself from a very tightly knit small-town extended family, most particularly a dominant mother. Thus the frequent moves her marriage to John entailed were both acceptable and difficult for Mary. Complications developed in the marriage when the second of two sons was found to have a rather severe learning disability necessitating placement in a special school situation and psychological help. Then came another move and a new search for the appropriate help for the boy. Furthermore this move placed John under the supervision of a particularly demanding and erratic district manager, who attempted to manage his close associates' private as well as corporate lives. John soon began to drink much too much at company parties. Husband and wife began to quarrel with greater frequency and the whole life situation of the Browns rather quickly moved toward crisis.

Careful analysis of the Browns' situation reveals both what we are here calling emerging and intrusive factors. Somewhere in the surrounding systems of direct but distant influences on both John's and Mary's selfhood lies the multinational corporation with its corporate policies regarding both promotion and life-style of its lower and mid-range executives. These influences intrude devastatingly into the more intimate life space of the Brown family, setting parameters around their freedom to work out family problems and self-integrity that are experienced by the Browns as so given as to be existential. Likewise, the style of management of the district manager intrudes on both John's self-perception as an aggressively self-reliant person and his need for approval. But emerging factors are also present to influence the shaping of the crisis experience. John's desire for success has blossomed over the years of his working life. The coming of children has altered the relationship between John and Mary as she has become more and more invested in the care of the children, most particularly the younger, handicapped son. The crisis experience for both John and Mary therefore can be seen as multidimensional and the result of a complex network of interactions along several vectors or avenues of interchange in their life space.

The schema of Figure 3 not only facilitates visualization of the formation of crisis experience; it also is useful in recognizing the manner in which the circles of influence which surround the self may provide or withhold those supportive and growth-producing influences that make for healthy and creative management of crisis on the part of the self. The relative importance of a single one-to-one relationship between the self and, for example, the pastor, as over against the nurturing of a community, should be readily apparent from this schema. Both individual and corporate modes of ministry that open up channels of communication and influence between self and world are necessary if the understanding of crisis as taking place within life space is to be taken seriously.

Chaos and the Ordering of Human Experience

"Creation and chaos belong to each other." Thus Tillich characterizes the organic polarity of the random, haphazard confusion and the ordered, purposeful formation of finite existence. This we cannot with any clarity put into a visual schema or even verbal picture. But I would suggest that it is a useful game to let your mind go into free wheeling or high gear for a few moments and imagine the schema of Figure 3 greatly multiplied. Imagine ever larger and more complex systems of interaction, relationship, influence, and communication. Envision, if you can stretch your imagination widely enough, myriads of individual ego-centered systems like our diagram constantly bumping into one another, communicating, blocking, grouping, flowing through time and history in streams shaped like communities, nations, and cultures. Reflecting upon that crazy-quilt picture, whether you focus upon the individual, a family, a community, or (if your imagination is large enough) the whole human community or situation, what sensation do you experience? I experience anxiety, as if there hovered in the background the possibility—the imminent possibility—of utter and complete chaos.

Here we have encountered one facet of the anxiety of existence, that vague and undefined awareness that just behind the outward appearance of reasonable, comprehendible human experience lies the black and formless void of chaos, absurd and illimitable.

To press the fantasy one step farther: when you experience the imminent chaotic possibility, what is your first impulse when you think of coping with it? Universally the need for humans is for order; the chaos must be kept back by an ordered structuring of existence.

"In the beginning God created the heavens and the

earth, and the earth was without form and void" (Gen. 1:1). Thus is recorded biblical humanity's first experience of God as the one who brings order out of chaos. So also the self, the creator, structures its world to make it manageable, comprehensible, to keep back the chaos. Thinking in these terms presents the possibility that the various avenues of interaction between self and world represented by the vector lines in Figure 3 are to be understood as structures of ordered life put together by the self in interaction with the environment. The circles of Figure 3 may then represent levels of organization made necessary by larger and larger systems of interaction, the outermost circle of which represents the bounded structure of finite existence itself. At the opposite extreme of the centered self, following the structural theory of Freud, the self may itself be considered as a system of interaction and exchange.

With regard to crisis experience, Figure 3 suggests that critical occasions of experience occur largely in one of three ways: (1) Crisis may occur when one or more channels of communication or avenues of interaction becomes blocked, and the open flow of interaction is interrupted. John Brown's problem with his new district manager is a good example of this kind of blockage, as is in a different sense the alienation in his relationship with Mary as a result of their child's learning problem. (2) Crisis may occur when interaction along one or more channels of communication interferes seriously with established patterns of interaction along other avenues. The pattern of acceptance of frequent moves by John Brown which begins to interfere with the pattern of coping with the son's learning difficulty is a good example of this kind of dissonance between patterns of interaction. (3) Crisis occurs at the interfaces of levels of organization represented by the circles when changes in the established order of organization at one level interfere seriously with the order of organization at another level. This may be seen clearly in the friction between the corporate policy regarding promotions and employee life-style of John Brown's employer and the organization of family and neighborhood life in his home.

The Vital Balance

It should be apparent by now that we are looking to the developing body of "systems" or "organismic" theory for a framework for understanding ways in which human experience is structured by persons, institutions, and communities. Space and our purpose in this writing do not permit the full elaboration of these theoretical concepts. For the purpose of crisis ministry, readers are referred to Karl Menninger's book *The Vital Balance* for a helpful approach to applying systems theory to the understanding of crisis experience and personality dysfunction.[14] One additional concept of systems theory is, however, of such crucial significance for understanding crisis experience that its importance deserves underlining, namely, the concept of equilibrium or homeostasis. Menninger's term for this concept is vital balance. Concerning it he says:

We have submitted that all behavior, that of cells and organs and the total organism, may be defined as a continuous attempt to preserve or enhance organismic integrity by some degree or type of adjustment to disturbed balances. We must define the steady state in a broad sense, not just as physiological constancy or just a psychological steadiness, but as the integrated operation of all constancy-maintaining partial systems of any kind comprising the total personality, and even the environment in which it moves. Changes in the balance of one partial system may reverberate throughout the system and may sometimes grossly affect the steadiness of other partial systems.[15]

The importance of the concept of vital balance for crisis ministry is perhaps obvious. Simply put, we may say that a crisis, seen through this perspective, may be understood as what happens when the equilibrium or vital balance in the life space of an individual, family, or community is disrupted or interrupted by some more or less drastic change in the dynamic relationships within the system.[16] Crisis ministry may then be seen as that intervention into the system of organization of a self, family, or a community that brings about restructuring or restoration of the system at the most creative and human level of functioning. It is recognized that the terms "creative" and "human" are value-oriented terms, the qualification of which is determined by the total theological frame of reference of the persons involved in the system, or the ministry being brought to bear on the crisis situation.

One further thing needs to be said about the human community as a system or series of levels of systems. Humans have a long history of ambivalence and vacillation as to whether they want their life to be an open or closed system. Obviously, the more the human inclination is in the direction of a closed, fixed, homeostatic state of affairs in our life, the more difficult will crisis experience be for us and the higher the potential for destructive rather than creative outcome. On the other hand, our structuring of our existence can become so open and temporary as to lose continuity and border on the chaotic. So persons and communities are presented with a two-horned dilemma at all levels of life. Between fixed and static structure that leads to decay and a closed life and open-ended change, people must find a middle ground that makes for both growth and continuity with the past. In times of crisis this dilemma becomes both visible and crucial and the opportunity for ministry correspondingly more significant.

A Theological Perspective

It is again right at this point that the theology of hope stance for ministry we have suggested and are testing offers a potential solution to the two-horned dilemma between too closed and tight a structuring of human reality orientation on the one hand and utter randomness and chaos with the absurdity that brings on the other. Wolfhart Pannenberg in his *Theology and the Kingdom of God* surveys the history of the human struggle for a linchpin by which person-oriented values and the meaningfulness of things can be secured and argues that there can be no securing center, no human order within existing reality. The power of the future alone makes all things cohere. Every effort to secure things as they are is destructive of human life and therefore sinful, which is the unwillingness to entrust oneself to the future rule of God proclaimed by Jesus.[17]

The pastor who embraces this theological perspective will have a firm but open-ended basis for encouraging persons in his or her care to sustain a self system open to the world and to the changing configurations of reality and self as both move into the unknown future. A life stance built upon eschatological trust in God's promise of his coming kingdom is provided with a basis for trust that is not dependent upon the stubborn continuation of a statically constructed life.

Approaches to understanding crisis experience are many and varied. A perspectival approach that takes into consideration a wide range of perspectives seems therefore necessary. While the pastor will always venture into other perspectives with one foot firmly placed in the theological perspective we have suggested, his or her work will be greatly enhanced by the perspectives set forth in this chapter. The usefulness and validity of such a multi-perspective approach remains to be demonstrated in application to specific categories of crisis experience. It is to this task we turn in the next and subsequent chapters. Our effort is to consider a typology of paradigms, each suggesting broader ranges of human experience. If crisis is to be seen fundamentally as any threat to the ultimate meaning of things, then the primary paradigm or model of models is the crisis of death and dying. We therefore turn to consideration of this, the final boundary time of finite existence, to begin the specifics of our exploration.

CHAPTER III

Death and Anguish

Death: The Primary Paradigm
of Crisis Experience

We have already indicated that the method of our exploration of crisis experience is to be one of in-depth consideration of several prototypical models of crisis experience and establishing some coherence among crisis ministry practice, contemporary social science theory, and theological reflection. Our definition of crisis as the extreme or boundary situation in which persons become aware of their finite existence compels the selection of death and dying as the primary paradigm. Death is that outermost boundary of finite existence, even as time, which in its movement takes us toward death, is the most immediate. To live in time is to live toward death.

Obviously death will have different meanings for different persons. The patriarch of eighty who dies with his children gathered about him in love and respect for what he has been and the heritage he leaves behind will have a vastly different experience than the man who dies lonely and alone in his high-rise apartment for the aging. Death is a very particular experience shaped by all the factors discussed in our last chapter. We know that the dying and the bereaved experience many emotions running the gamut from anxiety to anger, from fear to guilt. Some of these emotional experiences have an aura of psychopathology about them. We know, for example, how feelings of dependence and helplessness can become distorted in the agony of death. But deep within the experience at its core, the experience of death is existential. It is a boundary experience. If we are to

74

minister to persons on this boundary we must understand what that boundary experience contains.

In my search for a word that points to this universal and primary boundary experience of death, the word that seems most apposite, if taken in its root meanings, is the word "anguish." In its common usage, of course, anguish refers to acute pain, suffering, or distress. In its Latin rootage, however, anguish carries a connotation of a narrowing, strangling experience that has about it a certain angry torment. To experience anguish is to experience that excruciating distress of having life's boundaries pressed together about the self. One's very life is being squeezed out, tightened down. No angry wrenching loose will avail; the strength of life is dwindling, and all that remains is that helpless and angry torment—the anguish of death.

The Human Life Cycle and Its Finite Boundaries

The diagrams of Figures 4, 5, and 6 represent an effort to schematize in a very general and unspecific fashion the way in which the inevitability of anguish is structured into the individual's experience of finite existence. Figure 4 suggests that, when objectively and rationally conceived, the anticipated normal life cycle will appear somewhat like a convex lens with the points of the lens signifying the beginning and ending points of birth and death. During childhood and adolescence the horizons of life are widening at a relatively rapid rate. The child experiences his or her life as primarily becoming or growing, not only in physical stature but also in the manner in which he or she moves out into wider and wider ranges of experience and exercise of his or her capacities. Exploration and "out-growing" are primary modes of child life. Adolescence continues the process of widening horizons accompanied now by a growing need to test limits, both social and existential. Pushing back, breaking out, trying out are the modes of adolescent life.

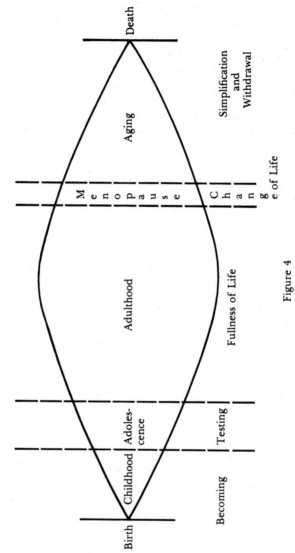

Anticipated Normal Life Cycle

Rationally Conceived

Birth

Childhood | Adolescence

Adulthood

Menopause

Change of Life

Aging

Death

Becoming

Testing

Fullness of Life

Simplification and Withdrawal

Figure 4

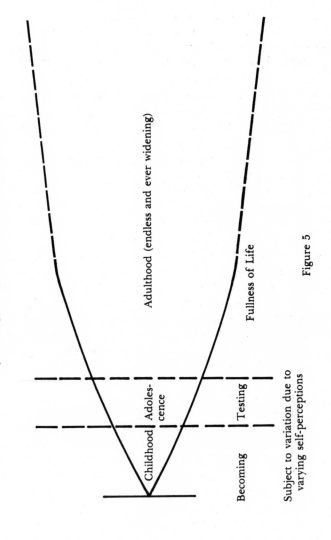

Psychologically Anticipated Life Cycle

Adulthood (endless and ever widening)

Fullness of Life

Childhood | Adolescence | Testing

Becoming

Subject to variation due to varying self-perceptions

Figure 5

The Phenomenology of Anguish
in
Aging and Death

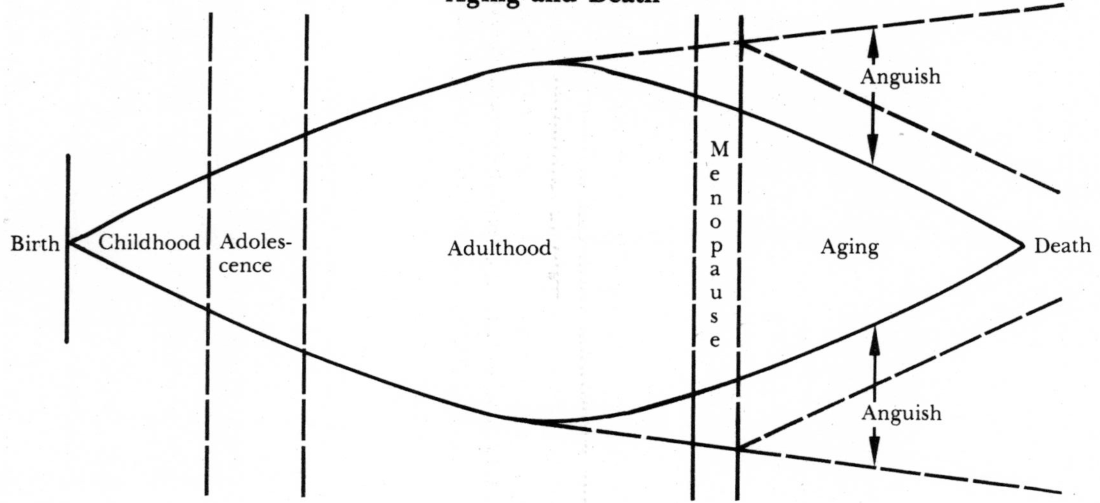

Figure 6

It is in adulthood that persons experience both the fullness and the realistic limits of life most completely in a kind of tension between what is possible and what is desirable. (Adults experience both the fulfillment of many of their life expectations and the need to compromise their dreams in order to live realistically) Just as responsibility and care are the tasks of adult life, so also are commitments and limitations the boundaries with which the adult must come somehow to terms. With the menopause comes the time of "change of life," when biological and physical strength begin to wane, bringing with that visible change the shifting family and social realities of aging. The process of narrowing has begun, inexorably and unrelentingly moving the life cycle of the individual toward old age and death. Instead of building up, life begins to contract. (The concept of self must now be adjusted to the narrowing realistic possibilities) Eventually withdrawal from one activity after another becomes inevitable; life must be simplified.

If the human experience of existential boundaries were subject fully to the control of the rational faculties, the ability of the person's thinking processes to adjust to changing reality would exercise control, and the human life cycle would perhaps be experienced free from the anguish of death. But paradoxically, human self-awareness and the ability to reflect upon life experience open up to us another level of selfhood. Intertwined with and underlying human intellectual capacities for objective, rational understanding of the boundaries of life lives another side of human nature which, in a broad sense, may be labeled emotive or, if you will, the realm of the wishful, the world of fantasy. This side of human nature, while much more subject to the vicissitudes of unique individual life experience, seems with relative consistency to have quite a different perspective on the human life cycle. Figure 5 is an attempt to visualize that perspective schematically. For this emotive side of our nature childhood and adolescence are marked by an impatient

79

awareness of boundaries. (The push against the limits is both persistent and pervasive.) It is as if, in the fantasy life of the child, to be an adult is to be without constraints, free in an ever-widening world of limitless horizons— limitless, that is, save for the freedom and power to fulfill the potentials of the self. Limits are experienced largely as those imposed by the adult world, a world which, when adult control is gained, can be transformed into the fulfillment of one's dreams. This is not all the child or adolescent experiences of the possibilities of life, to be sure. (The other side of the coin is the anxious, sometimes shameful anticipation that the individual will not be able to measure up to the boundless possibilities of life.) But the fantasy of ever-widening horizons and endless fulfillment nevertheless sets the stage for a fundamental contradiction between the rational perception of the life cycle and that psychologically real, emotionally subjective anticipation of what life will be.

Freud's psychoanalytic analysis of the most primitive beginnings of the infant's sense of self is, even if not taken too literally, helpful in clarifying the roots of this emotionally anticipated boundless and endless life cycle. In Freud's view the infant begins life outside the womb without the realistic sense of self as separated from non-self. Self and world are one. It is only as this primary narcissism is contradicted by the impingements of parental demands, the inability of the self to control its world to its liking, and the helplessness of pain and hunger that the infant begins to acquire a sense of self as separate from the world. But there lingers in the unconscious ego processes that fantasy that wishes the power of omnipotence and that the world can be made in the mold of desire.

Robert Jay Lifton, in his study of death symbolism in persons who underwent the unbelievable trauma of the atomic bombing at Hiroshima, adds an important dimension to Freud's thought.

I believe it is more nearly correct to say that our own death—or at least our own dying—is not entirely unimaginable but can be imagined only with a considerable degree of distance, blurring, and denial; that we are not absolutely convinced of our own immortality, but have a need to maintain a *sense of immortality* in the face of inevitable biological death; and that this need represents not only the inability of the individual unconscious to recognize the possibility of its own demise but also a compelling universal urge to maintain an inner sense of continuous symbolic relationship, over time and space, to the various elements of life. Nor is this need to transcend biological life *mere* denial (although denial becomes importantly associated with it): rather it is part of the organism's psychological quest for mastery, part of an innate imagery apparently present in man's mind since the earliest periods of his history and prehistory.[1]

Upon reflection we are reminded that some of the common expressions we use, particularly concerning the future, point to this unconscious anticipation of what life will be. We say: "Well, that will get better tomorrow." "One day I'm going to get that all straightened out." "There's always tomorrow." All these expressions seem to say that the future is really open-ended and boundless. Likewise, conversations with many relatively unsophisticated but faithful grass-roots Christian laypersons suggest that for some such persons the Christian hope for life after death has been so blended into the affective anticipation of life as endless that the denial of the narrowing boundaries that inexorably move us all toward death is reinforced. Even the Christian funeral, at least in its traditional American form, has more often than not been an all too premature celebration of resurrection so that the bereaved are reassured of endless life before they have been enabled to assimilate the reality of death and loss.

The contradiction between our rational and emotional views of the boundaries of finite life is graphically illustrated in Figure 6 by superimposing the schema of denial of Figure 5 upon the more realistic picture of Figure 4. Here we see schematically the suggestion that it is in this contradiction that the anguish of living toward death is to be found. The angry dawning of the realization that the boundaries of aging and death are indeed narrowing is like the unwilling entrance into the tight place! Over time the aging person is forced to come to terms with objective reality. Little by little the boundaries narrow. How the resulting anguish will be experienced will, as we discussed in the previous chapter, be shaped by all the factors, personal, social, and historical, that go into the formation of a given individual's experience. The core of the experience however, is existential; the anguish of aging and death is the anguish of contradiction concerning boundaries. (*of our existence*)

The psychologist who has made the most careful study of the psychological processes of aging is perhaps Robert Kastenbaum.[2] In his studies he picks up on a similar theme of contradiction in his dialectic between "engrossment" and "perspective." To be engrossed in life in one or more of its aspects is to be completely absorbed in the lived experience of the present moment. It is as if there were no boundaries, no time save the present, no pairing off of this experience with other experiences. This is the here-and-now dimension of human life. Perspective, on the other hand, involves the comparison of *this* experience with other experiences, *this* time with other times. It concerns itself with antecedents and consequences, with past and future. "If engrossment may be regarded as complete psychological involvement in one unitary situation, then perspective may be regarded as simultaneous involvement at two or more points in the life-space. The quality of engrossment vanishes when we compare, judge, plan, seek to explain."[3] Kastenbaum goes on to suggest that engrossment and perspective point to two parallel psychological processes both of which are necessary for mature human functioning. To live is to be in tension between these two processes.

(In the course of human life the aging process brings about a shift in the way in which the engrossment-perspective tension is balanced or lived with by the individual.) In the earlier years of life on through the productive years before menopause, the balance is most often in favor of engrossment.(But time and perspective seem to come together so that there is a toning down of the level of engrossment, a certain objective distancing from the engrossment of the moment. With the onset of aging, this process is further complicated by the diminishing powers of the individual to do and be everything he or she wants to do and be. As Kastenbaum puts it: "The basic problem for the aging individual is how to find meaning and satisfaction in life as he becomes increasingly less able to keep everything going at once. He can select one of several 'parts' for sustained involvement; he can try to preserve the 'whole' at the expense of the 'parts'; or he can vacillate between these solutions. 'Disengagement' is one rather popular solution to this underlying problem."[4]

Consider the many and varied ways in which the aging person is reminded constantly of the narrowing boundaries of his or her personal existence. Dr. W., the surgeon experiencing the transition from adulthood to old age described in chapter 2, was reminded of that narrowing by the crick in his shoulder. As I muse about that, I am reminded of a recent experience in my automobile when, after another motorist and I narrowly missed colliding, he leaned from his window and shouted at me, "Why don't you watch where you are going, old man?" The insult was sharpened considerably by his word choice. I was painfully reminded that someone saw me as "old." Not only that, but the jibe forced me to consider at least for a time that he might be right—at least to the extent that my slower than previous reflexes may have been in part responsible for the near accident. For just a moment the narrow, tight place of aging became visible, anguishingly, angrily visible.

The person who has lived into the seventies and

eighties has, of course, lived through many such experiences. One by one, choices have been made to simplify and adjust the expectations of the self to the now quite visible reality of narrowing boundaries. Repeated reminders over years of adjustment to aging probably account in large part for the relative lack of fear and anxiety concerning death common among old people. I recall a death-and-dying seminar I once conducted in which a panel of old people all past eighty were invited to talk about their thoughts and feelings concerning death. Several had recently lost their mates to death. From them came expressions of loneliness and loss. But in none of the nine participants could there be detected fear of death. They talked of death almost as of an old friend with whom they had lived for some time! One said: "Well, in my eighty-four years I have muddled through a lot of tight places. I guess I can muddle through that one." Acceptance of limits was a common theme of most comments of the members of the group.

Pastors should not, however, assume that this adjustment to finite limits will always be the case with aged parishioners. I recall another pastoral conversation with a woman of eighty-two lying in a hospital bed in a cardiac ward. Her medical records indicated that she was rapidly dying of heart failure. Her appearance, however, evidenced the extent of her denial of her condition. She was dressed in a frilly pink bed jacket, her nails freshly polished and her hair carefully set and colored that blue-white color that one often sees on older women when they are attempting to look their best. In a tiny but strangely seductive voice she talked of her past independence, the business she formerly owned and managed, the automobile she drove until she came to the hospital. As we conversed I became so impressed with her obvious denial of the tightening boundaries of her situation that, when she asked me to pray, on impulse I quoted Paul's Corinthian letter: "Though our outer nature is wasting away, our inner nature is being renewed every day" (II

Cor. 4:16). With that I said my good-bye and turned to leave. Whereas she had been speaking in a tiny voice, she now shouted at me, "But my outer nature isn't wasting away!" Within forty-eight hours she was dead, refusing the anguish of death until the end.

The analysis we have just made of the anguish of aging in living toward death opens up a way of conceptualizing the anguish of living toward death suffered by the person who becomes aware of the possible presence of a life-threatening illness or injury at some point in the life cycle prior to what is normally considered old age. Much of what takes place in the experience of such persons can be understood as analogous to the aging process though in a highly compacted form.

Figures 7 and 8 attempt to depict the analogy between death by terminal illness or accident and the living toward death of old age. Figure 7 presents schematically the nature of catastrophic, sudden death. Here life is literally cut off. There is no ending process, no anguish except perhaps the momentary awareness that something catastrophic has happened and is happening.

I am reminded here of a tragic situation in which I once attempted to minister in a large emergency hospital. Three young men ages seventeen, nineteen, and twenty-one had been driving along an expressway in an old delapidated truck. They had stopped for gasoline and filled the tank under the truck seat until it overflowed. Subsequently while they continued on their way one of the young men lit a cigarette, and the spilled gasoline caught fire and exploded. In the ensuing crash the driver, the oldest of the three brothers, was pinned under the steering wheel until his brothers could, at the cost of painful burns to themselves, pull him free. He was brought to the emergency clinic with 95 percent third degree body burns. Only his face and the soles of his feet had escaped the charring flames. With nerve endings largely destroyed, he was quite conscious and aware of his condition for most of the four or five hours that he lived.

Catastrophic Death

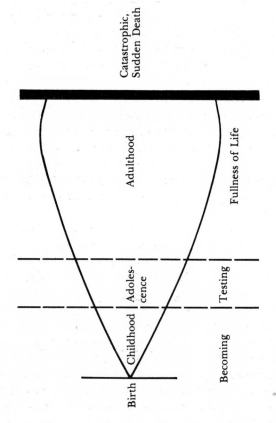

Catastrophic,
Sudden Death

Fullness of Life

Adulthood

Testing

Childhood Adoles-
cence

Becoming

Birth

Figure 7

Death by Terminal Illness

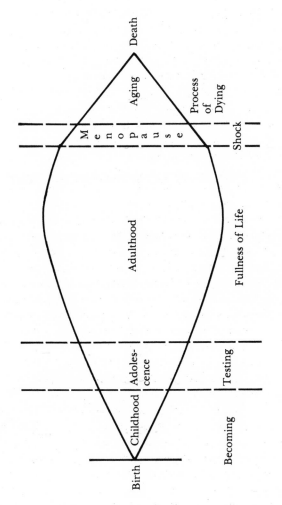

Figure 8

Sitting with this family while the oldest son was dying was one of the most anguished times I have ever experienced in ministry. Much of the fragmented frantic talk that went on between son and parents, brother and brothers could, upon recall and reflection, be seen as a highly compressed effort to bring the life story of this young person to meaningful closure. The sudden, catastrophic closing in of the limits of his life, made so apparent by the appearance of his blackened body, forced a tumbling and terrified effort to accommodate to the hard and raw boundaries of the situation. Never have I seen a family thrust so brutally into the tight place of death.

More often the awareness of the threat of terminal illness comes more gradually in a form more readily recognized as compacted aging. This more extended, though still highly compacted, process is schematized in Figure 8. Here we can begin to distinguish a series of stages or intertwining levels in the process of living toward death quite analogous to the stages or levels that can be seen in the normal aging process.

Elisabeth Kübler-Ross, a sensitive and compassionate psychiatrist, was the first to suggest that the dying go through a process of coming to terms with death that has recognizable stages or levels.[5] Dr. Kübler-Ross finds typically five stages in this process, though individuals vary considerably in the way in which they proceed through these stages. Stage one involves denial and an effort to isolate the thoughts and feelings related to the threat of death. Stage two is characterized by feelings of anger that may be focused or diffused and displaced on various persons and structures in the environment. Stage three finds the person bargaining with the illness—bargaining for time, for favor from God or persons close to the patient. Stage four Dr. Kübler-Ross calls depression, a time when the terminally ill can no longer deny the illness nor does the bargaining function to ward off the painful awareness of impending death. The result is the overpowering feeling of loss and defeat. Only as this stage is worked through can the person enter the fifth stage of genuine acceptance of the inevitability and appropriateness of the coming of death.

Terminal Illness and Finite Boundaries

If not taken too literally and prescriptively (as I sometimes fear has been done by the popularization of Dr. Kübler-Ross' work), (the notion of stages in the process of dying is a useful one for reflection about pastoral work with the dying.) From the perspective of living toward death as a process of coming to terms with narrowing finite boundaries analogous to the process of aging, I would suggest another possible schema for interpretation of observations. This schema suggests an interlocking set of themes or questions and a process most appropriately described as coming to terms with narrowing boundaries.

Coming to terms with an actual or potential life-threatening illness is marked in its beginning stages by an experience akin to that of the menopause or change of life.) Sometimes suddenly, often more slowly, there comes the dawning awareness that life has changed. Something is happening to one's body that reminds us that we are mortal. As in the menopause this comes as a shocking experience. Something is happening to me over which I do not have control. What is true for others may also be true for me. I am vulnerable to illness and death. I am a finite creature who ages and sickens. It is this signal of finitude that the person suffering from either a life-threatening illness or the normal changes in the body in menopause wishes to deny.

Denial and the Need for Rescue

Denial in the menopause is a common, perhaps even universal experience. The man who at forty-five buys a new sports car and the woman who suddenly buys an expensive new dress after missing her first regular period when the menopausal changes begin both are involved in denial. More tragically, the husband who suddenly leaves his family to escape into an extramarital affair with a woman much younger than himself is likewise involved in denial. Parenthetically, it should be said that in recent years, as images of liberation become more potent among middle-aged women in our society, we are observing not only men but women deserting families of small children in a frantic effort to deny the aging process.

So also with denial in the onset of life-threatening illness:

Joe M., a 46-year-old businessman is suffering from lymphatic cancer, a condition which gives him statistically a 50-50 chance of living two years. Three years prior to the onset of the illness, Joe lost his business that had brought him an income of $100,000 per year in the recession of the early seventies. Not long after that calamitous event he and his wife were divorced, a separation Joe initiated. He now dates the onset of the cancer to the time of his depression following the double loss of wife and business. He recalls having felt a mass in his abdomen for months before going for his long overdue annual physical examination. Having now gone through chemotherapy which has successfully reduced the size of the abdominal mass, Joe speaks in confident terms of being "cured," though his doctor has told him the facts concerning his illness. He also has begun a new business which he says is prospering.

Joe has also renewed his interest in his church, an interest which had waned in the ten years of successful business life prior to his business reversals. Though he remains highly optimistic about his future, he acknowledges that life for him has changed. No longer does he want to be a millionaire. He is content with a more modest income and values more highly the friends he has made at his church. One of his most meaningful activities is taking one of these friends, a terminally ill cancer patient, to the hospital weekly for radiation therapy. He speaks of trying to help his friend remain hopeful but to accept that life doesn't last forever.

Here we see a man in whom there is the intertwining of themes relating to both the menopausal stage of life and the stage of life-threatening illness referred to by Dr. Kübler-Ross as denial. Certainly Joe M. seems to be denying the reality of his illness and its life-threatening potential. In a sense he is also denying his aging as he begins a new business. (But beneath both outward appearances one catches glimpses of a man who is in the process of coming to terms with the limits of his finite life—a man in the anguish of entrance into the narrow place.) One can even suggest that for him the two processes of coming to terms with aging and coming to terms with life-threatening illness are interlocked and that the reaction to his illness has greatly compacted the process of the change of life it symbolizes.

One theme that emerges quite commonly from this first level of encounter with the anguish of entry into the tight place of narrowing boundaries is the theme of rescue. Many, if not most, persons suffering from life-threatening disease relate to their physicians with a spoken or unspoken request for rescue from the predicament the illness imposes. Recognizing the child-like qualities in these relationships, physicians often respond with the parenting reassurance that "everything possible will be done." Or, sensing the capability of a more mature and adult potential for realism in the patient, the doctor may respond with statistical percentage predictions about the common course of the illness. In neither case has the central existential experience of the patient been responded to helpfully. It is at this point that the contemporary trends in American culture described in our earlier discussion of the heroic image of coping with crisis can very readily be seen. The "mature" expectation is that the "adult" patient will somehow cope with the "facts" of his or her situation. The less mature must be reassured. Some more theologically grounded basis for coming to terms with the threat of terminal illness must be found that takes more clearly into account both the radically open-ended threat of terminality and ultimate human vulnerability in the face of death.

Pastors, too, receive some pleas for rescue from those persons caught in the narrow place of anguish whose consciousness remains within a natural-supernatural frame of reference. The pastor is asked to invoke the power of the transcendent God who, having set the boundaries of finite life, surely has the power to set those boundaries aside, to make an exception in this case. Pastors, too, can fall into the trap of offering the prayer that supports the childlike response. Some pastors can even be matter of fact and implicitly statistical in their refusal of such requests.

Coping with the Vulnerability of Dying

With persons who have been impacted by the modern desacralized consciousness, however, the pastor will more often receive either outright denial of stress or some vague plea for more strength to cope. To the extent that God language is used, it is appropriated to shore up the person's psychological and emotional strength to endure stress heroically. Like the doctor, the pastor may be tempted to use whatever theological language tools he or she possesses to shore up personal coping capacities. In that case the price of reassurance is the risk that the person may not be helped to open himself or herself to a more profound and theologically warranted grasp of the mystery of God's activity even in the time of death.

What is needed here by way of firm theological ground on which both the pastor and the parishioner can stand? Of course, the sensitive pastor will nearly always want to respond to the existential shock, acknowledge the interruption of life story that lies just beneath the plea for rescue or the request for psychological support. But a more solid base for pastoral response that does not close off the frightened groping for the promise that can hold meaning together even through the tight place of death must be found. Final human vulnerability in the face of death needs at some time in that groping to be acknowledged. Trust in God's future, mysterious and unpredetermined as that is, must be made possible. A firm grasp of the radical futurity of God's promise and the provisional quality of all humanly constructed hopes on the part of the pastor will assist him or her in walking that narrow path between too easy reassurance on the one hand and mere psychological bolstering of heroic selfhood on the other.

Sometimes, rather than the plea for prayers of rescue or for heroic support, the pastor will be confronted with what can only be described as theological denial. Confronted with the fresh threat to his or her existence contained in the possibility of terminal illness, the person may attempt quickly to leap over the threat with what amounts to desperate affirmations of trust. "I'm just trusting God!" "Jesus will see me through!" Such responses as these, when accompanied by signals of anguish and stress, more often than not point to the wish to deny what is happening. Again the response that quietly opens up the possibility of confession of fear, anguish, and wish for rescue will generally be more efficacious than the unction of theological reassurance. To attempt to leap over the anguish of Good Friday into the joy of Easter morning belies the necessity of moving through the tight place of vulnerability.

Exploration of Death's Meaning

For the person who has been able to work through the initial phase of shock and denial in awareness of vulnerability to death there begins a process of exploration of the full meaning of what is happening. As in the aging process of the late forties and fifties, this process will be touched off by incidents of reminder that inescapably present the harsh reality of narrowing boundaries. The pervasive quality of this level of living toward death is that of loss. The person is confronted everywhere with the possibility of losing what has made life meaningful. The mother must come to terms with the loss of her children, not only her children as they are now, but her children as they will be in the future. Beneath these losses in significant relationships lies the even more difficult to accept loss of self and self's future. The story of one's life has been interrupted. The long years that seemed to stretch out ahead have been foreshortened. The illusions that have been entertained in the secret recesses of the self about one's indestructibly immortal selfhood must be given up.

Much of the bargaining to which Elisabeth Kübler-Ross refers may be understood as an effort to exercise some continuing control over the degree and rapidity of loss experiences as the dying person is encountering one loss after another. If the mother cannot forestall the loss of her children's future, perhaps she can prevent the loss of seeing her daughter's marriage or her son's graduation from high school.

With the courage to confront the experiences of loss that are experienced more and more as both inevitable and specific, the dying person begins to confront likewise the questions of faith and the threat of loss of faith. The faith that has been linked to the specificity of desirable outcomes must either give way to a more realistic and less wishful faith that is not dependent on the illusion that one is an exception to the rule of mortality or regression toward denial and pleading for rescue will most often follow. In the person of mature religious faith this personal exploration of death's significance can precipitate what often appears to the observer to be a somewhat detached, even philosophical time of reflection about life's mysteries, its rich and contradictory ambiguities.

Anguish and the Threat of Forsakenness

But for all persons who are able to share the feelings of loss that death's threat brings there is the anguish of narrowing boundaries. For some the anguish is felt as forsakenness. It is as if one has been left to die. Here the symbol of Jesus' words from the cross, "My God, my God, why hast thou forsaken me?" is richly expressive. What the dying fear more than anything else is to be abandoned to their fate. The fear applies to loved ones and professional persons such as doctors and nurses, as well as to God. Here the question of God's presence or absence becomes crucial for the dying person. Unquestionably the theological question most often asked by the dying, sometimes directly, sometimes more implicitly in the disguise of an affirmation, is the question, Where is God?

It is as if the God whose presence is taken for granted or experienced as "with us" in the everyday flow of life has so altered his relationship that he has removed himself and is now over against us. The human purposes that informed and shaped ordinary life which are always a mixture of realistic and wishful considerations and for which God's blessing had been invoked are now being lost and found of no account. Where is God in this new and anguished situation? The wish to deny the reality of what is actually taking place leads toward the wish to invoke the rescuing God of one's wishes. The dawning reality of the situation, however, presses toward the question of God's absence, his indifference, his distance from one's human purposes. The result can be a helpless feeling of having been forsaken by God.

Though these feelings and thoughts are highly subjective and the quality and degree of their expression will vary enormously from person to person, they contain a very genuine theological problem. The often unconscious fusion of images of private, individual human hopes—hopes and expectations that did not include death—with God's purposes must somehow be disconnected, or else God must be unmasked as the one who in the end forsakes us. Trust in God's larger future that includes one's own death must be found. The helpless human vulnerability before death needs to be acknowledged and a final resting place of trust in God's future embraced. Here the pastor is faced with a delicate twofold task. He or she will want to relate empathically with the person's feelings of being forsaken, encouraging their expression. Yet the pastor will also want to represent that understanding of God's purpose that includes the Cross, that going through the tight place of death, and includes trust in God's promises. The degree of his or her own openness to both the pain of forsakenness and the trust of God's promise of the ultimate coming together of all things, that hope which has since Paul been called the hope of resurrection, will be operative in the manner of his or her presence in relating to the time of anguished forsakenness.

Just as indifference breeds contempt, so the feelings of forsakenness can breed a kind of nameless, pervasive hostility. Feeling abandoned and alone, the dying patient may be unable to stave off impulses to strike out at anything and anyone who represents those others who do not share the predicament of living toward death.

A theological student visiting on a cancer ward reported the following conversations with a fifty-five-year-old woman entering the terminal stages of widespread cancer:

(My first visit with Mrs. L was cut relatively short with the arrival of the patient's daughter and other guests. Impressions of that first encounter, however, appear significant. The telephone, newspapers, and magazines were on the bed forming an outline around the patient, almost as though they were either pushing in on her or purposefully kept within easy reach. The patient was markedly hostile about something that apparently had happened before I arrived.)

C-1: I'm the chaplain on this floor. I wanted to introduce myself to you. How do you feel today?

P-1: No good. I have so much pain. They cut me here and here. *(She indicated with her hands that she had had extensive surgery.)*
C-2: I understand.
P-2: About what?
C-3: About your having a great deal of pain.
P-3: Do you really understand?
C-4: No—not really. No one can understand another's pain completely. But I do understand that you are having pain. And I'm sorry.

(There was a rather long, awkward pause at this spot. She looked away from me toward the window. I resisted the temptation to fill the void with small talk.)

P-4: I just don't know.
C-5: About what?
P-5: About anything. I don't seem to be making much improvement this time. It's taking so long.
C-6: It's natural to be impatient sometimes. I have that problem too, you know, wanting everything to hurry.
P-6: I am a teacher. I'm used to doing and keeping busy.
C-7: I was a teacher too. What is your field?
P-7: English. What did you teach?
C-8: English.

(The daughter arrived at this time. Mrs. L seemed very happy to see her. She introduced me to her, and I excused myself, indicating that I would return for another visit. I also stated that she could call me if she needed me.

(On subsequent visits I found the patient with the same hostility, which does not appear to be directed toward any one person. Rather, it seems to be directed toward everyone and everything—life itself.)

(In a later visit, the following dialogue ensued. The blinds were drawn this time, the telephone, magazines, and newspapers no longer on the bed. The patient looked much worse than during the earlier visit described above. In the interim she had fallen. Questioning the nurse about this, I found that the patient was getting out of bed and had passed out.)

C-9: How are you again today?
P-8: Come around to this side so I can see you. *(She seemed to be unable to move her head easily. I moved as she requested.)*
C-10: I heard you fell.

P-9: Yes. I can't get up any more. It's taking so long this time. I've never been so low for so long. Look at my arms. *(They were black and blue.)* I don't have any more veins. The doctors don't know what to do. Turn off that TV set. I don't want it. The nurse *(special duty nurse)* keeps it on.

(I sensed a great deal of hostility directed toward the nurse. I turned the TV off.)

P-10: Come here closer. I want to tell you about what I have been thinking. I'm trying to write a poem. Listen to this. You're an English teacher. Think about this: "All our todays are yesterdays tomorrow." Think about that. I don't think I'll be having any more tomorrows in teaching.

C-11: Mrs. L, one thing about a teacher. Nobody can ever take our classroom away from us. We carry it with us. You're teaching now—here. I'm teaching. I appreciate what you're teaching me. I appreciate your sharing your thoughts with me.

P-11: What am I teaching you?

C-12: Your thoughts, being patient. I'm learning from you about how not to hurry.

(The special duty nurse entered the room at this time, putting a six pack of coke on the table.)

P-12: Oh no! Take that away! I can't look at all that. Get it out of here. *(To me)* She's forcing me to drink. I know it's all to keep me alive, but I can't see it all at once.

N-1: Well, the reason I brought it here is so I wouldn't have to keep running down the hall every time you needed one. *(She put all but one can in the bathroom, then sat down on a chair and began reading a magazine.)*

(I felt hostility on the part of both the patient and the nurse. Mrs. L did not seem as talkative after the nurse came.)

C-13: I'll go now. I'll be by to check with you again.

P-13: Think about what I told you. See how many things you can apply it to every day.

C-14: I will. Goodbye.

Mrs. L immediately signals her sense of having been forsaken in her response in P-2. With irritation she questions whether the young student pastor could really understand her pain. Strikingly, when he acknowledges that he indeed cannot understand her pain completely she begins to warm to the possibilities of a relationship that might bridge her lonely, vaguely angry, forsaken state. At least the young pastor is honest. Perhaps he does want to understand. She then is able to share a bit of her anguish in the tight place of death. "I don't seem to be making much improvement this time." Here we see the pastor presented with a tough choice. Will he reassure, attempt to soften the harshness of her awareness of her anguish? Or will he open himself to it and enter the tight, angry, and terrifying place with her? He elects to reassure: "It's natural to be impatient sometimes."

Then the fortunate kinship comes to light. They have both been English teachers. By this slender thread of kinship the relationship that may overcome, at least for a time, the forsaken, bitter aloneness begins to take shape. At this point there is an interruption. Mrs. L's daughter arrives. Again the pastor is presented with a choice. Will he stay in the room for a time to see if he can facilitate a relationship between mother and daughter that will counter Mrs. L's forsaken state? Or will he elect to keep his and the daughter's relationships to Mrs. L private? This is an important pastoral choice that can be made either way depending upon the pastor's sensing of the possibilities for in-depth sharing of the experienced reality of the tight place of anguish by both mother and daughter. Many relatives of the dying cannot tolerate the pain of their loved one's anguish. They, too, must reassure and shut off the sharing, thus reaffirming the forsakenness. Our pastor here elects to go it alone with the dying person—at another time!

The relationship tentatively begun in the first visit has, by the next visit reported on, begun to flourish. Mrs. L has continued to share her pervasive, generalized hostility, and it has not driven the pastor away. She elects to share more directly her fear of loss of her future, her despair at not getting better. Bidding the pastor to come closer (an important invitation) she shares her efforts to come to grips with her situation in a poem that expresses the reality of finite boundaries: "All our todays are yesterdays tomorrow." "I don't think I'll be having any more tomorrows in teaching."

Here the pastor seems truly to lose his nerve. He cannot tolerate the starkness of her expression of anguish and loss. He must reassure. He must himself deny what is happening. It is not so. "You are teaching now—here." The result is that Mrs. L is pressed back into her angry, bitter aloneness. She strikes out at the nurse, though she admits the nurse is actually trying to help. "I know it's all to keep me alive, but I can't see it all at once."

[handwritten margin note: reassurance is not always best.]

How Is Ministry to the Dying to Be Empowered?

If it is true, as much of the research carried out by Elisabeth Kübler-Ross and others seems to demonstrate, that what the dying person fears most is abandonment by those around him or her, then the most crucial question of pastoral methodology is here presented to us. On what basis or with what empowerment can the pastor (or others, for that matter) open himself or herself to the stark and unrelenting pain of living with the other toward death? Press that question even harder and the ultimate question of forsakenness by God enters our horizon of concern.

The common current response to this question in much of the popular literature on death and dying is that the prerequisite that will enable persons to open themselves to the anguish of death of another is that they have somehow come to terms with their own death. Here we see reflections of the heroic humanism referred to in chapter 1. Only the person who has heroically felt and thought himself or herself into the anguish of his or her own death in some kind of anticipation can have the courage to enter that tight place with another.

From a theological perspective this seems indeed an inadequate proposal. Freud was probably right in saying that human defenses against death are such that none of us can really imagine our own death. A more solid basis for a willingness to open oneself to suffering death with another needs to be found. (Heroic humanism, particularly as embodied in ministry, rather than overcoming the denial of death, tends to conceal it in its fullest anguish) For the pastor that basis clearly needs to emerge from a thoroughly integrated theological stance drawn from that most powerful of all Christian symbols of death, the cross. How then can a theology of the cross be appropriated in such a way as to enable both pastor and parishioner to live toward death with openness to that death-dominated future and the threat of forsakenness it holds?

Jürgen Moltmann, in his reinterpretation of a trinitarian theology of the cross, opens for us a possible avenue of faithful ministry in the situation of anguish that takes into account both the forsakenness of the dying one and the suffering with another of the pastor. In Moltmann's interpretation, the doctrine of the Trinity is a symbol pointing to the event of Jesus' death on the cross. It is an event "in God." God the Father forsakes, abandons God the Son, who becomes thereby the crucified God. (But God the Father suffers in his abandonment of Jesus to his fate.) Thus both the suffering of abandonment and the suffering of love in the act of abandoning are joined together in the event that takes place "in God" in the cross.

For Moltmann this trinitarian interpretation of the event of the Cross breaks through the traditional monotheistic view of God as the otherworldly, all-powerful God who, because he refuses to rescue the dying from their anguish, is experienced as absent or over against us.

Anyone who suffers without cause first thinks that he has been forsaken by God. God seems to him to be the mysterious, incomprehensible God who destroys the good fortune that he gave. But anyone who cries out to God in this suffering echoes the death-cry of the dying Christ, the Son of God. In that case God is not just a hidden someone set over against him, to whom he cries, but in a profound sense the human God, who cries with him and intercedes for him with his cross where man in his torment is dumb. The one who suffers is not just angry and furious and full of protest against his fate. He suffers because he lives, and he is alive because he loves. The person who can no longer love, even himself, no longer suffers, for he is without grief, without feeling and indifferent. This apathy is the sickness of our time, a sickness of person and systems, a sickness to death, to personal and universal death. But the more one loves, the more one is open and becomes receptive to happiness and sorrow. Therefore the one who loves becomes vulnerable, can be hurt and disappointed. This may be called the dialectic of human life: we live because and in so far as we love—and we suffer and die because and in so far as we love. In this way we experience life and death in love.[6]

Moltmann goes on to say that the "God of theism is poor. He cannot love nor can he suffer." But the trinitarian God who both suffers the forsakenness of the cross and the suffering in love of the Father is the God who can sustain us in our own suffering, whether that be the suffering of our death or the death of another whom we love.

This avenue opened to us by Moltmann's trinitarian interpretation of the event of the cross presents, to the pastor who can integrate that interpretation into his or her own manner of presence with the dying person, a more reliable basis for sustaining the relationship with the dying than simply one's own ability to face death. Here is presented a potentially powerful elaboration on the incarnational pastoral care tradition in which the pastoral relationship is seen as analogous to the incarnation in Jesus. Moltmann's interpretation undergirds both the pastor's identification with the suffering of forsakenness experienced by the dying person and simultaneously his "forsaking" of the dying one in that he or she must in the end walk away and leave the dying person to his or her fate.] Thus there is a peculiar ambiguity in the incarnational motif in ministry to the dying, as perhaps in ministry to all who suffer. The pastor must identify himself or herself with the suffering, the forsakenness of the other. Without that the other remains forsaken in the relationship. But in a real sense the pastor identifies himself or herself with God the Father, who loves and suffers with the other but remains outside that suffering, allows it to be, does nothing, indeed can do nothing to prevent it. The pastor's faith is that both the suffering of forsakenness and his or her own pain of having to leave the other to suffering are "in God" just as the event of the cross was "in God." Human courage is needed, to be sure, in ministry to the dying. But human courage, in and of itself, will falter. A theologically grounded stance for ministry rooted both in the human capacity to love and a thoroughly integrated theology of the cross gives the pastor firm ground on which to walk both in entering into the suffering of the dying and in walking away from that suffering, as in a real sense the pastor must.

How Am I to Suffer My Death?

Hidden in the dialogue with Mrs. L is another question with which many persons at this stage in the anguish of death must struggle. It is as if they ask of themselves and those who will listen to them, What must I do with what is happening? Sometimes this question is asked theologically: How does God expect that I should suffer death? Behind these questions lie images of the good and faithful death and the moral ought of dying bravely, with courage and faith. More often the question remains implicit in the vague, unexpressed question as to whether the person is to give in to anger and despair, become preoccupied with depression and loss, or avoid the whole business—"turn away the reproach which I dread" (Psalm 119:39).

CRISIS EXPERIENCE IN MODERN LIFE

In more articulate persons the question of how one is to die is linked to what has given meaning to life. The past is reviewed through story and memory (and thus meanings that have sustained the person in the past are brought out and tested in the fire of this most extreme of crises in finite life.) Whatever the symbols used, whatever the metaphor of communication, the question as to how one is to suffer, how the work of anguish is to be done, presses for expression and sharing that the dying person might not feel abandoned, forsaken. Persons who in one way or another find the way through that tight place of anguish begin to find an integrity in living toward death that overpowers both the wish to deny and the anger of loss. In the most profound sense such persons become open to the future of both their life and their death. Their faith takes on a quality of eschatological trust.

The resolution of the question as to how one is to suffer with integrity seems for many persons in the final stages of death to open up (a new level of concern for the welfare of significant others that moves beyond preoccupation with loss and forsakenness.) Parents express concern for what this death will mean to children and sometimes even plan for their care. Husbands and wives move both to comfort and prepare their spouses for the separation and loneliness of grief. Future scenarios without the dying one's presence are fantasized and discussed openly with a kind of selfless concern that both acknowledges the imminence of death and the ongoing life of the loved ones. One is reminded here of some other words of Jesus from the cross: "Woman behold your son. Behold your mother." (Here we see not only what Elisabeth Kübler-Ross calls acceptance, but also a quality of care for the living that the dying person may have had prior to the terminal illness but which was lost or pushed into the background by the preoccupation with the threat to selfhood contained in the narrowing boundaries.)

Mabel V. was such a person. At age forty-two she discovered a lump in her breast and was immediately scheduled for surgery by her doctor. As Mabel's friend and pastor I went to the hospital to be with her husband during the surgery. From the recovery room the word came that the surgery had been only partially successful. The cancer had extended to the lymphatic system, and cobalt therapy would be necessary to combat what appeared to be a rapidly spreading and life-threatening disease.

Mabel V. was a strong and self-reliant woman. With a salesman husband she had learned to make most of the family decisions herself as she reared three children now fourteen, twelve, and nine. Given to a rather matter-of-fact straightforwardness in her communication with others, she called me from the hospital to say that she thought she would be "needing a pastor" to cope with all she saw ahead of her. Thus began a very intense and purposeful pastoral relationship.

In the early stages Mabel vacillated between intense anguish and anger and denial of her plight. In the tightened-down moments of anguish, she expressed her profound disappointment and anger over not being able to finish the task of raising her children. Floods of anger made her call God unjust and unreasonable for making life so patently unfair. Why had she been selected for this tortured foreshortening of her hard work to fulfill her life's purpose? Her anger spilled over on some of her acquaintances who, having everything anyone could wish for, still complained and felt sorry for themselves. Long years of quietly managed anger at her largely absent husband who left her to make all the decisions now came forth as feelings of having been cheated by him and by God. At other times all these tortured feelings gave way to talk of her own ability to handle things and her wishful fantasies that the doctors were probably wrong and she would outlive everyone who now thought of her as dying. In this period my pastoral efforts were mostly directed at listening and accepting the flood of unwanted and unacceptable feelings. I agreed with her that it did seem unfair and that in no way did she seem to me to deserve what was happening to her. I also listened to the wishful fantasies of denial and told her I admired her for being a fighter who would not give up easily.

Midway in this anguished struggle to accept and cope with what was happening to her, Mabel received a letter from her mother, who lived some thousand miles away. Mabel had struggled over the question as to whether or not to tell her mother of the seriousness of her illness. The relationship between them had not been a warm and understanding one since Mabel's adolescence, when she had rebelled against her mother's religiosity and control. But finally Mabel decided that she must be honest with her mother and call her with the truth of her condition. The response was a letter in which the mother emphatically expressed her belief in faith healing. The closing paragraph of the letter read as follows: "Mabel, I believe in miracles. The miracles of Jesus followed the laws of God not man. If you will desire to be well and follow these ideas of life and living, I believe that you will demonstrate complete healing in a short time. Do as the doctor tells you but also use the power of God in you."

If Mabel had been a weaker, less self-reliant person, her mother's letter might have thrown her back into denial of her situation. Given the dynamics of that relationship, it had, however, the opposite effect. For the first time Mabel seemed fully to accept what was happening. She still suffered the anguish of loss and depression, but now her efforts began to turn toward the work to be done in preparation for her death. She began to talk realistically about the problems of leaving three children behind with a father whose work and temperament made him largely an absentee father. She began to accept that as a given in her situation. But still she wrestled with what to do about her mother. Old memories of the estrangement and difficulty of that relationship haunted her—memories which I gently encouraged her to share with me. The feelings of having been cheated by God were very tentatively linked to old feelings of having been cheated by mother and husband.

What now must Mabel do? How was she to live toward death, given the particularity of her self-understanding and her understanding of her situation? Her first resolution of that dilemma was, in spite of her now considerably weakened condition, to make the trip to see her mother to see if she could help her mother accept her impending death. Though I did not discourage her from making the trip, I tried to reflect a note of realism before her departure by reminding her that her mother had been who she was for a long time. Her response was that she knew that, but that she had to make one more try at redeeming the relationship.

Mabel returned tired and depressed. Her mother had been just as she always was. Her refusal to accept and support Mabel in her dying was beyond changing. (That relationship would have to be accepted for what it was.) Our prayer together that evening was an act of closure and commitment of the separation between mother and daughter to God's care and keeping.

One week later Mabel came for our weekly conversation with plans for carrying out the work that remained to be done before her death. She had cleaned out the closets and thrown or given things away that were hers and would no longer be needed after her death. She laid plans for placing an ad in the paper for a housekeeper who could care for the children when she became too ill to cook and do the other housework. The major qualification she would look for in applicants was ability to mother the children. She wanted to assure that for them in the first months after she was gone. The next few weeks were exhausting but satisfying ones for her. A housekeeper— "a good-hearted country woman"—had been secured. The mending of the children's clothes was getting done.

One final act of care for others remained for Mabel. She talked at length of her husband's inability to come to terms with her dying. He had returned to his traveling, saying that there would be bills that must be paid. Acceptance of her death for Mabel meant also accepting her life with Alfred. This is the way it had been, and she would act out her acceptance of that by doing for him what she could do to ease the time of her dying. She went to the funeral home, selected her casket and, accompanied only by the funeral director, went to the cemetery and selected a lot under a lonesome pine tree at the edge of a knoll overlooking a busy street. The evening she told me of what she had done we also spent a brief time talking about her funeral, which she decided she wanted to be a simple graveside service with scripture and a prayer of thanksgiving for her life. "You will know what to say, Charles. I don't have many religious questions. I believe in God and know whatever happens will be all right."

Mabel was now ready to die. The next time I saw her she was in bed and greeted me with: "You don't really need to come anymore unless you want to. Our work is done and there are others who need you more than I do." She seemed tired and distracted. Before I left she asked me to pray with her that she would die that night. I did. She lived another few days, largely sleeping peacefully.

It should be remembered that few persons will be able to struggle as openly and purposefully with all the dimensions of suffering as they move toward death as was Mabel V. Mabel's open and action-oriented style of both coming to terms with her dying and seeking pastoral help with that process were authentic expressions of her selfhood. But the basic themes of her dying will, with infinite variation, be present. The process is one of anguish with narrowing boundaries particularized by the specifics of each person's self and its situation. Pastoral ministry means being available to respond to the person as the crisis of death and anguish develops and hopefully comes to closure. Sometimes the time will be short and the process blunted. Sometimes the suffering is long and the process complicated by tangled personal and interpersonal dynamics. But in either case the task is the same. It is the task of shepherding an anguished process of movement into the tight place of death.

CHAPTER IV

Bereavement and Loss: Attachment and Separation

The logic of our paradigmatic approach to the exploration of crisis experience suggests that our study of death and anguish be followed by an in-depth examination of the human experience of bereavement and loss. In a broad sense bereavement and loss may be seen as the counterpart of death and anguish. Because persons, relationships, projects, and even cultures die, humans must constantly sustain the loss of something or someone valued as significant for their life. Time flows, and with it life cycles end, relationships are broken, and bereavements are sustained.

There are, of course, many kinds and levels of bereavement which persons experience. Bereavement comes not only with death but with all varieties of separation. Persons grow up and away from those to whom they have been attached in the bonds of family. Persons leave places, and there is the loss of a sense of place as well as the loss experienced by those who have been left behind. Relationships tear asunder; marriages end in divorce and there is loss and bereavement. In fact, one can view the entire process of the human life cycle as made up of a series of attachments and losses.

Reflection on this theme suggests that there is a double structure of bereavement and loss in human life. On the one hand, just as the narrowing boundaries of aging and death are built into human existence, so the bereavements that come with narrowing boundaries, aging, and death are structured into finite life. But intertwined with that existential structure of attachment and loss is another,⁽²⁾ humanly constructed structure of loss, that related to human choice and the inability of persons to sustain their attachments or alter them appropriately with the passage of time without sustaining bereavement and the loss or failure of relationships. At the experiential level, therefore, the structures of bereavement and loss contain a peculiar mixture of anxiety and fear having to do with coming to terms with life's inevitables, on the one hand, and guilt, hostility, and shame related to the imperfectibility of human relationships, on the other. Loss not only threatens the ultimate meaningfulness of an existence that contains inevitable bereavements, it also threatens the sense of self as able to sustain changing relationships.

Bereavement and loss, when thus viewed structurally, contain in a much more profound sense than is acknowledged in most of the psychological literature about bereavement, (the fundamental questions both of the ultimate meaningfulness of finite existence and of human freedom and desire.) The crisis of bereavement and loss is therefore to be seen as encompassing fundamental religious questions and not simply natural processes that can adequately be dealt with in psychological terms.

In order that we may examine in some depth both of these theological dimensions of the experience of separation and loss, I have chosen to divide our consideration of this theme somewhat arbitrarily into two chapters. In the present chapter we will explore the dynamics of attachment and separation as they are built into the life cycle of the family in order to uncover the way in which bereavement and loss are structured into intergenerational relationships. In chapter 5 we will pursue further the crisis of bereavement precipitated by the loss of intimate relationships through death. The two chapters belong together and pursue related aspects of the same theme of loss. Our intention will be to examine first the ways that humanly constructed styles of forming attachments affect most dramatically the quality and degree of conflict experienced in both the inevitable losses that occur as children leave home and, in some cases, when traumatic death occurs. In the following chapter we will then move into more careful consideration of the crisis of bereavement as it is commonly experienced in the loss of what we will call a "centered relationship," a relationship central to the identity of the person. In terms of pastoral theology, we will utilize this crisis to consider the way in which the management of the grieving process can profoundly affect the life of faith defined as openness to God's future activity.

Attachment, Loss, and Growth in Families

It is important to keep in mind all that has been said earlier concerning the impact of the structure of flowing time as we consider now the kinds of crises experienced by family members undergoing a sense of loss because relationships within the family must change as children grow and parents age. Just as time forces changes in persons as they adapt to the changing boundaries of the human life cycle, so time also forces changes in family relationships as the intertwined life cycles of family members interact. One useful way that has been developed by John Bowlby and others[1] to conceptualize this process of changing relationships in the family is to see it as a continuous process of attachment and loss in which old patterns of attachment to significant other persons must be given up and new patterns developed to accommodate to the changing needs of persons as they grow and age. From the very beginning of life infants must move from a physical attachment to the mother to a psychological attachment, which then must in turn be replaced by a new attachment at a higher level of maturation. As the child grows, the full dependency on the mothering figure or figures must be given up in favor of both a more autonomous sense of self and new, wider ranges of varying attachments to father, siblings, playmates, and a growing circle of significant others. Loss of old ways of attachment and development of new, more mature ways is therefore structured into human maturation from the very beginning. (Individuation and the formation of self-identity are dependent upon the individual's being able to cope satisfactorily with bereavement and loss of familiar patterns of attachment.)

While both the Bowlby studies and Erik Erikson in his explication of the Stage One dilemma of trust versus mistrust make clear that some primary and therefore to a degree determinative patterns of both attachment and coping with loss are set in early childhood, the coming to fruition and visible crisis of these patterns takes place in adolescence. This is the time of most intense struggle with giving up old attachments and forming new ones on which a life separate from parents can be built. Daily life of the adolescent is thus punctuated by small but cumulative experiences of loss and the risk of new ventures in heretofore unknown levels of adult attachment relationships.

A small incident in the life of a seventeen-year-old girl is here illustrative:

While her parents were away on a trip, K., a seventeen year old, experienced a mild but nagging soreness in her throat. With her parents absent she was pressed to deal with the illness "on her own." Her question about what to do, presented to the single young woman who was staying with K. and her sisters, brought the matter-of-fact question: "Do you have a doctor you can call if you think you need to?" The phone call brought a prescription and the suggestion from the family doctor that if the swelling in the glands in her throat persisted, K. should come in to the doctor's office for a closer examination.

A week after her parents returned K. reported to her parents that the swelling continued. For several days she continued to complain of the soreness but seemed to be waiting for her parents to "do something." Her mother commented that it probably was a lingering of the cold virus that would probably go away in a few days. Dissatisfied, K. appealed to her father. He first commented that K.'s mother didn't believe in overusing medical treatment and that she was usually right about that. He then asked if K. was worried that the swelling might be something more serious than a cold virus. K. acknowledged that she was worried, and her father suggested she go ahead then and see the doctor. "But Daddy, I don't know where his office is. You or mother have always taken me." "You can drive yourself now."

Tears of anger and frustration soon were flowing. K. withdrew to her room for a time. Later she approached her father again asking how to get to the doctor's office. He quietly said that he could take her if she really needed him to but that she was old enough now to make and keep her own medical appointments. K. did not respond directly to that comment. Rather she asked for directions to the doctor's office and later made and kept her own appointment, even though it meant venturing for the first time into the center of the city in the family car by herself.

Here we see how the daily life of the adolescent is pervaded by small but highly significant experiences of loss of old patterns of attachment to home and parents and the frightening but necessary and even desired venture of trying new ways of utilizing attachment relationships to get one's needs met. These transitions are, of course, fraught with the possibility of failure, power struggle, and anger simply because the person is in process both of letting go and losing, on the one hand, and of trying new and unfamiliar ways of relating, on the other.

Not only must the patterns of childhood dependency on parental guidance of behavior be transformed into patterns of self-chosen behavior, but the primary allegiances to home and family must be replaced by new ties on a different level of intimacy and mutual compatability. If the cycle of generations is to continue, a new household must be formed and the relative independence so newly won from parental loyalties must be transmuted into the obligation and commitment of marriage and parenthood. Adolescence can thus be understood as a time of profound transition marked by bereavement and loss as childish things are put away and life on one's own is taken up.

But this critical time of transition must be understood also from the perspective of the parents and their bereavement. A marriage is formed by a process of two persons leaving their families of origin, with the losses that entails, and forming a new attachment that inevitably is entered into in part to replace or correct the patterns of attachment of the parental home. The style of that marital relationship will therefore be heavily influenced both by the kind of attachment the individual had with his or her parents and the way in which the separation (loss) was handled in their leaving home. Ways of letting go of children tend to be passed on from generation to generation in families, just as styles of intense family attachment tend to be transmitted intergenerationally.

The roots of many problems we see in young marriages are to be found in these intergenerationally transmitted patterns of dealing with attachment and loss, integrating and letting go in the families of origin of the two spouses. Likewise, the problems which a given couple will experience in regulating the quality of attachment they have with their children and the degree and quality of conflict when they in turn must let go of their children will to a considerable extent be influenced by the long-range intergenerational patterns a given family has developed.

Grace M., a thirty-four-year-old black mother of four presented herself and her family to a community mental health center because she felt she "could no longer handle" her oldest child, a boy of fifteen. The younger children were another boy, twelve, and girls, ten and seven. The younger son was described by the mother as a "good boy" who could be trusted to do his school work and "look after" his younger sisters. The two girls, shy at first in the family evaluation session, later began to twinkle and volunteer information about family relationships—most particularly their concern over their mother's drinking problem. Fred, the oldest, was *the* "problem" as far as everyone was prepared to tell, including Fred. He and his mother had recently begun having uproarious fights over his friends, his truancy, and his experimentation with pot and alcohol.

The absent father in this family had been driven away in a fight with Grace, his departure coming after she threatened him with a knife. Fred, who bore his father's name, was still deeply loyal to his father and visited him regularly at the rooming house where the father now lived.

An intergenerational family chart, drawn by the evaluating therapist on newsprint taped to the wall as the family talked about the extended family network, revealed, among other things, that Grace had run away from home at fourteen after having a series of quarrels and "cuss fights" with her mother. She had lived first with her grandmother and then an aunt before marrying her husband at nineteen. One of her quarrels with her mother had to do with the desirability of a job to support her family versus the security of welfare. The mother, a long-time welfare recipient, objected strongly when Grace applied for and landed a job at a local motor assembly plant just a few months before the serious problems with Fred began. Grace expressed great pride in the job, saying she was the only woman who had been able to handle it, according to her supervisor. On the other hand, she had great anxiety about the job and all her responsibilities, wondering aloud if she could really make it on her own.

Many things could be said about the problems of Grace M. and her children, but for purposes of our consideration of attachment and loss in families, it is useful to note the similarity between the struggle Grace was having with her oldest as he approached the age when he wanted to be on his own and the struggle Grace had with her mother. Grace wondered aloud in the evaluation session if she were trying to drive Fred off as had her mother with her when she was about his age. Patterns of attachment by means of tight control and rebellion as a style of separation seemed firmly established in this family)Grace spoke tenderly of her younger children, who remained strongly attached to her and expressed deep frustration that this kind of attachment no longer seemed viable with Fred. Observing, one sensed that Grace, despite her staunch pride in her own independence, longed for someone on whom she could depend as she attempted to force her children to depend on her. On the other hand, she candidly admitted that she no longer permitted her mother to come into her house, so thick were the walls of separation between them.

Fred, while admitting that he fought with his mother, seemed sad and depressed as the evaluation proceeded. On having his sadness acknowledged, Fred agreed that he was troubled and spoke of missing his father. Bereavement and loss lay just under the surface of his angry, defiant behavior. He hinted that he blamed his mother for his loss of a father and complained vaguely that he resented her expectations that he be the man of the house.

(Themes of highly conflicted attachment and wrenching separation and loss of deep dependency bonds are readily apparent in Grace and her family.)Observing the attractive and relatively happy faces of the younger children, one could not help wondering if the attachments in this family were not very close and lovingly satisfying so long as the children remained dependent and close to the mother. It was when Fred began to separate himself that trouble began both for him and his mother. One wonders if the troublesome conflicts will not again be repeated with the younger children as they approach the age when their mother had wrenched herself loose from her strong and dominant mother, though one could speculate that the patterns of separation adopted by the younger children will be altered as they profit from the negative experience of their older brother.

If our intergenerational analysis is accurate, then we

are presented in Grace's family with an eloquently suggestive example of the way in which the structures of bereavement and loss which are built into the processes of change that come inevitably with growth and maturation are intertwined with the complications of these processes brought about by human failure, idiosyncrasy, and choice. Furthermore, these complications are not simply the result of the here-and-now behavior choices and coping patterns of the present generation family members. Rather, present attachment relationship styles and concommitant characteristic styles of separation evident in one generation of a given family are deeply embedded in intergenerational styles of dealing with attachment and loss that to a greater or lesser degree can be observed in three or more generations. The fact that a given nuclear family is formed by the bringing together of two often quite disparate family styles serves to complicate the ongoing process of family myths and traditions concerning how relationships and their inevitable changes are to be managed.[2]

A Typology of Family Attachment and Separation Styles

The chart in Figure 9 presents in skeleton form a typology of styles of attachment in family relationships which I have developed to assist me in thinking both descriptively and normatively about how styles of attachment and separation affect family relationships as children mature and begin the process of leaving home. The chart also suggests a typology of what we will call time orientations to indicate ways in which families of various types tend to be oriented toward certain attitudes relative to time.

Type I Families

Type I families are marked by attachment styles that can best be described as symbiotic. To say that these families are closely knit does not express strongly enough the manner in which members of these families become fused to one another. Type I mothers tend from very early to communicate to their children that the child's survival depends upon his or her remaining attached to the mother in such a way as to be primarily an extension of the mother. Individuation is blocked in the child, as much because the mother needs the child as an extension of herself as the child is taught to need the mother's protection. Thus a pattern of clinging in order to survive and fear of the child's growing need to differentiate himself or herself and become separate develops. These mothers are typically overanxious and solicitous of their child's welfare, seeking to protect and shield the child from the inevitable pain and struggle for growth. The child learns from very early that the world is a potentially dangerous place from which only mother's care provides protection. Both mother and child begin to fear loss and change and to avoid situations that require a more adventurous, testing-of-limits attitude on the part of both mother and child. (Fathers in these families tend to be either weak and dependent on their wives themselves or quite uninvolved with their children. Alcoholic and/or absent fathers are not atypical.)

But the passage of time, physical growth, and social mores bring even these children to the time when they must begin the process of separation. With school age comes the societal requirement that they must leave home for a time each day and fend for themselves in a world mother does not control. School phobias and frequent absences because of illness are common with Type I children. The more shy and passive child will often seek a substitute object for his or her need to cling while away from mother. Sometimes such a substitute relationship with a teacher or friend provides a bridge to the larger world of relationships apart from mother. Not infrequently the substitute relationship will take on many of the same clinging, symbiotic characteristics as the

ATTACHMENT	SEPARATION

I. Symbiosis
   The life-or-death
    attachment
   Individuation blocked
   Typical behaviors:
    "I cannot live without
    you, and you cannot
    live without me."
    "I must know not only
    what my child is
    doing, but what my
    child is thinking."
    "It is not safe away
    from my parents."
	Rebellion or Panic
	   "To leave is like tearing
	    myself out by my roots."
	Typical behaviors:
	   School phobias
	   Attachment to a sub-
	    stitute
	   Running away
	   Rebellious symbolic
	    acts
	   Anorexia nervosa

II. Mutual Dependency (a
    Less Severe Form of
    Symbiosis)
   Typical behaviors:
    The mother who
    needs her children
    to depend on her
    and they take her for
    granted
    The father who buys
    his children's affec-
    tion with money or
    permissiveness.
   Oversolicitousness
	Reluctant Autonomy
	   Difficulty leaving home
	
	Typical behaviors:
	   Early marriage to parent
	    substitute
	   Delayed adolescence
	   Parentification

III. Mutual Control
    Attachment and con-
    trol of behavior
    become syn-
    onomous.
   Typical behaviors:
    Authority struggles
    Conflict over hours,
    limits, friends, etc.
    Relationship seen as
    either dominance or
    submission
	Manipulation to Get the
	   Other to Set the Self Free
	   "If my parents would just
	    quit telling me what to do
	    . . ."
	   "If Johnny (or Susie) would
	    only be more responsible
	    . . ."
	
	Typical behaviors:
	   Acting to get a reaction
	   Reactive new relationships

Bereavement in Family Process

BEREAVEMENT	TIME ORIENTATION
Refusal to Accept Loss as Part of Life Clinging Helplessness Denial of love Fighting	Past and its Perpetuation
Resistance to Acceptance of Loss and Change as Part of Life Covert dependency New relationships hampered by blocked grief Resistance to mature responsibility	Past and Present and Their Confusion
Loss and Change Fought Over and Fought For Grief disguised as negativity	Present and Future and Their Mutual Exclusiveness

Figure 9 (cont.)   **Styles of Attachment, Separation, and**

ATTACHMENT	SEPARATION
IV. Developing Mature Mutuality The process of separation and individuation is not only accepted, but nurtured. Typical behaviors: Activity growth oriented Joy taken in developing adult to adult sharing and mutual responsibility	Negotiation of Freedom A process of moving through developmental stages toward autonomous relationship for the pleasure and responsibility of sharing in mutual concerns. Constant restructuring of expectations and responsibility. New relationships have their own intrinsic worth.

relationship learned so well at home. In more extreme cases, such psychosomatic "solutions" as anorexia nervosa (inability to eat and retain food) will appear which symbolically express (both the desperate need for separation and the deathly fear of it)

More aggressive, angrily dependent children will attempt to wrench themselves loose from the symbiotic relationship with behavior at home or at school marked by rebellious hostility, demandingness, and other predominantly negative behavior. As adolescence approaches, these children must try more and more explosive and sometimes even violent means of separating themselves from home and mother's protection, often doing so in ways that covertly invite the parents' intervention to "save" them from a situation they have created with some outside system such as the schools or courts. For some the only way to separate is to run away.

As is readily apparent from what has been said of Type I families, recognizable crisis sometimes does not appear until early or middle adolescence, though for some, school and behavior problems in children precipitate a

BEREAVEMENT	TIME ORIENTATION
Loss and Change Recognized and Welcomed	Past, Present, Future in Their Wholeness and Open-ended Process *(flow into each other)*

crisis at an earlier time. (But for all such families crisis experience hovers in the background from early in the family life cycle as the struggle over losing the earliest relationships of mutual attachment between mother and child begins.)

In all these Type I families there appears to be a virtual war with change, growth, and the expanding world of the child's future. The safe ways of infantile mother-child relationships must be perpetuated, even at the cost of blockage of growth and separation processes in the child. It is as if what we are calling the built-in bereavements of maturation must be denied and the loss of past patterns of attachment prevented at all costs. But, of course, the child must, sooner or later, break out of the symbiotic relationship, either with violence, rebellion, fighting and the denial of love, or with substitute objects for his or her clinging and helplessness.

Reflecting in the framework of our theological stance taken from the theologies of hope, we can see Type I families as wittingly or unwittingly caught in a pattern of refusal or failure to trust the promises of God concerning his presence and activity in the future. Future and danger are synonymous. The faithful life is the life lived in the safety of childlike dependence on one's earthly parents. Absent is any genuine sense of hope in the future which is experienced as containing only potential danger and loss. All bereavements, even the bereavement of losing one's child in order to gain a maturing son or daughter are, most often unconsciously, experienced as life-threatening to both parent and child. Innovation, openness to the future, and novelty in human life are fraught with great anxiety. Insofar as faith in God is sought, it is sought to provide safety, stability, and security rather than change or growth.

Crisis ministry to such families, while extremely difficult, is most beneficial when in very concrete and specific ways it is focused on helping parents to accept the reality of separation of children from parents as they grow and mature, and encourages children to venture more responsibly and autonomously on their own. The fears of loss and danger need to be aired and recognized as resistance to the flow of life's unfolding with its new opportunities for altered, more satisfying and promising levels of relationship between parents and maturing children. Family conferences which recognize the needs of the parents for assurance of responsible, trustworthy behavior on the part of the child as well as the needs of the child as he or she tests abilities to make choices and self-manage behavior will most often be the best structure for pastoral care and counseling with such families. The more severe Type I families will more than likely need referral to a family-counseling or children's services agency, since deeply entrenched Type I patterns will most often require more intensive and time-consuming therapeutic help than the pastor is prepared to give. Type I attachment and separation patterns can, however, be to a great extent prevented and meliorated by sensitive pastoral work focused on support of risk-taking and trusting of the future of children's growth and maturation. Working with such families within a pastoral frame of reference that sees their struggles as containing the frightened, desperate effort to stave off life's inevitable rhythm of attachment and loss, bereavement and new relationship, the pastor can give concrete expression to a theology of hope and future.

Type II Families

Type II families are those who tend to exhibit a less severe form of symbiosis we will call mutual dependency. While the relationship between mother and child is less totally binding than in Type I families, yet a perpetuation of mutually dependent patterns marks the process of growth of children and separation from parents. In these families mother tends to become the caretaker whom everyone takes for granted as the one who can always be counted on to put the needs of the children ahead of any other priority in her life. Her whole life tends to be wrapped up in seeing that her children have all the advantages that can be provided. Whether it be doing the laundry, seeing that the children's homework is done on time, or driving the car pool, mother provides what is needed. The result is that these children tend to take mother and her care for granted and only reluctantly and slowly develop ways of expressing their own need for separation and autonomy. Mothers in this group tend to encourage their children to try new things and excel in school. For whose sake and out of whose desire the accomplishments of the children are to be attained, however, remains at best ambiguous.

Fathers in Type II families vary considerably in their pattern of relating to their children. Some Type II fathers are highly achievement oriented and encourage their children to be likewise, while covertly they may be deeply dependent on their spouses to provide the strokes of encouragement and care they need in order to achieve success in the world. Some Type II fathers have great need for admiration and affection and may tend to purchase the affection of their children by overindulgence of their wants and permissiveness in regard to their behavior. Other Type II fathers are distant and largely unavailable to their children, leaving their care to the mother, who must then face the growth and "giving up" of her children without the helpful counterpoint of a fathering authority in the home and the affection she needs from a husband to enable her to need less affection from her children as they grow away from her.

From these brief descriptions of Type II family relationships one could anticipate that the style of separation that tends to develop in these families as the children reach adolescence is best described as reluctant autonomy. These are the children who will have difficulty leaving home, often returning several times even after months away before finally being able to establish themselves on their own. Adolescence, with its tentativeness and indecision about "who I want to be" and "what I want to do," tends to be extended well into the twenties in these families. Sometimes the difficulty in separating will be impulsively resolved by an early marriage to someone who, more than anything else, provides a kind of substitute parent relationship. (Parentification—here defined as the term is used in family therapy to mean the covert reversal of generational roles so that children are remaining close to home and parents in order to take care of them—is not uncommon in Type II families.)

The style of coping with the built-in bereavement of family maturation in Type II families is marked by the same reluctance that we observed in relation to autonomy. Loss and change are commonly accepted verbally but resisted covertly as patterns of mutual dependency are perpetuated beyond the time of usual separation. New relationships on the part of both parents and children tend to be hampered by the unresolved grief and disappointment that the close-knit family of earlier times cannot be perpetuated. Mature responsibility for self as well as for new relationships of commitment and obligation come slowly for these children, a reluctance that is matched by the parents' difficulty in letting go.

Time orientation in Type II families tends to be flavored with vague confusion between past and present. Nostalgia for times past "when the whole family was together" colors the reluctant effort to deal with present reality and changing relationships. While lip service may be given to anticipation of radically changed family relationships and a return to the two-member family, there remains a certain confusion of desire relative to time and the changes it brings.

Type II families generally will not come to the pastor's attention as families in crisis unless and until some critical situation arises as the time approaches when one or more children must ultimately leave home and become more fully autonomous. Conflict may arise over choice of marriage partner, vocation, or place of residence. Children may get stuck at the point of not being able to survive economically or emotionally away from the parental home, and a crisis develops as parents become aware that they have an adult dependent on their hands. But even where no highly visible crisis occurs, the pastor would do well to consider these families as involved in a quiet situation of prolonged bereavement and grief as children move into middle and late adolescence. Opportunities need to be provided for airing the feelings of loss and anxiety about the future that parents in these families experience. Family conferences, small group discussions with other parents, and pastoral support all can be useful to these parents, enabling them to discuss their ambivalent feelings about losing their children, think through their changing roles in relation to their children, and find new interests and relationships.

One of the common crises growing out of Type II styles of family attachment is that of depression in the middle years, most often on the part of the mother who is losing her children. When the mother's whole life has been involved in fulfilling the needs of children and home-making, she can become overwhelmed by a great sense of emptiness, uselessness, and loss as the children begin to send signals that they not only do not need but perhaps resent her continuing care. This is particularly possible with mothers who have successful or otherwise occupied husbands whose parental losses are cushioned by continuing job responsibilities in which others are dependent upon them. We are only beginning to realize the injustice done to many women in the past because of the sharp division of family responsibilities between the husband breadwinner and the wife housekeeper. Cultural value changes have added to the discomfiture of many of these women with the rising cultural expectation that women should have a career outside the home. Type II mothers can then begin to feel the double condemnation of not being needed at home and not having a useful skill in the outside working world. (Depression, blocked grief over the loss of a meaningful, identity-giving role, and hidden resentment over having been taken for granted or her husband's escape to work will be the result.)

In acute cases of Type II family bereavement such as we have described, the pastor will want to consider not only some extended pastoral counseling with the depressed, bereaved mother or, in more severe cases, referral to a competent psychotherapist, but also the possibility of family conferences with the entire family in order that the family's participation in the mother's grief process may be acknowledged and responsibility for the changing family situation shared. Without such family involvement in the grieving process, mother can be scapegoated by being identified as the person with the problem, whereas the truth is that the entire family is caught in a mutually dependent process of which mother is now the visible victim.

Type III Families

Whereas Type II families may be imaged as caught in the stickiness of human need and capacity for warmth and mutually dependent care, Type III families are those who from very early fight for control of a family situation experienced as lacking in warmth and care. Type III families tend to be preoccupied with deep hungers for greater family intimacy that is felt to be frustrated by the failure of various family members to behave as they should. Thus attachment and control of behavior of other family members tends to become synonymous. While these patterns emanate from parental needs for tight control over the husband's behavior by the wife and the wife's by the husband, the children learn very early to play the family game of solving problems and conflicts by getting the other person to do what you want them to do. Relationships within the family tend to be seen as either involving dominance and control of one by the other or as being submissive to the dominance of someone experienced as stronger, whose approval one must earn by conformity to that person's wishes.

Type III families tend to be preoccupied with exact descriptions of "right behavior," blame placing when things inevitably go wrong, and rules by which family members are to govern their behavior. Some Type III families are quite paternalistic, with father's word being taken as the law of the household. More frequently in recent years, the role of family lawmaker is played by mother either directly or by her management of the father's authoritarian relationship with the children. Older children tend to dominate younger children; one child tends to be pitted against other children by open comparisons of conformity to behavioral expectations, and thus competitiveness is added to the conflict among family members over who did what when and who was to blame. Behavior of children is most often managed by a system of rewards and punishments. Children are expected to grow in ability to take responsibility as they mature but in more or less tightly prescribed ways that keep them under the tight rein of parental control. Type III families thus tend to live by the law and the righteousness of their works!

As might be expected, the maturation of children in Type III families tends to be fraught with the appearance of authority struggles of all kinds with much family conflict over hours to be kept, household chores to be done, friends to be chosen, and other limits on behavior. Freedom, while increasingly longed for by adolescent children, tends to be seen only as something to be granted or withheld by whoever is in control of the family system. For that reason the style of separation typical of these families involves much manipulation and bargaining in order to get the head of the household, acknowledged or more covert, to grant the freedom that has been withheld. Children in these families will tend to find children of other Type III families with whom to ally themselves in their rebellion or efforts to get the restrictions on their behavior lifted. Separation must always be accomplished in some sense against the parents' wishes. Mutual "if only you would" accusations are the daily stuff of parent-child communication. Acts are committed in order to obtain either a desired reaction or to demonstrate that the undesirable behavior will inevitably follow from the other. New relationships tend to be formed as reactions against what children feel to be oppressive relationships with their parents.

In more healthy Type III families the attachment-separation process is managed by the parents, as one parent put it in a family workshop, "by holding a tight rein until it is time to turn loose completely." Even in these families the separation is therefore accomplished at the initiative and decision of the parent, who must remain in control to the last moment until it is time to let go.

That Type III families struggling to control or get free from the control of one another are experiencing loss and bereavement is usually not readily apparent. These families seem so locked to each other by the ties of control and conflict that, sitting in a family conference with them, the pastor can find himself or herself wishing that he or she could help them separate from one another. [If children are still in the preteen or early teen-age developmental stages the pastor will often have feelings of wanting to side with and support parents who are struggling with their children who threaten to become unmanageable. If the children are older the pastor may have the urge to side with the youngster and help him or her in the fight for freedom. Though either of these pastoral responses may in some cases be appropriate and even useful, seeing the family conflict as a process of grief and loss disguised as negativity in which the built-in inevitabilities of separation and change are being fought and fought over will help the pastor to see particular behavioral manifestations in a larger context and thus prevent him or her from getting caught up in the family pattern of accusation, counter-accusation, and blame placing.]

Type III families seem caught up in a peculiar war with the passage of time. Children seem to experience the present as preventing them from realizing their future, while parents fight to hang on to the present for as long as possible. Both seem to recognize that at some future time the family attachments must change, but that time is not yet and when it is to come must be fought over and argued. [Thus present and future are experienced as mutually exclusive and in conflict rather than as an open-ended process that can flow smoothly as change is embraced and separation and altered attachments accepted.]

Crisis will become visible in Type III families most often at those times in the family life cycle when the control of family process and behavioral standards is being either directly or indirectly challenged by one or more of the children or when disagreement over behavior management of children between the parents becomes intolerable. Frequently crisis appears when the oldest child, unable to win the struggle for freedom with the parents, acts out the conflict by getting in trouble with the authorities at school or in the community by truancy, petty thievery, or other delinquent or borderline delinquent behavior that in some way flaunts behavioral limits. Sometimes it erupts when the continuing family conflict evokes a family row that becomes visible when one or another family member, most often one of the parents, seeks out the pastor as an outside source of authority or assistance in restoring the family order. In these cases the pastor who listens to the complaining family member will often hear direct or indirect expressions of conflict between the parents over management of the children, blame placing, or other efforts to involve the pastor in the family's style of managing attachment and separation.

A pastoral decision will need to be made as to whether to allow oneself to be "triangled" into the family or marital conflict or whether to remain an outside resource to consult with the parents or the entire family as they struggle through their family crisis. Pastors need to keep in mind that changing a family style of controlling attachments to a more open, mutually supportive style is a long and difficult process to be undertaken only when the pastor or another professional helper has the time and skills to assist a family in making profound changes in their style of attachment to one another. Short of that, family interventions designed either to help the parents get the family situation back under control or, in some cases, to support an older child in separating from the family are often the only realistic possibilities.

Type IV Families

In developing the typology of family styles of attachment and separation as we have been describing them, it has probably become apparent that up to this point we have been emphasizing the negative, inhibiting qualities in Type I, II, and III styles of relating. This is, of course, not to say that everything about these styles of family attachment is bad or morally reprehensible. Rather it has been our purpose to highlight ways in which family styles of attachment develop out of a particular stance relative to the inevitable passage of time and the built-in bereavements of the human life cycle. What we have described are more or less "pure" types. Most families will fall somewhere between these types or manifest mixed patterns of two or more types.

It has also been our purpose to introduce in the typology a normative concern. Pastoral care can never be based simply on descriptive categories without serious attention to ways of constructing human relationships that comport with Christian norms as to how human relationships ought to be managed. The pastor's work must always represent a posture with regard to what finally is creative and supportive of human life and what is destructive or antithetical to the standards of the gospel.

From such a theological perspective the most fundamental problem with the styles of attachment and separation thus far examined is clearly that they tend to cling to the attachments of the past, distrust the flow of human development as persons move toward the future of their individual and corporate family life cycles, and express a stubborn human need to control and fixate patterns of attachment to prevent the losses that realistically are inevitable in life as we know it. One could say that the fundamental stance of Types I, II, and III is mistrusting of God's promises that, amid change and the unknown of time's flow, God will continue to be at work. Rather these families seem caught in attempts to preserve something that was experienced as good in family relationships of the past and/or preventing something from happening that threatens to alter the tenuous balance in family relationships as they now exist. In either case they become caught in styles of attachment that stand against the flow of human development and the changes that must come as separations are made and new and different attachments are formed.

Type IV families, on the other hand, are those families that seem somehow able to trust the human development processes that carry families into an unknown future of constantly changing relationships. There is both a clear and certain warmth and caring about this style of attachment and a certain looseness or acceptance of the need for constant change and formation of new, less dependent, less "managed" or controlled structures of parent-child attachment. The process of developing separation of children from parents and development of individuated identities in both parents and children is not only accepted, but nurtured and prized. The delicate balance between discipline and boundary setting, on the one hand, and encouragement of venturing and testing of limits, on the other, is monitored by the parents with the clear intention of fostering growth both in the developing of powers and competencies of the child and in the exercise of responsible and autonomous choice. Joy and delight are taken in the children's developing capacity for more mature mutuality with both peers and adults rather than parental pleasure being derived from either keeping the children immature and dependent or under the parents' tight control. As the children enter adolescence these parents tend to foster open-ended discussion of the realistic problems of living encountered by teen-agers as they explore and experiment in the larger world of relationships away from parents rather than prescribing specific standards of behavior and restricting choice.

The style of separation in Type IV families can best be described as mutual negotiation of increasing degrees of freedom—the children from parental control and dependency and the parents from full responsibility and care for the children. A process of movement through stages of relative freedom and self-direction toward a mutually pleasurable and responsible adult-to-adult relationship in which common concerns for the welfare each for the other becomes the norm is actively fostered. This means that expectations of children and of parents are constantly being restructured and renegotiated. Parents in Type IV families seem better able to trust to the point of almost taking for granted the processes of mutual identification that have gone on and continue to go on between children and their parents—a process in which children model after their parents and parents are reshaped by what they experience with their children. It is as if a certain promise had been made to both parents and children that, come what may in the open-endedness of a constantly changing future, that which is recognizable as family identity, values, and fundamental life style will be preserved and fulfilled. Certainly bereavements and losses of old and comfortable patterns of mutual attachment will be sustained and painful separations will come as children move away from the center of home and family. But the promise of new, more mutually mature relationships allows these changes and losses to be sustained without rupture or fundamental conflict that cannot be transcended.

Strange as it may seem, the pastor may find himself or herself being utilized more on an informal basis by families tending toward Type IV as a resource person to assist them in negotiating the inevitable minor crises that occur in all families with growing children than he or she will with families tending toward other types. Whereas Types I, II, and III families tend to be defensive and protective of their privately kept family secrets and conflicts, Type IV families will be more open and accepting of the understanding that family life process will involve problems and crisis times for which help may be sought from a trusted pastor friend. Ordinarily an approach to these requests for help that takes advantage of the openness of these families to discussion of feelings and different points of view, negotiation of new covenants of relationship, and realistic facing of change will be most beneficial. (An approach that emphasizes family pathology or focuses on some designated family member who manifests "the problem" will be less apt to assist Type IV families in working through the crisis in a manner that builds on their strengths as an open, growing constellation of individuals evolving new structures of attachment and separation with one another.)

Type IV families in their time orientation seem more able to value all three modes of time: past, present, and future. There is a certain wholeness and expectation that life is an open-ended process moving out of the past through the present and into the future that these families seem better able to trust than do Types I, II, and III families.

From the perspective of the theologies of hope, Type IV families may be said to have, at least implicitly and experientially, an eschatological trust in the total process of ongoing history and the movement of time, particularly as that process is being expressed in the unfolding development of this family and its individual members. The implicit faith of these families is not in some ordered life that must be maintained despite the contingencies and changes of ongoing life. Rather the implicit faith is in the unfolding process that is taking us into an unknown future. This comes close to Pannenberg's definition of faith as "the entrusting of ourselves to that power of the future which we are persuaded is trustworthy."[3] Whether or not that faith is explicitly articulated or connected to a specifically Christian theological orientation is another question to be asked concerning each individual family. The experiential basis for such a faith is, however, clearly rooted insofar as family life is concerned in Type IV styles of family attachment and separation.

Pastoral care of Type IV families presents in an interesting and significant way the question of the distinction between implicit and explicit faith and the relevance of that question for the work of pastoral care. One can observe, of course, that there are those persons and families whose lived life is an implicit expression both of a faith in the ultimate meaningfulness of things and a confident trust in the worthwhileness of the processes of life and changing human relationships, though there may be little evidence of a well articulated, intellectually appropriated faith being expressed. On the other hand, there are those persons whose more openly verbalized, explicit faith is contradicted by the mistrust and anxiety of their lived life. Pastoral care may then be understood as the effort to relate to persons in ways that assist them in developing their trust in the power of God to work for their good in the open-ended future at both implicit and explicit levels. Mature faith will evidence a degree of congruence between the implicit faith of lived life and relationships, on the one hand, and explicit, affirmed belief, on the other. Persons and families who do not evidence implicit faith must receive ministry at that experiential level before the language of explicit faith can be expected to empower them to live with trust toward their future. But even those persons and families whose lived life evidences implicit faith need ministry that helps them give significance to what they experience, so that their faith implicitly evident in their experience may be given expression and intentionality.

Here comes into view the manner in which the three theological modes of pastoral care methodology discussed in chapter 1 can each meaningfully be appropriated by the pastor who is sensitive to the level of faith functioning in the individual or family under consideration. Each of the three modes (pastoral proclamation through direct use of traditional biblical language, incarnationally modeled pastoral relationship, and pastoral search for signs and symbols of God's activity in life experience) has its appropriate function. The mode of pastoral care needs, however, to be adapted to meet the level of functioning faith evident in the individual or family at a given point in time and life process. Moreover, our analysis of family attachment and loss does suggest a certain priority to the process of engendering what we have called implicit faith. Without that level of faith experience, explicit affirmations tend to fall on deaf ears or to fail in empowering trust in God's promise for the future. Without, however, the eventual articulation or making explicit of that level of trust, fully mature faith that can be shared and given significance by the persons involved does not seem possible.

Considered from the standpoint of implicit and explicit faith, pastoral care may be seen as a developing hermeneutical dialogue in which what is implicit in the life stance of both pastor and parishioner and in the relationships under consideration is increasingly revealed, made explicit, and taken up for reconsideration. The sharing of both implicit and explicit levels of faith as trust (or mistrust) "of ourselves to that power of the future" is central to that process.[4]

Type IV families will by virtue of their implicit faith stance that is trusting of life process and open to the future, be more open to reception of an interpretation of God's providence as the fulfillment of his promise on an open-ended and radically contingent future. They are more open to eschatological trust. Families of Types I, II, and III, on the other hand, will tend to cling to a grasp of providence that assures them of continuity with the familiar and more tightly structured styles of attachment of the past.

Two incidents of ministry to different sets of parents, both of whom had tragically lost a teen-age son in an automobile accident, are illustrative of the profound difference in the way in which the concept of God's providential care is appropriated.

George and Betty Jones were called by the police to inform them that their son had been "badly hurt" in an accident on the motorcycle he rode to school at the county junior college. Upon arriving at the hospital they were met by the physician in the emergency clinic who attended their son and one of the chaplains of the hospital. Gently but matter-of-factly they were told by the doctor that their son was dead, having suffered massive head injuries in a head-on collision with an automobile. Mrs. Jones at first refused to believe what the doctor said, responding, "He will be all right, won't he?" Mr. Jones' first response was one of bitter anger: "I told him those cycles weren't safe!" Later, as the realization of what had happened began to dawn upon both parents, they wept bitterly. "How could God do this to us? He was a good boy and he was ours. We tried to protect him, but he would not be careful. God gave him to us. How could God take him away from us? He was our whole life, him and his sister."

The pastor's responses to George and Betty Jones were limited to brief words encouraging them to express to God what they were feeling: their anger with God and their bitter disappointment over their loss. He sensed that this was a family where there had been much struggle over the son's developing rebellious, reckless life-style as a teen-ager. He also sensed their guilt over having been unable to protect their son from danger and death. He attempted to respond to their bewilderment and covert anger over what they perceived to be the failure of God's providence to protect their child and them from their grief.

John and Sybil Rogers received a call late at night from the emergency clinic in a nearby city informing them that their son, age 19, had been badly hurt in an automobile accident along with several other college friends with whom he had been riding after a fraternity party. Before leaving by car for the hospital John called their pastor, asking if he would accompany the Rogers on their hurried trip. In the two hours it took to get to the hospital both John and Sybil expressed their grief and terrible fear over what had happened and talked openly of the question of their son's possible death. Tears were shed, but there were also long periods of thoughtful silence. The pastor was asked to pray for God's strength to enable John and Sybil to face whatever the end of the journey would bring.

Upon arrival at the hospital it was learned that Hank, though still alive, was not expected to live more than a few hours because of the extent of his head injuries. Hank lived an additional sixteen hours, during which time John, Sybil, and the pastor waited for what inevitably would happen. During that time, though the deep grief and loss continued to be expressed openly, much of the conversation dwelt upon the utter unpredictableness of human life, its uncertainty and mystery. "When you have kids, you take a gamble," John said. "You care for your kids and you let them go. The chances of their survival are sure not 100 percent. God didn't make life a sure thing." Sybil spoke several times of her gratitude for having such a fine son for as long as she did. "We had let him go on his own, and now we must let him go. We still have Tom [Hank's younger brother], but we must be careful not to make him make up for Hank's loss." The pastor and John at one point talked at length about the problem of theodicy, with John in simple terms affirming his faith in God despite what seemed such a meaningless, chance incident as had happened to their son.

Reflecting on these two incidents of parental grief, one is impressed with the radical difference in the crisis experience of these parents because of factors of both implicit and explicit faith. The Jones' grief is greatly complicated by their dismay that God had not seen fit to protect their son as they had tried to protect him. Anger, guilt, and bewilderment make their grief doubly painful. We can speculate that a family attachment and separation style marked by characteristics of Types II and III provide the experiential background in which their threatened loss of faith now takes place.

John and Sybil Rogers on the other hand, give evidence of Type IV family attachment and separation styles. Their grief, though deeply painful, lacks the bitterness, the utter dismay of the Jones' reaction. Their implicit and explicit faith seems oriented toward drawing strength from God to meet the reality of what is happening to them. Their grief is somehow cleaner, less marred by confused and contradictory feelings thrust into the situation out of the conflicts of the family attachment-separation style. They seem more genuinely open to facing and receiving God's promise for the future. Their grief is painful, but it is not hopeless.

The cases of George and Betty Jones and John and Sybil Rogers bring into full view the two aspects of the crisis of separation and loss with which we began our exploration at the beginning of this chapter. Separation and loss are built into human existence both in terms of the developmental process with its inevitable changes in human attachments and finally in the experience of loss of persons central to our existence as persons through death. Moreover, that existential experience is, for most if not all persons, greatly complicated and made more painful by the development of family styles of attachment and separation and the accompanying private meanings and emotions these relationships have attached to them. The work of bereavement, particularly as it relates to losses by death involves suffering with and working through the pain of both these aspects of separation and loss. It is to this process that we now turn our attention in the next chapter.

relational

loss thru death

CHAPTER V

Bereavement and Loss: Creative and Destructive Grief

The most common usage in speaking of bereavement by death is to refer to these situations as "the loss of a loved one." This euphemism is most often used to differentiate the bereavements suffered in the loss of a spouse or family member from other, supposedly less significant persons such as colleagues, business associates, neighbors, and acquaintances. Though that differentiation is in general an accurate one, for our purpose of more careful analysis of the crisis of bereavement we perhaps need a more exact designation. Let us then speak of centered relationships and the process of working through grief caused by the loss through death of any centered relationship.

A centered relationship is any relationship central to the meaning of who one is as a person, a relationship in which one's identity is centered. For most people this includes spouse and other members of the nuclear and, in varying degrees, extended family. But centered relationships may well include close associates in profession or business, neighborhood or church group. Persons draw their identity from those by whom they are identified, and in that way, as we commonly say, persons in whom our lives are centered become part of us. These relationships are central to us, and our lives are in a very deep-rooted way centered in them. To lose such a person, be he or she family member or old enemy, is to lose part of one's self, a meaning central to one's identity.

The Dialectics of Identity

The concept of centered relationships brings within the horizon of our consideration the dialectical nature of selfhood whereby one's identity is formed and maintained in a tension between autonomous, self-initiated qualities and those qualities attributed to the self by those by whom one is identified. Identity, being shaped in this dialectical tension, can in a given individual become more or less dependent upon one or another centered relationship for its maintenance. To the extent that this is the case, there is a "pull" in the direction of symbiosis or complete dependency of the self for its identity maintenance upon that relationship. To a greater or lesser degree this is true for all centered relationships. We are not necessarily speaking here of what in psychological terms might be called psychopathological, though psychopathology may be involved in any given relationship under consideration.

From a theological perspective we can suggest another dialectical tension, that between an identity drawn from one's centered relationships with other persons and that relationship by which one is finally identified, ordinarily referred to as one's identity as a child of God. Only in that ultimate relationship can the tension between unique, autonomous selfhood and selfhood through identification finally be resolved. God's relationship to persons is one that affirms and makes possible both uniqueness of self and selfhood through responsible relationship. In our identification as children of God we are promised a relationship in which we are both set free to be ourselves and bound into a community of faithful relationship.

Figure 10 is an effort both to schematize this dialectical perspective on identity formation and maintenance and to suggest that, to the extent that centered relationships move toward symbiosis, they become involved in idolatry. A relationship in which the identity of the self is centered, which is centrally important to the individual, though finite, tends to become of ultimate importance to the

Centered Relationships and Their Idolatrous Tendency

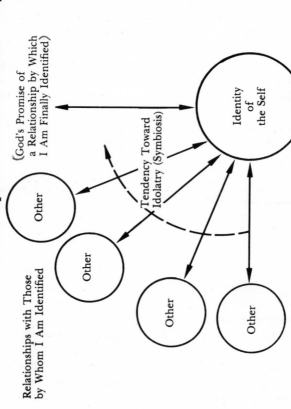

Relationships with Those
by Whom I Am Identified

(God's Promise of
a Relationship by Which
I Am Finally Identified)

Tendency Toward
Idolatry (Symbiosis)

Identity
of
the Self

Other

Other

Other

Other

Figure 10

person; to that extent that relationship tends toward idolatry. We are using the term idolatry in the Tillichian sense of "the elevation of a preliminary concern to ultimacy."[1] Tillich proposes three possible relations of the preliminary concern to that which concerns us ultimately: mutual indifference, a relation in which a preliminary concern is elevated to ultimacy, and a relation in which a preliminary concern becomes the vehicle of the ultimate concern without claiming ultimacy for itself.

When viewed in this fashion, our analysis of family styles of attachment and separation suggests that Types I, II, and III attachments are idolatrous to the extent that they involve symbiosis. Only in Type IV attachments—or, more accurately, to the degree that a relationship involves Type IV attachment—does the relationship become a vehicle of the ultimate concern, the fulfillment of individual identity as a child of God. Since all centered relationships have implicit in them the pull toward symbiosis, there is in all centered relationships the tendency toward idolatry, though the degree of that tendency will vary enormously depending primarily on the style of attachment.

Bereavement and Identity Reformation

The schema of Figure 10 is highly important for a pastoral theological perspective on bereavement and loss relative to the loss of a centered relationship by death or other radical separation. (Such losses necessarily pose a profound threat to the identity of the self such that there is a genuine loss of selfhood.) This loss of identity is frequently expressed by the acutely grief-stricken as a sense of emptiness or an imagined "hole" or hollow in the self. The long process of grief work may best be understood as a process of restructuring one's identity taking into account the profound loss that has occurred

Creative Grief

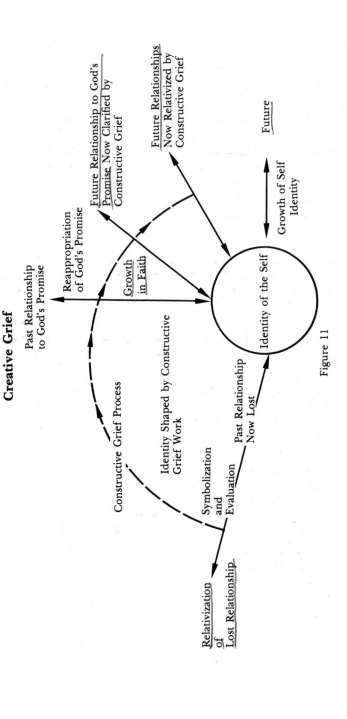

Figure 11

Destructive, Blocked Grief

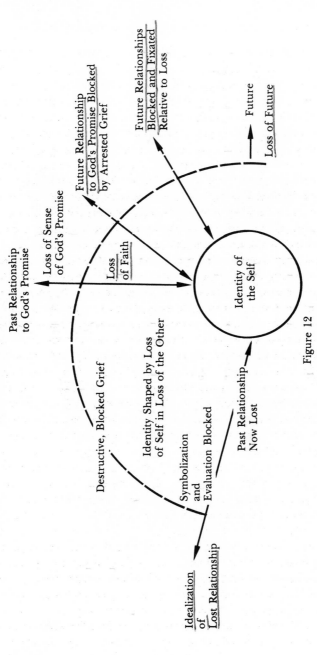

Figure 12

in the absence of the centered relationship by which one has been identified.

Figures 11 and 12 seek schematically to express phenomenologically how the process of identity reformation following the loss of a centered relationship takes place. Figure 11 schematizes the process of creative, constructive grief. The past centered relationship, now lost, must be given up and reincorporated into the identity of the self in a new way so that the new identity is shaped by the past identification with the lost loved one but also by the process of constructive grief work. This necessitates a long-term process of reevaluation of the lost relationship and its central importance to the identity of the self. Reevaluation takes place as, often in small and apparently insignificant ways, the relationship is symbolized in both its past meaning and its future significance in the new situation of its absence. The result of this long reevaluation and symbolization process is that the lost relationship becomes relativized in terms of its ultimacy as central to the identity of the self. The loss of the centered relationship is slowly replaced by the new symbolic meanings of that relationship, by a fresh sense of the self's ability to shape an identity in the absence of the centered relationship, and by new relationships which are themselves made relative by the constructive grief process.

At both the levels of implicit and explicit faith, constructive grief work involves a reappropriation of God's promise of a relationship by which the self is ultimately identified. We are here using the terms implicit and explicit faith in the sense discussed in the previous chapter. Profound bereavement by death or other radical loss necessarily poses a threat to this ultimate relationship. The quality of that threat will, as was seen in the cases of George and Betty Jones and John and Sybil Rogers, vary considerably depending upon the level of implicit and explicit faith that has been present in the past. Hopefully, the future relationship to God's promise will be clarified and given more secure grounding by the experience of constructive grief) Much here depends upon the presence or absence of a pastoral or other human relationship within which the painful and identity threatening experience of loss can be worked through. This ministering relationship must itself be one which, in Tillich's terms, "becomes a vehicle of the ultimate concern without claiming ultimacy for itself."[2]

Destructive Grief and the Loss of Identity

Figure 12 schematizes what can occur when the process of creative, constructive grief work is blocked so that it becomes destructive to the identity of the self. In these cases the lost relationship, rather than being painfully reevaluated and symbolized anew, is idealized. The loss to the self's identity in the loss of the centered relationship becomes itself the center around which the new identity is shaped. (At implicit and/or explicit levels the idolatry contained in the lost relationship is confirmed.) The growth of the self through the painful process of mourning and reinvestment of the self in new relationships is arrested. Future relationships will tend to gather to them the fixated needs of the person relative to loss rather than opening fresh possibilities for new identifications and reformation of self-identity. Thus, blocked grief brings a loss to the self of a sense of future.

At the level of relationship to God's promise of an ultimate relationship by which the self is identified as God's child in an open-ended future, the person suffering destructive, blocked grief will tend to interpret his or her loss as containing a loss of a sense of God's promise. It is as if the person's faith in God's providence has been so bound to the promise of continuity of the lost relationship that its loss threatens to destroy the faith of the bereaved in the promises of God. There is a loss of eschatological trust.

Persons suffering destructive, blocked grief must be

helped to confront the loss of self-identity they have experienced and offered a relationship of trust and hope. Within that relationship they may begin the painful process of relativizing and resymbolizing the idolatrous relationship, the loss of which they have permitted to so dominate their sense of who they are as persons that other avenues of growth and identification have become arrested. At the deep emotional level this means facilitating the surfacing of the disappointment, the feelings of abandonment, the anger at desertion that most often are buried beneath an outward appearance of long-suffering and despair. The reality of existential boundaries between past, present, and future must be gently but firmly kept before the grieving person with the implicit and explicit invitation to come to terms with what is lost and now past and to open the self to the new possibilities of the future. Thus God's providential promise can in an incarnationally patterned relationship - w/ the be slowly reinterpreted to open the way toward faith in paster? "that power of the future which we are persuaded is trustworthy." Beginning, often feeble efforts to move beyond self-identity defined by loss and grief must be encouraged, nurtured, and blessed.

More than anything else, ministry to those suffering from destructive, blocked grief requires great patience coupled with the capacity to enter into the despair of the grieving person and get beneath the covering facade of apparent faithfulness to the lost-centered relationship. The reluctant turning from preoccupation with the past and its losses toward the future and its possibilities must be quietly and insistently nurtured. A temporary dependency on the pastoral relationship needs some-times to be tolerated, while yet pointing the person toward other, more mutual and growth-oriented rela-tionships that present themselves. For some a group experience with others who are experiencing grief or have successfully done so in the past will prove more helpful than a one-to-one relationship with the pastor, with its temptations for symbiosis. The central task, *(in ministry to those of destructive grief)* however undertaken, is that of facilitating the turning of the grieving one from the past with its losses toward the future and God's promise of faithfulness in it.

Grace Burton was an ambitious but deeply dependent person in her forties. Married to a successful and equally ambitious businessman, she had developed an identity as the attractive wife of an upwardly mobile, hard-driving man and mother of three fine children. Her house was a symbol of the family's success image: large, in a fine neighborhood where her children would have every opportunity to make the most of the relationships to children of upper-class families that were available to them. The fact that her husband, Jim, was so involved in his work that he had little time for the family was somehow rationalized in both Grace's and her husband's minds by the priority given his success that made possible the family's advantages. Grace became an active club woman, becoming chairperson of one important charitable board and a member of several others. She, too, felt successful and competent.

Two events of bereavement radically altered Grace's life and threw her into a profound identity crisis. Her youngest child, a boy of six, developed acute leukemia and, within 18 months, was dead. In the early stages of the illness, Grace refused to accept what was happening, frantically taking her son from one clinic to another in an effort to find someone who would make a more hopeful diagnosis. She kept up her club and civic activities in an equally frantic effort to maintain a "normal" life. Later she was forced to abandon everything except her care of the boy, now hospitalized and critically ill.

After her son's death Grace returned to her old and familiar pattern of life, but her dependency on her husband increased markedly, involving going with him on business trips, attempting to draw him into more involvement with the two remaining children, now teen-agers, and generally needing his full and complete presence in her life) Jim, sensing Grace's need since her bereavement, responded with gestures of affection and reassurance, though his primary emotional investment remained with his business.

Then, just a year after her son's death, Grace suffered her second bereavement. Her husband fell dead from a heart attack at his desk at work (Grace's primary source of identity, support, and meaning for her life was gone.) Grace's reaction to this second devastating loss was at first to maintain a facade of success and strength. Her husband's insurance program had left her relatively financially independent. She plunged into renewed civic and church work, enrolled her two girls in a private school and in general attempted to carry on "the life Jim wanted for us." But soon that balloon collapsed, and Grace became lonely, bitter, irritable with her children, and began to speak of her life being over. She resigned from most of her civic and church activities, began to be preoccupied with her health and soon was involved in a battle with her daughters to get them to spend more time with her and less at the country club with their friends. But all Grace had to talk with her children about was her unhappiness and dissatisfaction with their choice of friends, activities, and new morality values. Her children began to resent her.

Desperate for the idealized support she fantasied she had enjoyed from her dead husband, Grace impulsively made a potentially disastrous decision to remarry. Her second husband was, on the surface, as successful and strong as her image of her lost mate. But Frank was not a strong man. Though older than Grace, he was the youngest child in his family and had long been dependent on his older brother, with whom he was a business partner. He was looking for someone to take care of him, as was Grace. The marriage soon degenerated into bickering, complaints, and mutual efforts to get the other to be stronger.

Grace is a tragic example of a person whose blocked, destructive grief over an idolatrous, symbiotic, lost relationship continues to dominate her life and color all her efforts to rebuild her life. Pastoral counseling with her did not begin until after the second marriage, when the process of identity reformation as the victim of tragedy, the one whose life was over, was already well established. She strongly resisted all efforts to get her to reevaluate the first marriage. Jim had been the ideal husband. Without him life was empty. Frank was nothing but a poor, inadequate substitute. She alternately blamed him for her unhappiness and felt sorry for him for being the weak, inadequate man he was in her mind.

Pastoral counseling with Grace was, to say the least, a long and difficult process that achieved only modest results. She was able to share her bitter disappointment and sense of desertion over her first husband's death, her shame and disappointment in herself for not being strong enough to build a happy new life for herself, and her anger toward God for not fulfilling her dream for her life. Some progress was made in helping her to accept Frank for who he was, a man with limitations but with many admirable qualities who deeply wanted to care for Grace if she could only accept that he could not and did not want to take Jim's place. Grace gradually accepted that her children needed to live their own lives, that her sacrifice for them was no longer needed or wanted. She began renewed interest in her church and began to pray for guidance in rebuilding her life. (But her primary identity remained centered around her bereavement and the self-understanding that her real life was over.) What was left of her life was only a tolerated and less than happy existence.

The reasons for Grace's arrested grief and the reformation of her identity around her loss experiences are, of course, complex. The fact that her relationship to her husband harbored deep tendencies toward symbiosis while outwardly she was strong and self-reliant probably forms the core of her psychological problem. The illness and death of her child, during which her competent, strong self-perception was shattered by the refusal of his illness to yield to her efforts to cope with and overpower it, took a heavy toll on her strong self-perception. Her more dependent self became more predominant as she sought to cope with her loss by moving more symbiotic-ally toward her husband. If he had lived she might well have eventually made a good recovery from the loss of her son and reestablished her identity as a strong and competent wife and mother. But the second loss of the central relationship of her life was too much for her to cope with; she had no one else in her life who could replace him. Her older children were in process of turning away from rather than toward her. Another bereavement was in process. [Thus Grace's restructuring of her identity "as the bereaved one whose life was over" began to take shape.] Her second marital choice was but one expression of that already reformed identity, though it also paradoxically represented a desperate effort to restore the lost equilibrium of the past.

Throughout her bereavement, Grace's relationship to God and his promises of faithfulness were being heavily impacted by the developing themes of her self-identity reformation. Her prayers during her son's illness were for God's miraculous cure of the boy's illness. That disappointed, she pled that God would have mercy on her weakness. The husband's death brought the onset of prayers of resignation, disappointment, and thinly veiled anger. But through the entire crisis process she sought, sometimes desperately, sometimes more quietly and searchingly, to find a final resting place for her dependent need for symbiosis. (Only occasionally and less strongly could she turn toward God for help in looking toward the future and new relationships.) The disappointment in Frank evoked prayers for his strengthening so that he could better care for her. Only after much hard work in the counseling relationship was she able spontaneously to begin praying for courage to accept and love him as he was.

Fortunately, though the loss of a centered relationship always initiates a crisis of identity at the most profound levels, the degree of the crisis depending upon the relative centrality of the lost relationship, most persons are more able than was Grace to restructure their identity, taking into account the loss and gains made by the self in encountering it. For those persons the grief process can over time bring about creative changes both in personhood and faith orientation.

Stages in the Process of Grief Work

As we observed was the case in coming to terms with impending death, so also there are in the bereavement process recognizable stages which tend to blend together but which it may be helpful to delineate.

The first stage is one of shock, often accompanied by denial of the reality of what has happened and overpowering feelings of impending chaos. The pastor who has had occasion to be with families at the time of death of a family member will have observed the sometimes bizarre ways in which chaos and denial are manifested. In the first impact of loss, often a family drama of acute grief will take place, most often focusing around the bereaved person recognized as having had the most central relationship to the dead family member. Various roles are taken in the drama of grief, frequently roles that in some way relate to the role the person has overtly or covertly played in the family structure. Some will be comforters and direct supporters of the focal grieving person. Others will take lesser roles of errand runner, telephone messenger, and coffee bringer. Someone will take charge of whatever needs to be organized, giving instructions to others, calling the funeral home or the pastor, sometimes even making a list of what now must be done. Some will withdraw into themselves or feel compelled to leave as if what has happened is too much with which to cope except in the loneliness of isolation. And, like all dramas, the drama of grief will attract spectators, those who simply gather to watch and share the grief at a proximate but safe distance.

Denial and chaos in acute grief also have their physical manifestations. Fainting, numbness, inability to stand or walk and other bodily phenomena point to both the chaos and denial themes as well as to the literal impact of loss on the bereaved person.[3]

Denial and feelings of impending chaos will often persist in bereaved persons for several weeks or even months following the loss of a centered relationship. As the fuller realization of what has happened takes shape, another stage of identity crisis begins to emerge, that of awareness of the threat of disintegration of the self. An overpowering feeling of inability to go on without the lost relationship threatens the self. There is acute awareness of loss of a future with the lost one. Not infrequently this phase of grief is accompanied by thoughts of suicide, fears about the possibility of terminal illness, and wishes to die. The desire to give up and submit to what is experienced as a mortal blow to the self becomes at times almost irresistible.

Intermingled with these early stages of grief process are to be found almost invariably struggles with guilt relative to the death of the loved person. Preoccupation with ideas that "if I had only . . ." then maybe death would not have happened or would have happened differently or later are very common. The origin of these unrealistic feelings of responsibility for another's death are difficult to sort out. Certainly they have their roots in the feelings of mutual responsibility and accountability found at some level in all centered relationships. Any mutual commitment brings a greater or lesser sense of responsibility for the welfare of the other. Another, perhaps less well accepted and understood root of guilt in bereavement is that of the primordial ambivalence in all finite human relationships. Because of the dialectical tension between what we have called symbiosis and freedom in all centered relationships, from the beginning they are fated to contain a positive and a negative pole, or, in the Freudian understanding, to involve both love and hate, life and death wishes. The positive pole of that tension has in grief rituals and conversation with others about the loss, ample opportunity for expression. The darker side of the lost relationship has, however, little opportunity for socially acceptable expression. It is therefore converted into guilt, the irrational feeling that the bereaved is somehow responsible for what has happened. That the centered relationship has become integral to the self-identity of the bereaved only seems to reinforce this vague sense of being guilty.

As time passes, bringing with it the growing need to put what has happened into perspective, to restructure the meaning of selfhood in the absence of the lost relationship, gradually the work of grief begins. This involves for most persons repeated painful efforts to review the meaning of the lost relationship with the accompanying temptation to idealize and make ultimate the meaning it had for the bereaved one's life. In the relatively healthy person that temptation is matched by the pressing need to restructure the self-perception, to pick up the broken pieces of self and move on into what is experienced as a lonely and unknown future. Sometimes temporary substitute relationships are sought or efforts made to fill the emptiness with another centered relationship as, for example, the young parent who has lost a spouse and turns toward one or another of the children for the kind of intimacy and support once shared with the lost spouse. I recall one such young mother who came to the painful realization that she was looking to her six-year-old mentally retarded son for the love she once had with her dead husband. (It was an important step in her bereavement process when she became aware of what was happening and began to come to terms with the depth of her loss and the tasks of building a new life that now lay before her.)

The resymbolization of the lost relationship is a slow and unplanned process that takes place as one incident after another occurs that reminds the bereaved of the lost loved one and the altered situation brought about by his or her absence. Each of these reminding occurrences, often superficially relatively insignificant, serves to trigger both memory of and reflection about some facet of the meaning of the lost relationship. Something old that was taken for granted must now be reconsidered and given a new meaning in the altered situation of bereavement.

I recall one new widow who called me as her pastor one evening to come to her home because she had a problem with which she couldn't cope. Expecting a major crisis, I hurried to her home only to find that the problem was that the "johnnie" in the master bedroom bathroom wouldn't stop running! "Bill always took care of these things. What am I going to do?" There followed a brief but important conversation about the possibility that she had been more dependent on Bill than she realized and that she now wanted to become more independent. This brief snatch of identity restructuring and resymbolization was, of course, interspersed with some very practical talk about the inner workings of bathroom commodes!

This incident, small as it was, served as one among many such little crises that together began the process of relativizing the lost relationship of this woman with her dead husband. Important as the relationship had been to her, she was learning that she could survive without the relationship; it was not finally of ultimate importance to her survival. A new identity could be shaped without this once centrally important figure.

It is at this point in the bereavement process that many persons find themselves feeling strangely angry at the lost loved one. The anger springs not only from the awareness of having been "deserted" by the one who has died, but also from the dawning awareness of the hidden idolatrous qualities that may have been in the relationship. If aired in a pastoral or other relationship of acceptance so that the hasty urge to bury the anger under fears of being disloyal to the lost one can be resisted, these feelings can give impetus to the desire to restructure the self-identity in the direction of growth and exercise of greater self-direction.

In cases of long illness preceding the death of the loved one, these struggles with the anger of desertion and idolatry may be experienced in anticipation of the death.

CREATIVE AND DESTRUCTIVE GRIEF

Beverley Bowie, a sensitive and desperately honest man who died of cancer leaving a wife and several young children, writes of his wife's feelings about his impending death:

> She took the verses at a gulp,
> Dubious but possibly constructive medicine,
> And gagged.
> "Very gay, very debonaire, and very false.
> Who is this Death you seem to be on such good terms with?
> You drop his name about with careful spontaneity,
> And yet I do not recollect him as a guest of ours
> Nor, as a matter of fact, his advance press-agent,
> That rather nasty fellow, Pain.
> One thing I'll tell you:
> You never met them in *my* company.
> It must have been on one of those
> Haphazard trips of yours,
> To some unfinished corner of the globe
> —Anywhere, so long as it's a thousand miles
> From home, and with no telephone.
>
> And now you want to go with them again,
> These raffish, no-good bums I've never even met . . .
> A matter of necessity, you say. Business. An urgent call.
> You'd rather stay with the family, with me,
> You'd rather revel in my cooking and my bed,
> Apply the diaper and blow the flowing nose—
> My foot! You mouth your pretty speeches
> But go on packing your valise.
> No, I know you. You're off again,
> It doesn't matter where or
> With what unsuitable companions;
> The main thing is to go,
> And go without me.
>
> I'll tell you one thing more:
> If a card comes drifting back,
> Postmarked from Hell or Lethe or Death's Other
>   Kingdom,

I'll not read it to the children
Nor prop it proudly on the mantlepiece.

I'll stuff it up your effigy."[4]

With persons who can articulate their deeper feelings and questions about their bereavement crisis experience, the pastor will most often need to listen for expressions of ultimate concern about the question of God's providential promise. Persons who have been steeped in the biblical tradition of the Christian faith will most often express these concerns in that language, more often in the form of affirmations about which they seem to need reassurance than in the form of questions. Pastors will need to tune their ears to the nuances of meaning in these expressions of tentative faith if they are to be able to respond to the underlying doubts and questions that signal the need to make a new appropriation of God's promises of faithful care in the new situation of bereavement.

Persons whose lives have been heavily impacted by the modern consciousness will sometimes be timid and embarrassed to share their religious concerns directly in the traditional language. They sometimes reveal these concerns at the implicit level in testing the pastor to see if he or she is open to the doubts and questions of one whose religious concerns do not fit what is felt to be the traditional mode. If the pastor meets the test of openness to a more unconventional religious quest, the deep needs for some intellectually and emotionally acceptable access to the resources of faith may be shared. Pastors who are to help these persons make a new appropriation of the faith must be able to speak in the metaphors of communication that come naturally to the seeking person, resisting the need to speak of God and his faithful promise only in traditional language. Bereavement is a time when, pressed by the deep need to make some kind of ultimate sense out of what has happened, these persons are most

meet them where they are...

open to ministry, but it is a time that requires of the pastor great sensitivity and flexibility. Heavy-handed application of religious cant will not meet the profound questions of faith with which the bereaved grapple.

Gradually, sometimes after months, often not before the traditional year of mourning has passed, the person who has engaged in creative, constructive grief work will begin to recognize that his or her feelings and self-perception have changed and are changing. A new identity tested in the fire of life's most painful loss is beginning to emerge. This awareness brings new choices to be made, the possibility of experimentation with new modes of living and new relationships. The person slowly begins the process of reinvestment in new activities and, more important, in new centered relationships shaped by what has been experienced of the self and the hazards and values of relationship in the loss that is now past.

For the person who has done the work of bereavement well and faithfully, the future begins again to open, undergirded by a renewed trust in that power of the future which the person is more firmly persuaded than before the loss occurred is indeed trustworthy. Hope is renewed. God's promise has been reappropriated. It remains a promise. The final word of God's faithfulness remains to be spoken. Hope carries uncertainty within it, as the bereaved have painfully and forcibly learned. But the restructured identity of the self is now supported by eschatological trust—the trust of God's future.

CHAPTER VI

Suicide, Hopelessness, and Despair

Our exploration of crisis experience has to this point quite properly focused on those aspects of finite human existence that are built into our nature as creatures of time with a limited life cycle. The anguish of death and the painful separation and loss of bereavement are experiences that in one way or another all must sooner or later undergo. They are existential though they are infinite in their variation from person to person because of the unique ways in which persons develop styles of coping with life's existential boundaries. Our exploration of styles of attachment and separation in families only serves to illustrate the manner in which crisis experience is thus shaped by the way life's realities are perceived and constructed by persons in styles that are both characteristic of cultural communities and highly particularized by individuals who assign events and relationships private meanings. Crisis experience is not therefore simply existential, though at its core it is most often triggered by the necessity of coming to terms with one of finite life's inevitables.

Our theological perspective has suggested to us that one of the key ingredients in the ability of persons to meet existential crisis successfully is the ability to grasp finite human life as open-ended, contingent, and sustained not by the promise of continuity of things as they have been, but by the promise of God's continuing activity in the very open-endedness and futurity of ongoing life. Following Wolfhart Pannenberg, we have sought to establish the primary criterion of faith in God's providence as trust in the future which the person is persuaded is trustworthy.

We turn now to the task of further testing of this theological hypothesis and extending our exploration of crisis experience by examining closely the experience of persons who have entered the crisis of hopelessness and despair, the experience of loss of a sense of future in which the person can have any confidence or sense of expectation. These are the desperate, the discouraged, the disheartened—those whose perceived human condition is such that the very sense of life or "liveliness" is threatened. There seems no way out, no viable future, no possibility of coping with a situation that is experienced as growing more and more impossible.

The primary paradigm of despair is probably to be found in persons who have considered or are considering suicide. When one loses all hope of the possibility of a lively alternative to one's perceived situation, the alternative that presses for expression is that of death as the only way out. Death then becomes not the boundary of finite life to be avoided or postponed as long as possible, but rather the boundary beyond which an impossibly desperate situation may not pursue the person. Death is invited or courted as the alternative to a "fate worse than death." Faced with the impossibility of sustaining the meaningfulness of human cares and expectations, the despairing turn toward self-imposed death as a final act of desperate integrity. Thus suicide is both a self-imposed condemnation and punishment for failure at living, on the one hand, and a defiant act of taking one's future into one's own hands, on the other.

Recent Interest in Suicide

In recent years in the West there has been a remarkable resurgence of interest in the "problem" of suicide. Beginning with the publication of Emile Durkheim's classic sociological study of suicide, first written in 1897 but not published in English until 1951, the suicidal person has received increasing attention as an index of the social and cultural conditions of the Western world.[1] Western society has been seen as a world in which themes of meaninglessness, absurdity, and despair have become increasingly dominant in literature and other writing about everyday life. The social condition of Western persons has thus been seen as one of increasing anomie.

Durkheim was primarily concerned with utilizing his studies of suicide to demonstrate the preponderance of sociological factors in determining behavioral patterns in social groups. He therefore proposed three types of suicides: egoistic, altruistic, and anomic. Egoistic suicide occurs in the person who has been inadequately socialized into the structure of a group. This type of suicide results from what Durkheim called "excessive individualism."[2] Altruistic suicide, on the other hand, occurs as a result of oversocialization in that the person commits the act of suicide out of what is perceived as a sense of duty or obligation to the society or group of which the individual is a part—"where the ego is not its own property, where it is blended with something not itself, where the goal of conduct is exterior to itself, that is, in one of the groups in which it participates."[3] Anomic suicide, the type becoming most common in contemporary Western society according to Durkheim, "results from man's activity's lacking regulation [by the society] and his consequent sufferings." The individual lacks the necessary checkreins on individual passions and is thus thrown too much back upon his or her own individual resources and restraints. Such persons have difficulty sustaining themselves in the face of the usual vicissitudes of living.[4]

While Durkheim's pioneering sociological studies of suicide do much to establish the central importance of factors of individualism and social integration in determining the broad expectation of despairing experience in given social groups, they have limited value in helping pastors and other helping persons predict or recognize despairing experience in their parishioners beyond those broad generalizations. More recent studies by those whose work has been with individuals suffering from despair of suicidal proportions will prove more useful in equipping the pastor for work with the despairing. The development of suicide prevention programs in many urban centers in this country during the last two decades has produced a substantial literature concerning both the more proximate or psychological causes of suicidal behavior and the intervention of helping persons into the life experience of the despairing. Although most of this literature either builds upon Durkheim's basic hypotheses or develops a psychology of suicide, there are also a number of studies which consider the problem of suicide from philosophical or more broadly humanistic perspectives. A selected list of these writings has been included in the bibliography.

Two Theories of Suicide

As a background for our further exploration of the crisis of despair, I want to draw particularly from two recent studies of despairing behavior, one by a psychologist, the other by a theologian. Maurice L. Farber, professor of psychology at the University of Connecticut, in his book *Theory of Suicide*,[5] speaks of suicide as "the disease of hope." Despair and hopelessness go together, and the absence of hope leads inevitably in the direction of that ultimate despair of life itself, the wish to suicide. But hope is not itself an "ultimate particle of psychology."[6] Rather hope is itself an outcome of two factors, one in the personality and the other in the situation of the person. Farber calls the personal factor competence, by which he means the basic pervasive feeling in the individual that he or she has the resources within the self to cope with the demands of living. The situational factor is the "degree of threat leveled against the individual's being able to sustain a minimally acceptable existence."[7]

165

Farber, following Erikson and other ego psychologists, finds that the degree of competence in a given individual is greatly dependent upon the presence or absence of a certain quality of nurturance in the early development of the person which either makes for the ability to cope or for a degree of vulnerability to situational threat. In the language of chapter 4 above, the development of competence in growing children will depend upon the degree to which families are able to sustain Type IV styles of attachment and separation. Types I, II, and III families will tend to develop children who lack a basic sense of competence in situations that fail to reproduce the tightly structured conditions of the family of origin.

But hope, the great counterforce to suicide, is not simply a psychological possession of the individual; it is a social phenomenon that to a greater or lesser degree pervades the atmosphere of a community or a society. It cannot be sustained by the individual alone, but depends upon the availability of succorance and hopefulness in the social situation in which the individual finds himself or herself.

Farber goes on to develop a general theory of suicide which he condenses into the following formula:

$$S = f\left(\frac{\text{PIC, DEC, DIG, TS}}{\text{Su., HFT}}\right)$$

S = Probability of Suicide
PIC = Personalities Injured in Sense of Competence
DEC = Demands for the Exercising of Competence
DIG = Demands for Interpersonal Giving
TS = Tolerance of Suicide
Su = Availability of Succorance
HFT = Degree of Hope in the Future Time Perspective of the Society

In Farber's formulation, therefore, the potential for suicide in a given individual is in direct proportion to the degree of injury suffered by the individual to his or her sense of competence, the demands made by the person's social situation for the exercise of competence, the demands of the social situation for interpersonal giving, and the degree of social tolerance of suicide as a "solution" to problems of living in the society. The potential for suicide is in inverse proportion to the availability of succorance to the individual and the degree of hope in the future time perspective that pervades the society in which the individual must live his or her life.[8]

Farber's general theory of suicide is important and useful for our study of despair at a number of points. From a strictly social scientific perspective he supports our designation of hope and expectation as the central thrust of that sense of security necessary for the person to sustain confidence in the worthwhileness of making the effort to cope with life's contingencies (a secularized way of speaking of what in theological terms we have called faith in the trustworthiness of God's promises concerning the future). Farber also emphasizes the corporate social responsibility for providing those conditions within which the individual may develop a sense of competence for living and sustain hopefulness about the future. Persons who experience the crisis of despair tend to be those who have been injured in their sense of competence by a social situation that continues to demand both competence and interpersonal giving of its members. Thus social norms established by the community in which the person lives his or her life, including even the norm as to the acceptability of despair and suicide as a "solution" to life's problems, set the context in which the person is either enabled to embrace a hopeful, lively stance toward life or is pressed toward despair. Likewise the primary counterforce that can restore a sense of competence and hope in despairing individuals Farber sees to be the availability of a caring, succoring community that nurtures hope in the future time perspective.

Thomas Oden, writing in his book *The Structure of Awareness* from a stance that combines phenomenological analysis and theological assertion, relates despair to the struggle for authentic selfhood.

In despair I wish, despairingly, to be something other than I am. I am convinced that there is no hope for a new self-relation in which I could affirm myself as finitely free. No ray of hope remains for the real self to be brought back, redeemed, repurchased. I experience myself as "sold" to inauthenticity, a condition well known in Scripture: "The whole head is sick, and the whole heart faint. From the sole of the foot even to the head, there is no soundness in it" (Isa. 1:5-6).[9]

Oden further quotes from Paul: "I am carnal, sold under sin. I do not understand my own actions. For I do not do what I want, but I do the very thing I hate. . . . So then it is no longer I that do it, but sin which dwells within me." (Rom. 7:14-17.)

In Oden's phenomenology of despair, he relates the experience to the three modes of time: past, present, and future. In relation to a sense of past inauthenticity there is the experience of despairing guilt; in relation to the present inauthentic selfhood there comes the awareness of despairing boredom. In relation to "the threat that the self will continue in bondage to inauthenticity in the future, as far as the imagination can see," there comes the threat of despairing anxiety.[10]

Oden's theological assertion concerning despair is that "it is impossible to despair over ourselves before God, if God is understood as the one who addresses us as his covenant partner ever anew in the now. The psychological experience of despair is now perceived to be rooted in an ontological impossibility, however much I may experience it as if it were a response to reality. Insofar as I stand before the God who speaks freshly in every now, there is no time or ground for despair. My task is to learn to identify myself in a new way, on the basis of God's own naming of me as son."[11]

Oden draws his theological assertion in large part from the classic work of the nineteenth-century theologian and father of existentialism, Søren Kierkegaard, on the crisis of despair, *Fear and Trembling; and, The Sickness Unto Death.*[12] Kierkegaard's fundamental position is that persons in their human condition are, without God, all condemned to ultimate despair. Despair is related to human finitude and the fantastic human wish for infinity.

For the self is a synthesis in which the finite is the limiting factor and the infinite is the expanding factor. Infinitude's despair is therefore the fantastical, the limitless. The self is in sound health and free from despair only when, precisely by having been in despair, it is grounded transparently in God.[13]

Although Oden's theological stance taken from Kierkegaard has a much more neo-orthodox flavor than the more open-ended process theology of Wolfhart Pannenberg or Jürgen Moltmann, on which we have developed most of our theological reflection thus far, there seems to be a basis for some compatibility between the different theological perspectives. In all three the basis for faithful selfhood that overcomes despair is in the confidence placed in God's continuing identification of the self as his child with all the hope for future authentic selfhood that confidence entails. The self is not simply dependent upon its own psychological well being as a bulwark against the threat of despair and meaninglessness. God's activity in human affairs in the ongoingness of time provides the solid basis for hopeful engagement of the problems of living in the human situations that threaten to engulf the self in absurdity, inauthenticity, and finally despair.

By bringing into a kind of double focus the social scientific perspective on suicidal despair of Maurice Farber and the phenomenological-theological perspective of Thomas Oden's elaboration of Kierkegaard, we are offered a useful interdisciplinary approach to the development of a pastoral understanding of despair and the care of despairing persons. The pastoral task that comes into view through this double focus is a multi-faceted one that relates to a broad spectrum of the pastor's work and not simply to his relationships with the despairing individual, important as that work is. If hope is a quality that exists or fails to exist in the climate of a social group, making possible a hopeful outlook on the possibility of competent coping with life's exigencies, then the engendering of such an atmosphere of hopeful expectation in a community of believers becomes a crucial, if not sharply defined, task. If a sound basis for hope must finally be grounded in trust in God's promise of continuing activity on human behalf in an ever-changing and contingent future, then the work of the pastor as spiritual leader in engendering such a climate of faithful expectation is specifically relevant in countering those forces in Western society that press contemporary consciousness toward anomie and the threat of absurd, meaningless existence. The fostering of communities of persons that provide what Farber calls succorance for those who suffer from the threat of despairing situations of living and threats to competence in being able to cope with life's threats becomes a primary responsibility of the church and its leadership. These general tasks come clearly into focus, though much more careful reflection and sifting of detail needs to be done before the specific methodologies of pastoral work either with the despair-ing or with the larger community that must support a hopeful outlook can be set forth.

Themes of Despair

Before taking up the task of developing a pastoral methodology in the care of despairing persons, it is necessary that we first probe more deeply into the experience of despair and uncover some of the common themes of that experience. As with death and bereavement we must try to see despair from the inside as it takes hold of people's lives and colors them with the dark colors of desperate hopelessness. We must see if we can grasp with greater clarity some of the dynamic forces that create the despairing, deadly situation.

We begin with the notion that the sense of life or liveliness (as opposed to deadliness or desperation) is dependent on a certain lively sense of integration of the self within itself and in relation to the significant others of the self's social situation—what Oden calls authenticity. This sense of liveliness must be sustained in the ebb and flow of changing relationships, the new tasks of the life cycle, and those chance, contingent threats that to a greater or lesser degree come to persons in the uncertain business of living. Some of us are more protected than others from these threats; some are in situations that provide little nurturant support for this sense of authentic liveliness. Others are more fortunate. The rate of flow of experience, of interpersonal communication, of stimulus to lively response will vary enormously from person to person and social situation to social situation. As we suggested in chapter 2, persons are presented with the continuing necessity of restructuring and reevaluating their past experience while at the same time prestructuring and preimaging their future life expectations. This entire process requires a lively, flowing, interactive engagement of the self with itself and its social situation. To be alive and authentically human requires this kind of lively, dynamic process, which, as Farber has suggested, is a function both of the person and his or her social situation.

Such a dynamic flow of experience involves a continuing process of interpretation and evaluation of events, of nuances of communication and relationship, and an assignment of significance to what has occurred or may occur. It is in this process of interpretation that the qualities of hopefulness, a sense of personal worth and

171

competence, and faith in the worthwhileness of living are maintained or, on the other hand, are threatened. Persons develop certain characteristic ways of "tending" to their experience that become habitual. At the unconscious level these ways of "tending" express dynamic patterns of conflict and identity formation that reach back into the early developmental periods of the person's life process. Selective attention and inattention patterns develop. Through these configurations of perception, interpretation, and evaluation, a gestalt of authenticity or inauthenticity, liveliness or deadliness, hope or hopelessness emerges and is maintained.

Inevitably for most of us—more for some than others—certain discrepancies develop in our interpretation of events and nuances of relationship. Self-perceptions and the individual's perceptions of others' interpretation of his or her behavior or interpersonal events do not always coincide. Discrepancies develop between the person's evaluation of his or her behavior in a particular event and the self's ideal of what one's behavior should be. Sometimes direct threats or attacks on the self's evaluation of itself come from significant other persons whose esteem is highly important for the maintenance of a sense of authentic selfhood.

Most of us most of the time are able to integrate all these discrepant interpretations and maintain a relatively constant self-evaluation of authenticity and integrity while feeling hopefully and expectantly engaged with life around us. But when these discrepancies become too great to manage and our interpretations begin to take on a consistently negative cast, we begin to be threatened with despair over the possibility of maintaining authentic selfhood and a hopeful outlook. Our "tending" to our experience begins to take on a deadly, desperate, despairing quality.

Viewed in this manner, despair can be seen as occurring when the discrepancy between, on the one hand, the person's perception of himself or herself and his or her relationship situation and, on the other, his or her understanding of what the self and its situation should be is so great and consistent as to be unbridgeable, beyond integration. Such a person begins to feel a loss of the self in both its authenticity and its competence to cope with living.

Myra: An Attempted Suicide

The chaplain of a large metropolitan hospital was called by the medical social service worker in the emergency area of the hospital to talk with Myra, a white woman in her late twenties or early thirties. The social service worker said that she had spoken with the patient briefly, but that she had been able to elicit very little from Myra about the attempt on her life she had made before being brought by the police to the hospital. The social worker said that she had called the family and that the father-in-law was on the way to the hospital. As the chaplain entered the emergency area the surgical resident on duty smiled and said: "She didn't do such a good job, preacher. She just nicked herself pretty good with a 32. She won't say much about it. Maybe you can make some sense out of it."

When the chaplain entered the treatment room, Myra was on a stretcher wearing a hospital gown, lying on her side with her back to the doorway. It was difficult to tell her age. She seemed young, yet looked strangely old and tired. Her hair was bleached and silvered very becomingly and her face looked immature, yet careworn. She looked the chaplain over very carefully as he spoke:

C-1: I'm Chaplain C. You're in a pretty tough situation, aren't you?

M-1: Yes, I am. I'll be all right though, I guess. *(She spoke with very little animation throughout, as though detached.)*

C-2: You sound as though you're not sure that's the way you wanted it to turn out.

M-2: Well, it's a shame I didn't succeed once I got my nerve up.

C-3: You feel sort of like you muffed a good chance, 'cause it takes a lot to get to the point of doing it?

M-3: Yes. It takes a lot.

C-4: Pretty rough?

M-4: Yeah.

C-5: Want to talk about it?

M-5: *(Changing her tone to a very light, sarcastic quality)* Oh, I have a good husband, a nice family, and a good job. We have enough money to get by on. It's just crazy, I guess. *(Pause)*

C-6: It's hard to talk about personal things to a stranger.

M-6: Yes. I don't know if you're going to do like all the rest and go out and tell everything I tell you. That woman called my family and I didn't want them to know.

C-7: Don't know who you can trust, is that it?

M-7: No, I don't! *(Pause)* Who did you say you are?

C-8: I'm the chaplain—the minister.

M-8: Then you won't have to blab what I say, will you?

C-9: You feel your confidence has been violated before?

M-9: It's my business what I've done, and besides, my family wouldn't understand how it is with me now any better than they ever have.

C-10: It is hospital regulation that relatives be notified, but you feel you would rather go it alone right now?

M-10: That's the trouble. I don't want to go it alone, *(beginning to cry)* but I know I have to. I always have. I said I had a good husband. I do—a good, fat, dumb, easy-going, sweet, stupid husband who couldn't understand anything about this. We make a good living. I make about $100–$125 a week as a waitress, and he has a good salary. He is a gang foreman on construction work. I have a full-time maid who takes good care of my children—better care than I could. So that's not the reason. We get along better than lots of people. But that's not important. You need to have someone who can understand and talk to you sometimes.

C-11: There's something more than just getting along? And you feel you don't have it?

M-11: Yes. I want someone to listen to the things that bother me, some companionship and understanding. Oh, I have the kind of company a husband provides in bed or a rough-and-tumble childish brute who brings all his decisions to me to make for him. But he thinks he's the only one who has problems and he doesn't know what it means to be worried or unhappy. He thinks I never need to lean on anyone, that nothing ever bothers me.

C-12: It's sort of a one-way process, huh?

M-12: Yeah, all give and no take. He's just like one of my children. But that's just like everybody else I know. I don't know anyone who could really understand me when I want to talk about the things I've seen and know. You are the first person I've ever talked to like this. Do you know what it's like to be alone?

C-13: You felt that there wasn't anyone who could hear you and it just got to be too much.

M-13: Yes. *(Long pause)*

Here she described how she had gotten drunk in order to shoot herself and had driven for hours as she became inebriated. Then she parked behind the night club where she worked at about 3:00 A.M. and finally shot herself once. A policeman came to the car to see what she was doing there and, seeing a bloody spot, said, "Did somebody cut ya?" The policeman failed to see the gun on the car seat. She replied, "Do me a favor, will ya?" "Yeah?" "Get lost!" When he left she shot herself again, less superficially than before. The chaplain commented that the policeman was someone who might have listened.

M-14: Yes, even if that old cop had just sat down with me and listened a little bit I would have stopped the second shot. But most people are like that. They don't give a damn about anyone else beside themselves, and that kind of life isn't worth living to me anymore.

C-14: You do feel all alone, don't you?

M-15: Yes, and I don't see any way to change it.

At this point the interview was interrupted by the arrival of the operating room personnel coming to take Myra for surgery for her gunshot wound. The chaplain walked down the corridor with the stretcher and told Myra as she was wheeled into the OR that he would see her later in the day.

Later in the day the chaplain went to the surgery ward and found Myra alone just after her parents had left. She seemed hostile and depressed. In a few moments Myra's husband, Butch, came into the room to see Myra for the first time following the suicide attempt. He had come directly from work in a nearby city. He looked bewildered and was breathing hard as he burst into the room.

175

B-1: Honey, why did you do a thing like this? Were you doped up or crazy or something?

M-1: Yes, Butch, I was drunk. You just wouldn't understand.

B-2: Well, there's something more to this than meets the eye, and I'm going to find out what was going on. I'll turn hell upside down if I have to.

M-2: It was me, Butch, just me. I'm tired. Can you understand that? Tired!

B-3: *(Turning to the chaplain)* How can anyone want to do a thing like this just because they are tired?

C-1: It's hard for you to understand how anyone could do this unless something forced them to, like dope or being crazy?

M-3: He can't understand. He doesn't know what it means to be tired inside.

The chaplain reports no further conversation, since there was an interruption by the entry of a nurse at that point. Since her wounds were fairly superficial, Myra was discharged from the hospital the next day. Although she was given an appointment to the out-patient psychiatric clinic, she failed to keep that appointment.

The discrepancies in Myra's perception of her self and situation are blatantly apparent in these two brief interviews following her suicide attempt. She begins to communicate this despairing interpretation of her life in the sarcastic tone of her comment in M-5. In M-9 more of the discrepancies begin to emerge. She has parents who should, but she feels do not, understand her. What's more, they never have. In M-10 the discrepancy between feeling utterly alone and having a husband and children is bitterly expressed as is her self-evaluation as a poor mother. In M-11 and what follows, this discrepancy becomes a cry of despair and loneliness. Her suicide attempt had been both an act of self-condemnation and a desperate cry for help. In her hopeless state she had not been able to reach out to the one possible source of last-minute succorance. She had sent the potentially helpful policeman away.

In the second interview we get a brief glimpse of what is

probably characteristic communication between Myra and her husband. Butch, a blundering and insensitive man, wants desperately to know what went wrong that brought Myra to the "crazy" decision to kill herself. Like a construction worker with a sledge hammer, he aggressively asserts in B-2 his intention to extract an answer from Myra, from whom one senses he has for a long time taken his directions. In quiet despair Myra voices the exhaustion of her ability to cope competently with what has become a hopeless situation: "It was me, Butch, just me. I'm tired. Can you understand that? Tired!"

These two short but richly expressive conversations with Myra and Butch bring into focus some of the common themes in the loss of selfhood experienced by the despairing. Though these themes blend together and intertwine, for the purpose of reflection and analysis we can differentiate the following qualities in the experience of loss of self in despair:

(1) Loss of trust. Myra no longer feels she can trust her own ability to carry the burdened, lonely life she has come into, nor does she see anyone in her situation whom she feels can and will try to understand what she is experiencing. The one hopeful sign that emerges in the conversation with the hospital chaplain is in M-12 when she tentatively suggests the faint hope that she can "talk to" the minister. At least he may not "blab" what she says to others and multiply her problems of trust and acceptance as have others (M-8).

The despairing person can often, like Myra, begin to feel isolated and cut off from sources of acceptance, trust, and nurture. This throws the person more and more back upon his or her own depleted and rapidly vanishing resources. Myra's "tiredness" has come about because she lacks relationships of trust in which her depleted sense of self can be refreshed. The result is a slow or more rapid depletion of her very sense of being a self of value and worth.

(2) Loss of integrity. Myra's loss is not simply of

relationships of trust. She has begun to experience her own personal depletion as a loss of integrity as a self. In Oden's terms she has no avenue of expression of authentic selfhood. She is filled with despairing guilt over her inability to go it alone, be a good mother, and maintain her equilibrium and competence. She feels desperately burdened by her present situation and totally unable to carry it further. There is no positive connection remaining between the self she feels herself to be and her vision of what her life and selfhood should be. Integrity gone, she feels unworthy of even her own efforts to salvage a self she can value.

(3) Loss of mutuality. Myra's loss of a sense of authentic selfhood lies in part in the way her relationships with the significant persons in her life have become structured so that there is little sense of mutual give and take, mutual care in them. One can speculate that the relationships in her family of origin lacked this quality of mutuality. Myra hints of authority and control struggles with her parents. Her intense need for nurturance—"someone who understands"—suggests that there may have been a heavy atmosphere of dependency in her earlier family style and that she was ill prepared for the give and take (what Farber calls demand for interpersonal giving) of marriage and a family of her own. Certainly she voices in her desperate cries about her marriage the loss of mutuality she experiences there.

(4) Loss of fulfillment or opportunity for self-realization. Myra's life has become a hopeless treadmill. One senses that she feels little fulfillment in her work that provides only a meager income. The necessity of working, combined with her lack of lively engagement in the tasks of motherhood, have cut her off from that avenue of self-realization so important for most parents. Without such meaningful avenues of self-expression, she in large part lacks the possibility of having those everyday experiences by which her sense of authentic selfhood may be restored. She "tends" to her work and her home

life only through the interpretative lens of her loneliness and deprivation. Hope, to be sustained, needs the atmosphere of self-actualization, though self-actualization by itself, as Durkheim has demonstrated, cannot long sustain itself.

(5) Loss of future. One does not sense that, in the common phrase, Myra has "anything to look forward to." Rather her consciousness is pervaded by that hopeless, treadmill feeling that there is only the now of monotonous existence with no purpose, no future, no end. Stated another way, it is as if the context within which Myra experiences her life has become very, very small, encompassing only the flat, empty events of meaningless work, drudging home life, and deprived emotional life. There is no larger, hopeful, expectant context toward which she can turn for new experience, fresh possibility, or altered situation. Life has closed in upon her, and unless interventions can be made from outside that encapsulating context, she has little basis for hoping for change in herself or her situation.

Chronic and Acute Despair

Some persons, like Myra, seem to live in a relatively chronic state of despair. Usually these are persons whose life situation, both historically and in the present, is marked by extreme deprivation of adequate nurturance and of hopeful possibility that things might be better. Many of the poor and oppressed people of our great cities as well as in such rural areas as Appalachia live in such chronic despairing states. They, out of necessity, tend to develop a hand-to-mouth, one-day-at-a-time style of living in quiet despair. Often one sees in these persons a tenacious and cunning ability to survive on what amounts to starvation rations of nurturance of all kinds. The structures and systems that deprive these persons run the gamut from family and neighborhood to opportunities for meaningful employment. Often, deprivation at all levels has been the state of these families for generations so that the usual family dreams of upward mobility, personal fulfillment, and social usefulness have themselves long since given way to chronic despair that the family situation will ever change.

In similar circumstances others whose immediate outward situation may be as deprived as their chronically despairing neighbors may, through the grace of meaningful family, church, or work relationships, manage much of the time to live hopeful, even joyful lives though in difficult circumstances. Anyone who has observed or participated in an inner-city black church made up largely of the poor will have seen countless such faithful, joyful people. The ingredients in their lives that are missing in the despairing are, quite apparently, nurturing, succoring relationships, a sense of authentic personhood, and hope for a better tomorrow (often expressed in a commitment to a religious vision of a "better land" in another life beyond death).

Here, of course, the church is presented with the necessity of developing a theology and mission of liberation. Such a theology and mission will not only seek to provide the community of fellowship and faith that nurtures hope within the church itself, but also grapple with the larger systemic issues of a society whose structures of affluence and corporate indifference to poverty and oppression create the social situation of chronic despair for countless people. The pastoral perspective on the crisis experience of chronic despair will itself demand that a larger image of ministry than simply the one-to-one effort to intervene in nurturing, hopeful ways in the lives of those caught in large and complex networks of despair-producing relationships, inform the life and mission of the church.

Other persons whose total life situation and history do not evidence the elements of chronic despair to which we have alluded, may, nevertheless, experience acute crises of despair that can be equally as devastating to their ability to engage the tasks of living in a lively, hopeful manner. For these persons the crisis most often is related to an event or series of events that, in the interpretation given them, embody real or symbolic threats to authentic, competent personhood. Most often these interpreted meanings of triggering events will relate to one or more of the themes of despair we have discussed in relation to the case of Myra. Even chronically despairing persons like Myra will most often experience the acute stress of severe or suicidal despair when an event or events have occurred which are interpreted as threats to authentic selfhood. To get more deeply into these experiences of acute despair we will need to press our phenomenological analysis a bit further.

The Pit of Despair

We have already proposed that despair involves an interpretation of experience by the despairing one. To be in despair means to have put together the bits and pieces of one's experience, usually in a rather haphazard, unsystematic fashion, in such a way that the affective and cognitive conclusion drawn is one of hopelessness and desperation. In the language of hermeneutics we might say that a vicious circle of interpretation is generated that then becomes the hermeneutical circle by which perva-sively all continuing experience is understood. As was indicated earlier, this proposed understanding of despair is not meant in any sense to contradict the presence of underlying unconscious dynamic forces that may be pushing the person toward a despairing interpretation of his or her experience. Probing for and understanding these unconscious factors will be of great importance in any long-term counseling with the despairing. Alongside that more traditional psychotherapeutic approach, we are here proposing a phenomenological avenue to understanding despair. Our hope is that this approach may provide a possibly fruitful avenue for developing a

The Pit of Despair

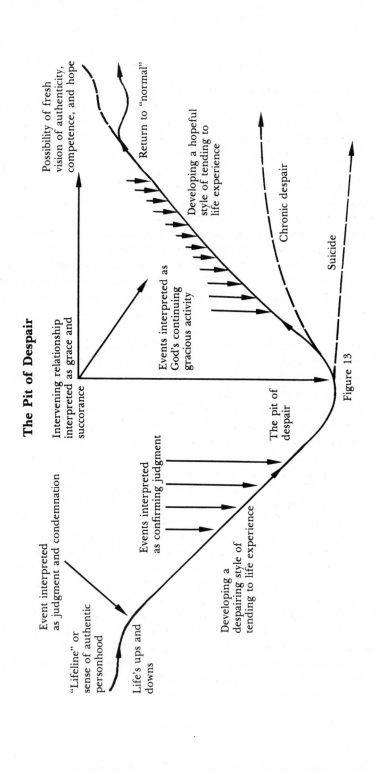

Figure 13

pastoral perspective and methodology for ministry to the despairing.

Figure 13 is an effort to present schematically both the way in which a despairing interpretation of experience develops and a possible approach to conceptualizing ministry to the despairing. The schema suggests that in the ordinary ups and downs of living, persons tend to maintain what we might call a "lifeline," or level of the sense of authentic personhood. This lifeline might be seen as in some sense analogous to what Karl Menninger has called the "vital balance."[14] It is to be expected that this level of liveliness will not always be constant, but rather that it will ebb and flow, move up or down depending upon what is happening in the everyday course of living and the interpretation being given by the person to these occurrences of experience.

The schema suggests that, whether we are speaking of the acute, suicidal despair of the chronically despairing or the sudden onset of despair in the person who most often is able to function with a fairly optimistic sense of authenticity and competence, the entrance into the pit of despair is most often triggered by an event or series of events that are interpreted as judgment and condemnation of the self. This event may be an incident of failure that triggers guilt and shame, an event of interpersonal rejection that brings feelings of abandonment and loss of self worth, or an event that throws into radical question the whole matter of the viability of the future for the person, thus triggering anxiety and the question of hope or hopelessness. Many different kinds of events can be interpreted as judgment and condemnation of the self.

Unless other events of a more positive, hopeful, self-affirming nature intervene to reverse the judgment and bring into operation a more hopeful hermeneutic, there will be set in motion the development of a style of what we have called tending to life experience that confirms and reinforces the judgment and condemnation of the self. Whether or not intervening events can reverse the process of entrance into the pit of despair will, of course, depend upon many factors, both personal and situational. Most of us, most of the time are able to have fresh experiences of self-affirmation so that our lifeline, though it has ups and downs, remains fairly constant. To develop over time, short or long, a despairing style of tending to life experience so that, through selective attention and inattention and the exercise of a despairing hermeneutic of interpretation, a primarily negative judgment of the self is confirmed, is to fall deeply into the pit of despair. Such a person becomes more and more caught in a downward spiral of despairing consciousness such that, insofar as the self is concerned, it becomes increasingly impossible to extricate oneself. The movement downward into the pit of despair becomes more and more deadly and hopeless. Suicide, or conditions symbolic of partial suicide (chronic despair being one of them), will follow unless something happens to intervene and alter the process.

If it is indeed true that entrance into despair is triggered by events interpreted as judgment and condemnation, then the importance for maintaining a hopeful, lively lifeline of implicit and explicit faith in that relationship with God by which the person is finally identified is of ultimate importance. Whether or not the traditional language of faith is utilized in interpretation of experiential events, the continuity of an awareness of one's acceptance by God despite one's unacceptability, to use a Tillichian phrase, is crucial in sustaining a hermeneutic of interpretation that avoids judgment and condemnation in the manner of one's tending to experience. It is just that sense of being understood and accepted despite life's ups and downs that the despairing have difficulty maintaining.

What then emerges from our reflection on the entrance into the pit of despair concerning what is most needed in ministering to the despairing? The schema of Figure 13 suggests that ministry to these persons must begin with a relationship that is willing to risk entrance into the pit of despair with the despairing person. The condition of being in the pit of despair means that the person is no longer able to interpret events or gestures from outside the pit of despair as offering hope and succor. Despairing patterns of tending to experience rule out such an interpretation. All efforts to cheer up the despairing, to remind them that their interpretation of experience is not the only possible one, that from someone else's perspective these events have another possible meaning, are to no avail. The condition of despair must first be shared by one who is willing to suffer the despairing condition with the other.

At this point the strand of pastoral care tradition that has drawn its analogy for the pastoral relationship from the kenotic image of the incarnation in Jesus becomes most relevant. As Jesus emptied himself, taking the form of a servant and became one with the human condition, so the pastor as God's representative must empty himself or herself of his or her own very different perspective on the events of judgment in the life of the despairing in order to understand and identify with the despair of the other. To the extent that the pastor is able to do this (always partial and imperfect), the way is opened for the despairing to experience the relationship as gratuitous, unearned, accepting despite the unacceptable, "condemned" state of the despairing. Reception of such a relationship of grace is most often acknowledged by the despairing through expressions such as one might expect to hear from Myra if her wish were fulfilled for "someone who understands." Only when such an unearned relationship which the despairing can interpret as gracious, understanding, alongside themselves in their despair, has been with some consistency and unintrusive intentionality offered and received can the despairing begin to feel some ray of hope for emergence from the pit of despair.

But simply the gratuitous offering of a relationship of

acceptance and hope will not in itself be sufficient to break the vicious downward spiral of despair. In fact, experience working with the despairing in pastoral counseling or group work with alcoholics, for example, would lead me to feel that, unless the pastoral relationship can move beyond mere identification with the sufferer in his or her despair, important as that is, prolonged identification with the despairing leads inevitably to despair on the part of the helping person, at least insofar as hope for help for this person is concerned. The vicious circle of a despairing tending to life experience must somehow be broken and in its place must be engendered a more hopeful, life-affirming hermeneutic of interpretation. Without that, either the relationship of grace and acceptance will be difficult if not humanly impossible to maintain, or the hermeneutic of despair will overpower the helping relationship as the despairing one has renewed experiences of judgment, condemnation, and hopelessness in other aspects of his or her life.

Reflection on the pastoral methodology problem conceived in the framework of the preceding paragraph suggests that the pastor must attempt to ferret out and bring into the community of awareness between himself or herself and the despairing person those experiences of other relationships, untended and overlooked events that may speak of hope, self-affirmation, and authenticity which can counter or contradict the despairing style of tending that has taken possession of the person's awareness. It is as if there are numerous allies to the pastor's succoring efforts that remain in the shadows of the person's life unresponded to and not given significance. New events that may offer the possibility of hopeful interpretation will occur. The problem is that of breaking the despairing hermeneutic circle so that an enlarged context of awareness and interpretation that includes forgiveness, acceptance, and a growing expectation of God's activity on human behalf can be fostered and a hopeful style of tending to experience engendered. Just how that process may take place and the nature of the pastoral methodologies involved should come more fully to light shortly as we look closely at a long-term pastoral relationship with a person in despair. It may, however, be useful to sketch out in general terms the elements that come together to make up the process of change. In skeleton outline they are as follows:

(1) The pastoral relationship is symbolically interpreted by the despairing person as representative of or incarnating the relationship of God to the self.

(2) A process is set in motion which involves an enlargement of and enlightening change in the context within which the person experiences the suffering of his or her despair. The pain of suffering is not removed, but the context of suffering, by being enlarged, loses some of its isolated, hopeless quality.

(3) A process is set in motion involving the bridging or gathering together in some greater wholeness of those splintered, separated aspects of self and life experience, i.e., the bridging of fantasy and reality, alienation and the desire for union or closeness, past and future, self and object world.

(4) The interpretation of new experience as God's activity seems to take place at points in the process that can best be described as "parabolic events" experienced "in the fullness of time" or at the right moment in the process. Interpretation of the parabolic event as momentous in the sense of involving God's activity seems to take place in retrospect.

(5) The process of finding new solutions to old suffering, a new and hopeful style of interpretation, is sometimes experienced by the person as a symbolic process of dying and being reborn. The intervening pastoral relationship is thus experienced as embodying both threat and promise eliciting both fear and resistance, on the one hand, and anxious longing, on the other.

It should be easily recognized that what we have been developing in this schema is a specific example of pastoral care as an expression of the third strand of pastoral care tradition set forth in chapter 1. From the standpoint of pastoral theology we are suggesting an approach to engendering a process of tending to life experience that is open to signals of God's continuing activity in fulfillment of his promise of unremitting care for his people.

Not all persons who succeed with help in developing a hopeful style of tending to life experience will, of course, interpret what they experience as God's activity. Some may simply return to their more customary pattern of ups and downs, more or less hopeful depending upon what they are able to carry with them of their experience of having been helped to emerge from the pit of despair. For some, however, as Kierkegaard has suggested, the experience of despair itself provides the grounding for a fresh vision of authentic selfhood, competence and hope precisely because their experience of acceptance and hope has become grounded transparently in God.

Despair is potentiated in proportion to consciousness of self; but the self is potentiated in the ratio of the measure proposed for the self, and infinitely potentiated when God is the measure. . . . Sin is: before God in despair not to will to be oneself, or before God in despair to will to be oneself.[15]

The self that has entered the pit of despair, and with the help of a gratuitous relationship been enabled to become aware of the sinful state of tending to life experience with a hermeneutic of despair, has put before itself the possibility of catching a fresh vision both of the self's possibilities and the ongoing activity of God in the self's behalf. Such a one will, through all of life's fresh ups and downs, find his or her life grounded in that more hopeful possibility that, with God's measure and succor, the self is potentiated in a process beyond itself.

Mrs. Reed: An Example
of Ministry to the Despairing

We turn now to a rather extended and careful consideration of one example of ministry to the despairing out of which many of the ideas presented in the previous section began to take shape. Here is a person who is readily identified as one who suffered from chronic despair for much of her life, though her coming for pastoral help was precipitated by an incident that threw her into acute despair of suicidal proportions. By sharing in some detail the story of her entrance into the pit of despair and subsequent involvement in an extended pastoral counseling relationship I hope to explicate in greater depth the process by which an individual found what was interpreted as divine grace and acceptance through a pastoral relationship and a series of events interpreted as confirmation of a new life grounded transparently in God.

I had not talked with anyone about Mrs. Reed prior to our first time together. She had called me at my office saying that a minister of my acquaintance had suggested that I might help her. The suffering of desperation was evident in her words, her voice, and the urgency of her request that I see her. Some few minutes after the appointed time there came a quick and faint knock on my office door. Being involved in writing something at my desk at the time, I called to her to come in. As I rose from the desk there appeared a woman who was, by everything about her appearance, the most pitiable example of human suffering and despair that I had encountered in a very long time. She wore an ill-fitting black dress that sagged to one side so that her underclothing drooped below it by several inches on the other. Her hair was disheveled as if it had received no care for several weeks. On her face were all the marks of suffering—fear, pain, a look of self-loathing and despair. Her eyes also communicated that suspicion and expectation of hurt that

189

spoke of having suffered much at the hands of her fellow humans.

At the moment during which I was taking in this blatant impression of suffering and despair, she, too, was trying to sense who this strange man across the room might be. Quickly she turned, as if to go as far and as fast away from me as possible. My response to this was quite spontaneous: "Don't go yet; there may be help for you here." She stood for the next several minutes in the door while I renewed my invitation to come in from across the room, fearing that if I moved toward her she would really flee in panic.

Those first moments of our relationship were excruciatingly painful both for Mrs. Reed and, in a sense, for me. Some twenty minutes passed before she, with great reluctance and much protest that she was wasting my time, finally sat down in a chair at some distance from me. In those first moments she introduced me to what were to be the two central themes of our relationship for many months to come: her desperate fear that still more condemnation and greater suffering might be the result of our being together and her overpowering and pervasive guilt, shame, and self-rejection. At the end of the hour I invited her to return the next week at the same time. Her first response to this was quite like her initial response at the door. Then, as if having decided something, she smiled faintly and told me that she had expected a much older man, at least someone past seventy! I replied that I could not change my age for her, but that the invitation to return still stood. I would reserve the time for her. Somewhat to my surprise she did come back, and we were together for an hour each week for approximately the next three years with three or four periods of several weeks during which she did not come, usually because something we had talked about was too painful or frightening for her to risk returning for a time.

Slowly over the first eighteen months Mrs. Reed's story of despair and suffering unfolded. When we first met she was approximately sixty years old, being the mother of two children now grown. Both children are married and have children of their own and, in addition, her family included several brothers and sisters with whom Mrs. Reed grew up on a farm near a small village in south Georgia. Her marriage, a short-lived affair, had ended in divorce not long after the birth of her second child. Since that time she had first supported her children and later maintained herself by working as an unlicensed practical nurse engaged largely in private-duty care either of new mothers with babies or very sick, often elderly patients confined to their beds at home.

Despair for Mrs. Reed began with her earliest memories, now encapsulated in two vividly painful recollections. One was of her father, whom she describes as a blunt and cruel man. The memory is of his looking at her in a new dress ready for Sunday school in the little country church and saying, "Well, if you had to be a girl, you might at least have been pretty." So she shunned him and feared him until she became old enough to leave home as a teen-age bride. The memory of her mother was likewise full of a more quiet kind of despair, though now muted by idealization. Mother was dutiful, but coldly unemotional, and the pain of recollection brought to mind in one of our conversations was of an occasion when she needed desperately to talk with her mother and could not. The tears that hovered in the back of her eyes with the telling of this spoke of disappointment, longing, and loneliness.

Though her black clothes and blackened conscience spoke deeply of shame and guilt, the event around which all this self-inflicted punishment and rejection clustered in Mrs. Reed's memory was not revealed to me for nearly two years. It became more and more clear that something so terrible as to be unspeakable had happened, but still the safety of the accepting relationship I attempted to offer was not firm enough to risk the sharing. Loss of trust had become a familiar yardstick by which Mrs. Reed measured all new possibilities in relationships. Finally, with all the emotion of a fresh and acutely here-and-now experience, the revelation came. When she was twelve and just beginning to experience the excitement of becoming a woman, she had been raped by "one of the men on the farm." Frightened and ashamed, she longed to tell her mother, but could not. She decided she must forever suffer her secret alone, and so an already lonely, disappointed, and insecure girl began to live a life of isolation and estrangement, interpreting all the experience of her life through the dark lens of her shameful defilement. She lived in constant anxiety lest someone find her out. Slowly she began to split her experience into two worlds. In the one she became, like her mother, dutiful and unfeeling, mechanically fulfilling what was required of her, even marrying and bearing children, but all without love or hate, meaning or purpose, save the bleak and arid purpose of dutifully living out her despair. In her other world she dreamed of love and beauty, travel and discovery, joy and peace. That world was like a fairy tale, complete with magic wands and princesses, white knights and love trysts.

By the time her children were grown, the splitting of Mrs. Reed's life as her only desperate means of coping with suffering had become fixed in a chronically stylized pattern that in the language of medical psychiatry would be called ambulatory schizophrenia. In her work as a practical nurse she was, as she described it, "not really there." She took care of people as her mother had cared for her, dutifully, without affect, without involvement. When she went home, which, when I first knew her, was a room in the home of one of her sisters, she entered her "other world," which, like the Garden of Eden before the Fall, had no knowledge of good and evil. Here she was beautiful and innocent; she traveled and knew intimately many people, all of whom loved and admired her. Most of all, this world was safe from pain and suffering, a world without despair. All the stories had happy endings.

Although Mrs. Reed did not complete elementary school, she developed a pattern of writing her thoughts and feelings, her fantasies and wishes, while alone in her other world. These writings she never shared with anyone. Only after more than two years in our relationship did she begin to share these writings with me, and then only during our times together, always making sure that she had them back when she left the office.

The event that brought Mrs. Reed to me, I gradually learned, was another intervening relationship that, without her being aware of it, broke through the wall of separation between her two worlds and threw her into the pit of acute despair. By chance she accepted an assignment to care for a man recovering from a cardiovascular accident and was his nurse for a number of months. He was a gentle and learned man, without family, and therefore quite lonely. In the long hours after he regained his speech, he and Mrs. Reed began to talk about many things—he because he needed a companion, she because it was her duty to be pleasant to her patients. As the months passed, they become more and more persons to one another and, much to Mrs. Reed's surprise, when he was well enough that he no longer needed her as his nurse, she found she missed their conversations. The cataclysmic event of judgment came when, quite unexpectedly, he called her and invited her to go for an automobile ride with him, "so I can show you how well I can drive." The real purpose of his invitation was, however, to ask her to be his wife. The panic she felt at this suggestion became overwhelming when he casually, and quite innocently and appropriately, mentioned the sexual fulfillment that they could be for one another. With that she made him stop the car and literally fled back to her room. She never saw him again, and some three or four weeks later she came to me. In the intervening weeks she had been preoccupied with thoughts of suicide, her condemned state, and fear of punishment.

An atmosphere dominated by Mrs. Reed's hermeneutic of despair prevailed in our conversations from the beginning for many months. It was as if she brought with her into the counseling room the expectation and fear of condemnation and the guilty self-judgment that she deserved whatever suffering might come. Despair had been the context of her total life to this time and the acute despair she now felt was only a confirmation of what she had always perceived her fate to be. Despair provided the interpretative lens through which all her experience was filtered. The testing of the safety of the room accompanied by testing for rejection from me that would match her own self-rejection seemed ever present, though the levels on which this testing took place and the risks she felt free to take became deeper and more central to the core of her despair. This sensitivity to the context within which she shared her suffering with me was almost unbelievably acute. Facial expressions, clothing, what was on my desk, the presence one day of a new piece of dictating equipment—in short, all the verbal and nonverbal languages of communication—seemed to speak to her of the context in which we were together. There would be times when she seemed satisfied that it was safe and accepting; in these times she began to tell me freely of her two worlds. At other times she was frightened, elusive, or preoccupied with her "black heart."

Slowly and with many reversals, she and I both began to sense that the context in which Mrs. Reed experienced her suffering was beginning to change. She became more aware of objects and people around her that she had not noticed before. She would report on lively conversations she had engaged in with people on the bus on her way to my office. She talked less of her "other world" and of the pain of the past. She still, however, pressed me to agree with her that she was "too old to grow up," or "just a silly girl in an old lady's body," or in some way worthy of rejection. It got to be a game between us in which I would laugh and tell her she was doing it again, and she slowly began to laugh with me at herself. The context of her suffering was beginning to change. She was beginning to trust the pastoral relationship and the message of acceptance I was attempting to communicate.

As was noted earlier in our description of the second element in the process of emergence from the pit of despair, the quality and intensity of Mrs. Reed's suffering had not by this point significantly diminished. She continued to be preoccupied with feelings of fear and self-hatred. The acuteness of her sensitivity to the possibility of pain was, if anything, increased rather than diminished. The context within which her struggle with despair took place, however, was beginning to change markedly. Thomas W. Klink, in his *Depth Perspectives in Pastoral Work*,[16] points to the important distinction between pain that is meaningless and despairing, and suffering having to do with the integrative "work" of suffering that must be endured if meaning and hope are to be found. Our suggestion is that the intervention that makes possible moving from the pain of despair to the work of meaningful suffering has to do with the quiet, insistent effort of the helper to change the context within which the pain is experienced. The theological stance that informs that effort is one of representing or incarnating a relationship analogous to the Christian kerygma concerning the relationship between God and the self.

Indentifiable changes in the context within which the despairing one begins to experience his or her suffering seem best described by such words as "enlarged" and "enlightened." By enlarged I mean that the sufferer begins to experience the pain of despair as human pain set in the context of human life related to other human beings. Glimpses of "my pain" as congruent with and related to the pain of all humans seem to take place in the process of context enlargement. The pit of despair becomes less private and isolating. By enlightened I mean that the pain and anguish of suffering begins to shift from being a meaningless, empty experience of despair in the direction of becoming meaningful. The work of transforming the hermeneutic of interpretation by which all of experience has been understood has begun. This process was with Mrs. Reed a multi-faceted one pertaining to her own history, the clarifying of aspects of her pain, and the naming of those persons who had been her tormentors. Only much later did it involve a reworking of the symbols of religious faith that were Mrs. Reed's heritage. Here again we see evidence that pastoral work must first take place at the level of what I have called implicit faith before more explicit reappropriation of religious symbols can take place.

Though there were many incidents, both within the counseling room and in her life outside it, that were turning points for her, there was a series of three experiences over the first eighteen months of the relationship that were of such profound and changing importance to her that I came to think of them as being like parables that happened at crucial times in such a way as to be momentous for Mrs. Reed. Each of these parabolic experiences was brought up again and again as if it had caught up the whole of something that was happening to and within Mrs. Reed as a result of our work together. It was in the process of interpretation of these experiences that a transformation gradually took place in Mrs. Reed's style of interpretation. Her interpretations began to move in the direction of seeing events in her experience as evidence of God's gracious activity on her behalf, though only much later was she able to bring that interpretation clearly into focus.

The first of these parabolic experiences had to do with her outer attire that had for so many years spoken mutely of her inner life. For years she had worn nothing but black except for the white uniforms she put on to do her task as a practical nurse. Though I had never verbally called her attention to the way she dressed, after a time she began to refer to her black dress as expressing her "black heart" and the white uniform as expressing the way in which she did her work without fear or feeling of any kind. She invited me to make a judgment about the "goodness" and "badness" of this. I usually met these invitations only with a comment about the contrast and the harshness with which she had passed her own judgments on herself. The theme kept recurring.

The parabolic experience relative to her dress came one day after she left my office. She went downtown to catch a bus and, on impulse, walked past a department store that had window displays of women's clothing. Her eye caught sight of a red dress. As she described the experience several weeks later, she quickly looked away, but seemed drawn by the dress. She walked back and forth in front of the store several times feeling tremendously excited and yet without her old and familiar fear and guilt. Finally, as if in response to some new feeling, she went in and bought the dress in her size. By the time she got home, the "new feeling" had faded and she quickly put the dress away in a drawer. But in the days that followed it kept attracting her and on one occasion she put it on, but did not leave her room. Instead she decided to tell me of the experience the next time we were together. The following several weeks we spent exploring the meaning of what had happened and what she wanted to do about it. At one point I invited her to wear the dress to see me. The next week she did not come. Finally, however, she wore the dress and we spent the time talking about how she felt in it and what it would mean to be rid of her black heart. She wondered aloud if God had been involved in her impulse to go past that store. My response was to affirm that something of ultimate importance to her was in the experience.

The symbol of the red dress slowly became for Mrs. Reed a token of beginning acceptance of forgiveness and an awakening sense of wholeness in her personhood. The symbol also had, as we were to confirm later, another meaning relative to her unspoken desire for that which she so greatly feared. Taken as a whole, the red dress experience marked a significant change in the way Mrs. Reed held together the brokenness and self-condemnation of her life.

In the months that followed, Mrs. Reed moved to change her pattern of separation of her experience into two worlds. Not only did she stop wearing black, but she also began to bring to me observations of people and her own thoughts and feelings about her work. It was as if, having been blind to the world of reality around her, she was now beginning to see other people and give her observations an enlarged interpretation and significance. This process led to two other momentous experiences that, like the first, seemed to occur in the fullness of time and to gather together into some glimpse of wholeness some of the separated and broken pieces of her life.

One day, some months after the red dress experience, Mrs. Reed came to her appointment looking quite like a new and different person. Not only was she no longer in black, but her hair was quite becomingly arranged and tinted to highlight its gray and her cheeks were faintly and warmly pink. She could not wait to tell me what had happened. Again, on impulse, she had decided to go to a hairdresser, something she had never before in her life even thought of doing. She had noticed a little shop that had opened in her neighborhood and one afternoon after work she went without an appointment. The momentous thing about this experience, in contrast to the first, was that Mrs. Reed walked in and told the woman that she knew nothing about such things but was looking for someone who would take some time "with a foolish old lady" and teach her how to be as beautiful as one could be considering her age. Mrs. Reed described in a warm and tender way her gratitude that the woman did not turn her away or laugh at her, but matter-of-factly said she would be happy to try. "I think she was a Jewish girl, or a refugee of some kind. She did not speak English well, and I think she knew what it is like to be afraid and ugly." To Mrs. Reed the hairdresser seemed to provide some kind of bridge from despair toward a more hopeful, optimistic attitude toward herself and the future.

Following this experience Mrs. Reed began to talk now and again about her isolation from people. Simultaneously she also began to hint at some strangely angry feeling that she could no longer "get back in that other world" whenever she wanted to, alone in her room. She became at one point somewhat preoccupied with the suffering of other people and the painful price one had to pay to be aware of the world around one. During several hours she spoke of wondering if she really had been a "sinner" all these years because of her alienation from people, even though she attended church regularly. She confessed that she always went late so she would not have to shake hands and be friendly with people, and left during the final hymn for the same reason. In Kierkegaard's terms, she was becoming aware of her past refusal to will to be herself in relation to other persons. Her despairing, condemning judgment of herself had been altered by the new context the parabolic experiences had thrust upon her.

The matter of shaking hands became during that time a crucial concern for Mrs. Reed. This act of touching and being touched had powerful dynamic linkage with the long-harbored traumatic suffering of her childhood. Now she began to share with me little by little the story of her sexual assault and subsequent pervasive feeling of being unclean. Simultaneously I noted that in her own very subtle and hidden way, she was becoming more womanly and at times even coquettish in her manner with me. We were moving toward another crisis in our relationship when Mrs. Reed would have to make another momentous decision either to maintain her despairing style of tending to her experience or to adopt a more hopeful stance that accepted her experience as authentically her own.

The parabolic experience related to these issues came following a counseling hour during which Mrs. Reed struggled openly and literally with the problem of human touch. She spoke about how she could touch her patients without fear because it was only a mechanical act made necessary by duty. To shake another's hand was another matter. Finally I extended my hand to her across the desk and for the next twenty minutes she struggled with that invitation. At the end of the time she came and stood across the desk from me and reached toward my hand, drew back, and, after several minutes shook my hand quickly, said good-bye, and left.

The following Sunday Mrs. Reed went for the first time in many years to church before the time for the service to begin. As expected, when she entered the door, there stood an usher with his hand outstretched in greeting. She took his hand, murmured a hasty good morning, and started toward her usual place in an obscure back corner of the church. The usher, however, invited her to follow him and, strangely, she did not refuse. He took her near the front of the crowded church and seated her, of all places, beside a man who was obviously without companions. At this point, Mrs. Reed reported, she almost fled in panic. But something held her. Time came for the first hymn and the man held out the hymnal for her to join him. She started to refuse, whispering, "I can't sing." His response was for Mrs. Reed the decisive thing in the experience. He whispered back to her, "I can't either, but we can hold the book!" She took the proffered hymnal and later reported the next few moments as being a deeply moving time of being joined with a fellow sufferer.

The three parabolic experiences have been presented with some narrative detail in order that a number of concepts related to the process of emergence from the pit of despair may be illustrated. First, they reveal how the pastoral counseling relationship can become a bridge by means of which a growing circle of relationship possibilities may be tested and given transforming significance by the person. The acceptance found in the pastoral relationship provides the impetus for testing the altered self-understanding it offers in other experiences. These new experiences are then tended with the new hermeneutic the pastoral relationship has contained. Second, though there is a constant flow of experience being taken in by the person, some of which verifies the changing self-awareness while some seems to confirm old patterns of perception, certain events seem to occur which, because of their significance in relation to the dynamic questions at issue in the counseling process and the radically new interpretation given them, have transforming effect. Numerous other experiences, re-lated and unrelated, were shared by Mrs. Reed in the counseling room during this period, some more significant and affect-laden than others. But in the case of the three reported experiences, something of more profound significance was quite apparently present. Like the biblical parable, they had an "it is as when . . ." quality about them that gathered up in a decisive, momentous way the meaning of what was breaking into Mrs. Reed's experience. The very manner of her tending to life experience demanded altering. Each parabolic experi-ence was followed by a period of reflection, rethinking, and integration of the experience into a whole new gestalt by which Mrs. Reed began to perceive her existence. Always it seemed this involved some return to long familiar, but until now less potent or less well understood religious symbols.

Not long after the experience in the church Mrs. Reed's coquettishness with me became an open interest in discussing the whole matter of sexuality, with mounting indications that the wish contained in the red dress and transformed appearance was now coming strongly to the fore in our relationship. After waiting a number of weeks for some sign that Mrs. Reed was ready to put her wishes into words, I finally very gently suggested what I saw was happening. Immediately, Mrs. Reed leaped from her chair and ran out of the room, later to call me asking why I had to ruin everything that had happened between us. My confrontation had again brought to the fore her self-understanding as one who deserved judgment and condemnation. I reminded her of the many other things she had talked through with me and suggested that this, too, could be dealt with in a way that might bring her not more pain but deepened understanding.

After an absence of four weeks Mrs. Reed returned, and it was as if during her time away something old and deeply troubling to her had died and she was now beginning anew with hope and anticipation. She rather matter-of-factly told me that she guessed it was all right for an old woman to have young ideas, but that she knew I had a wife and children and that any wishes she had were only that. From that point on our relationship was openly warm and intimate, but the fearful, wishful, dreadful expectation of assault or seduction and the judgment that went with it were no longer present except in fleeting and clearly recognized flashes. Usually Mrs. Reed's comment on becoming aware of one of these moments would be to laugh and ask me if I thought she would ever grow up!

It is my experience that such times of critical, life-or-death change are not infrequent in the process of helping despairing persons. It is as if old and deeply buried wishes and fears form the nucleus around which the despairing style of tending to and interpreting experience cluster. The self-condemnation and judgment of the self holds these wishes and fears alien to the ego at bay beneath the level of awareness. As the helping relationship breaks through the hermeneutic circle of despair, these wishes and fears come to the fore and must be worked through in a different way to again form a nucleus around which a more hopeful, self-accepting hermeneutic is formed. It is as if something old and central to the self must die that something new may be born, and this poses both threat and promise. It is, of course, possible to approach these data from other frames of reference, as, for example, the psychoanalytic framework of the transference. The momentous, life-or-death decisiveness that surrounds the experience, however, coupled with the religious symbolism that frequently is brought to bear in the interpretative process, seems to warrant the use of the death and rebirth metaphor.

The Symbolization of Experience as Signals of God's Activity

Though much remains unshared of the pastoral counseling relationship with Mrs. Reed, perhaps enough has been related to give a flavor of the process by which she entered and then began to emerge from the pit of despair. What needs further clarification is the process by which the implicit faith connections between what she was experiencing and her religious faith became more explicit and open to reconsideration. I will call this the process of symbolization of experience as signals, glimpses, or signs of God's activity on behalf of the self.

My assumption about the process of symbolization is that, within whatever community of religious language is the heritage of an individual, there is at least latent in every individual the necessity of making ultimate sense out of what life brings to him or her and what the person's response to the ultimate significance of what he or she has experienced is to be. Langdon Gilkey has described religious language in this manner:

Religious language, and so its symbol of God, requires that some significant mode of ultimacy or absoluteness be latent within the object to which the symbol is applied, that the sacred transcend, and infinitely, the finite in and through which it appears. By the same token, however, since the sacred to which the language refers appears in the finite, illuminating and transforming it, the continuous relatedness of ultimacy to the finite is also implied. . . . Thus religious language, in a way that arises out of its multivalent form, is essentially paradoxical: it is referent to ultimacy and absoluteness, but through finite media.[17]

I have already alluded to the paradoxical manner in which Mrs. Reed interpreted what we have called her parabolic experiences so that both the immediacy and powerfully feelingful (finite) quality of the experience became real for her and the momentous quality (ultimacy) was reflected about and acted upon in subsequent experience. This brought about the new hermeneutic of hope and expectation. The momentous quality of the parabolic experiences was observable in process simultaneous with the reporting of the events outside the counseling room as well as in the counseling relationship itself. Heightened affect, a sense of excitement that something of great significance had taken place or was in the process of taking place, and an atmosphere of climax or fulfillment of something that had been in process for a time marked the parabolic events as of ultimate importance and decisive. Although the rhythm of involvement in the work of suffering and search, on the one hand, and reflection about the meaning of what had happened, on the other, characterized the entire counseling process, reflection leading toward a reworking of Mrs. Reed's religious symbols seemed consistently to take place in retrospect, most significantly subsequent to each of the parabolic experiences. Likewise, the process of reflection seemed consistently to take the form of associating the momentous experience with one or another religious symbol out of Mrs. Reed's own tradition, reflection upon the relationship between the fresh experience and the religious symbol, and restructuring of both symbol and understanding of experience. Thus the momentous, decisive experiences provided both the impetus for restructuring of religious symbols and were themselves integrated into a new and fresh understanding of the meaning of Mrs. Reed's existence as a whole. This interplay of experience, reflection, restructuring of symbol, and decision shaped the formation of a new hermeneutic by which Mrs. Reed began to interpret her experience, including her experience of God.

A letter from Mrs. Reed while she was away on her first trip outside her native state provides further illustration of the process of symbolization. The letter was written shortly after what I have called the death and rebirth experience concerning sexuality and the pervasive feeling of uncleanliness. In part Mrs. Reed writes:

Standing here in the midst of God's handiwork, I find my faith renewed or maybe the birth of a real faith, for I think now I never had any faith. I think in my dreamy world of make-believe I only grasped the things I heard that were useful to me. Standing alone under the stars and viewing the vastness of nature I very dimly understand what David meant when he said "The heavens declare the glory of God," and you feel as if the mist or dew of heaven can wash you clean and why cannot it be so? For the Bible tells us, "Though our sins be as scarlet He will make them white as snow; though they be red like crimson He will make them white as wool." And if you think He will do this for a hardened sinner who deliberately planned and sinned, would He not clean and make whole a person who was defiled and made to feel unclean all their lives by what was done to them by brute force when they were only an ignorant, unloved child? Standing here on a mountainside alone at two in the morning looking out on a sleeping world I feel that this is so; I feel as if I were being lifted up and for the first time since I was a child I feel pure and clean. . . .

Up here none can look at the vastness of the universe and doubt the reality of God, or read the prayer Christ taught his disciples and not recognize the fatherhood of God, for he taught us to say, "Our Father." . . . I have a strange feeling as if the place where I stand is holy and that it will be my Bethel, the well where I left my waterpot. O, if only it is! If here I can leave everything: my hurt, hate, anger, resentment and fears. If I can carry the peace I have found up here back with me I know I will be a different person. Though I am an old woman I will always know that I was really born on a lonely mountainside. . . . I wonder if I will be able to grow into a real woman. Will I have the time, live long enough, have the courage? I trust that I will.

Here Mrs. Reed quite clearly places her experience in the context of her relationship with God and focuses her decision and hope for the future in that relationship. The symbols she uses are biblical and consistent with her own religious heritage. The experience these symbols now contain is claimed as fresh, uniquely personal, and determinative of her future. Having faced and worked through her despair and claimed a new hermeneutic of hope and expectancy, her vision of selfhood is grounded transparently in God.

CHAPTER VII

Identity Crisis and Change

Our plunge into the crisis of despair has brought into focus the fundamental human need for a structure of meaning and interpretation by which the events and relationships of our lives can be ordered. Life must somehow make sense. Connections must be made. Meanings must be found that link together both the random and the regular events that occur to give them a quality of predictability and wholeness. To be without such a structure of interpretation is to find oneself threatened with chaos and profound anxiety. The hermeneutic of despair itself comes into being in large part because, given who the person is and the events that have occurred, it is the only interpretation that "makes sense" to the person. The suffering of despair, painful and paralyzing as it is, is more tolerable than the chaotic possibility that there is no meaning structure that can render what has happened intelligible.

Our study of despair has also revealed how closely tied together are the structures of interpretation of events and relationships and the self-understanding of the person. Who I am, how things appear, and what they mean are of a piece. Not only that, who I am and the meaning of what happens must have some continuity as one moves from time to time and place to place. Thus a hermeneutic of interpretation and an ongoing sense of identity are necessary for survival in a finite human existence within the boundary of ongoing time.

We cannot speak of identity in its modern psychological usage without acknowledging the cardinal impor-

tance of the work of Erik Erikson.[1] Erikson, a neo-
Freudian ego psychologist, proposes the concept of
identity as that cognitive and affective configuration of
characteristics that provide the self with a sense of
self-sameness amidst changing priorities in the tasks of
the human life cycle and changed external circumstances. At one level the concept points to a certain
continuity of style in being a person. This includes
everything from the habitual use of a certain turn of
phrase in speech or writing to body postures and modes
of relating to others. At a deeper level identity suggests an
unconscious striving for continuity of personal character
that brings automatic responses to new situations making
use of old experience as a kind of template of perception
and response. Identity means a certain idiosyncratic way
in which the individual ego performs its tasks of
perceiving, valuing, reasoning, compromising, and
choosing. At yet another level the concept points to that
maintenance of one's rootage in solidarity with a group's
ideals and corporate identity.

Throughout all of these functions of identity there
runs a tension between the need for continuity of
selfhood and the necessity of change. Time places a
boundary that sets a limit on the human desire for
continuity. But the self sets its boundaries as over against
the impacts of changing reality in order to preserve its
sense of self as recognizable to the self. Peter Marris, in a
remarkably useful book titled *Loss and Change,* based on
his experience with dislocated persons in a variety of
contexts on several continents, speaks of this human need
for continuity as "the conservative impulse."[2] By this
Marris means that humans survive and adapt to a wide
variety of circumstances only because there is in human
beings a deep-seated impulse both to consolidate
meanings and patterns of perception into a certain way of
seeing things and stubbornly to impose that mind-set
upon new circumstances even at the cost of overlooking or contradicting facts that may be apparent to an

outside observer. In this sense we are all profoundly conservative.

The conservative impulse implies, then, an intolerance of unintelligible events. For if we were to encounter frequently events on which we could not impose an interpretation, our behavior would become alarmingly disoriented. But nothing becomes meaningful until it is placed in a context of habits of feeling, principles of conduct, attachments, purposes, conceptions of how people behave; and the attachments which make life meaningful are characteristically specific. They cannot readily be transferred. Purposes which might be satisfied in many ways become associated with a particular relationship or setting, and cannot thereafter be detached from it without anxiety.[3]

Here comes into view a wide panoply of human crisis experiences that has come, since the widely appropriated work of Erikson, to be called identity crisis. Under that broad umbrella we would generally include all of those crises in which the existential tension between the continuity of identity and altered circumstances, changed tasks, and contradictory meanings becomes so stretched as to throw the person or group into a crisis of self-world understanding that threatens both self-perception and the self's hermeneutic of interpretation.

An Example of Family Identity Crisis

Franklin and Ann Harris, now in their mid-forties, have been married for nearly twenty-five years. They have two children, a boy eleven and a girl seventeen. Their marriage has always, until recently, been a stable and comfortable one. Both had been reared in small Southern towns, she as one of the middle children in a family of eight and he as an only child. Both families of origin had been steeped in Southern cultural values that included respect for one's elders, family solidarity, genuine religious commitment, and hard work.

As an only child, Franklin had been both indulged and sheltered from financial hardship by his parents. Ann on the other hand, had known what it meant to have too large a family and not quite enough space or food. She was proud of her husband's modest but secure position as office manager in one of the mills in their county seat hometown; he rather took his work for granted and enjoyed being close to the mill management.

The event that precipitated an identity crisis for both Ann and Franklin as well as other members of their family was the somewhat unexpected retirement of Franklin's parents because of his father's declining health. A long illness took most of the parents' accumulated savings and with what funds were left they, at Franklin's suggestion, built an addition to Franklin's house to provide a spacious bedroom for the parents. No real discussion took place as to how much of the rest of the house the elder Harris' were to share with the rest of the family, and slowly over a period of months they "took over" the family room and kitchen because both enjoyed television and the elder Mrs. Harris liked to cook. Ann, meanwhile, decided to get a job, since there did not seem to be as much for her to do at home as before, and besides, they now needed the money, what with the daughter's approaching college and the added expense of having two more adults in the house. A pattern developed in which the younger Harris family began more and more to "live" in the bedrooms upstairs while the retirees took over the use of the main floor of the house.

Within a year the marriage that had been so stable began to deteriorate. Petty bickering over inconsequential things began to erupt at times into violent arguments. Ann began to suspect that her husband was being unfaithful to her with another woman in his office. For his part, Franklin was increasingly feeling caught between his loyalty to his parents and his desire for some privacy in which to restore his marriage. This was symbolized for him by what seemed constant running down stairs to "spend some time with the folks" and hurrying back upstairs to placate Ann. In his view she suddenly had changed from a pleasant, supportive wife to a suspicious and complaining woman who spoke frequently of wanting to leave him "if it weren't for the children."

The strands of identity continuity with accompanying strain in the context of changed circumstances run in several directions in the Harris family. Franklin, whose identity and interpretation style was strongly colored by the childhood experience of being able to take the care of his needs for granted, had stumbled into the stressful situation of having his parents take over his house. He had taken for granted that his wife and children would be glad to accommodate to his and his parents' need to shelter them as they had sheltered him. Now the stress that his decision had caused was unintelligible to him. Why was everyone so unhappy? But the switching of roles that had taken place between him and his parents was also a strange and new experience for him. Suddenly their needs became his responsibility. He must be the shelterer instead of the sheltered. In relationship to his parents, that seemed right and proper. He could accept that role change, though it made him anxious and unsure of himself. But what had happened to Ann? He had always been able to count on her for support and encouragement. Now she only complained and argued. His insistent interpretation was that for some unintelligible reason she no longer cared for him.

For Ann the changed circumstances brought painful feelings of dislocation. Someone was literally pushing her from her own house. Having had a secure and comfortable marriage in which she found her identity as homemaker and mother of her children, she found herself working at a job she didn't really want and unable to get to her own kitchen to cook a meal because her mother-in-law had already prepared it. Old childhood interpretation patterns having to do with too many people under the same roof and not enough to go around began to reassert themselves and she strangely found herself thinking about "getting out."

The behavior of Franklin's parents likewise indicates the tenacity of old patterns of identity and interpretation in a drastically altered situation requiring change. Now aging and increasingly dependent upon their son and his family, both Mr. and Mrs. Harris in their quiet but insistent "takeover" in their son's house are perpetuating their image of themselves as the providers. Meanwhile the priority of their own need for a household of which they are the senior parental members has become dominant in the changed living situation in which this is no longer appropriate. More recently they have become aware of the growing unhappiness in the home and have asked their son to "tell us if we are the problem," but have done so in such a way as to invite his quick denial. The question has strangely devolved into talk about whether they should come upstairs in the evening to talk to Franklin and Ann or whether it is "the children's responsibility to come down and talk to us." Here we can clearly see the degree to which old patterns of identity and interpretation persist—an extreme which appears so ludicrous as to border on the bizarre to the outside observer. The elder Harris' growing discomfort with the situation is apparent in their having recently gone to their pastor to talk about their concern for their son's marriage. They seemed at that time to the pastor to be vaguely aware of their role in the family conflict but helpless to alter their adaptation to the changed circumstances of their lives.

We see in the Harris family the way in which individual identity crisis and family crisis are often intertwined. Both at the individual and family levels the Harrises are experiencing in their own idiosyncratic way the inevitable changes of the individual and family life cycles. From what we know of the history of the family, at an earlier time when the elder Harrises had their own home and relatively comfortable income, both families and the individuals in them were functioning fairly well with no more conflict than many families in which underlying issues of dependency versus autonomy play a central role in determining family style. The separate residences of the two families and consequent occasional times of being together provided enough space and freedom in their separate lives to make comfortable accommodation to each other's needs possible. For Ann, having her own house and family provided the security she needed that there was a "place" for her. The tension between dependency on parents and an identity of his own was for Franklin held in a comfortable balance, with his taken-for-granted supportive relationship with Ann providing the nurture that he needed to feel secure and self-sustaining. Separately the two Harris families were thus able to live relatively healthy, well-adapted lives.

In retrospect it appears obvious that the shift in the direction of identity crisis for all four Harrises began with the decision, forced by the breakdown in the elder Mr. Harris' health, to consolidate the two families under one roof. Here loyalty to deep cultural traditions about families "taking care of their own" came into play to rule out the option of a retirement home in a nearby city for the elder Harris couple. Another family, more adapted to an urbanized, nuclear family social structure might well not even have considered adding a room for the retirees. In that case the identity crisis would have been largely borne by the elder Harrises as they were transplanted from a home of their own in familiar surroundings to a retirement complex in the city. Here we see how the dynamics of societal change interact with individual and family life cycle change to shape identity crisis in certain ways depending upon whether and how much a given family remains loyal to traditional cultural values.

Once the Harrises had made the choice to live under the same roof, the identity crisis in the family was set in motion because there existed an apparent tacit assumption by all concerned, with the possible exception of Ann, that life could go on as before without significant identity changes for anyone. The combined household became for the elder Harrises "their" household, and the younger couple, by their actions at least, accepted that. They moved the center of their activity upstairs, thus within the confines of one house persevering in the attempt to manage the family relationships by means of separate space. Ann took a job away from home. Franklin became again the son who wanted deeply to please his parents and keep their nurture of him flowing. A full-blown identity crisis for all four was in the making. Franklin and Ann, seemingly forced to accommodate to the insistent preservation of old identity patterns by Franklin's parents, were largely the ones who bore the pain of the crisis that actually involved the whole family.

As is often true in such cases, the conflict between the generations in the family became displaced into a conflict between the marital partners. Franklin and Ann began to quarrel and felt increasingly alienated from each other. Ann, sensing Franklin's increasing preoccupation with his relationship to his parents but unable to confront that directly, began to suspect his involvement with another woman. Franklin, thrown back into an old and painful dependency conflict with both his parents and his wife, floundered and felt unloved and unsupported—a condition that, of course, left him open to the very extramarital involvement that Ann suspected.

I have not mentioned Ann and Franklin's two children, not because they were not involved in the family crisis but because in this case they tended to play a peripheral role in the family conflict. In another family that might not have been the case, with the possible result that one or both of the children might have been scapegoated for the family problem. It was apparent that the children quietly resented the dislocation their grandparents' presence created. They, too, gravitated to the upstairs and their own rooms. But there were compensations: grandmother was a good cook who liked to ply the children with kitchen goodies!

A Theological Perspective

Thus far our analysis of the Harris family situation has been largely descriptive and phenomenological. We have seen how changing realities brought about by aging of individuals and families create the necessity for identity changes that are resisted by the conservative impulse. Old identity patterns tend to persevere at both conscious and unconscious levels. Family systems theory and ego psychology both provide some useful descriptive tools for understanding the dynamics of identity crisis as it appears in persons like the Harrises. What then of a theological perspective? Are there facets of the Harris' crisis that come more clearly into focus by means of theological reflection?

Theological reflection is potentially useful in formulating a pastoral perspective on problems such as those of the Harris family at several levels. First, when considered theologically, identity and identity crisis point to a tension between being and calling. Embedded in the process of creation and history, each of the members of the Harris family has about him or her certain givens having to do with having been born into a particular time and place and family constellation. The givens of that historic situation are very real and cannot, except within fairly narrow limits, be altered. For example, what it means to be born as an only child of parents like his in a particular sociocultural situation is a given in Franklin's life that affords to his life a certain destiny. The same is true for Ann's having been born a middle child of a large family in the circumstances of her family of origin. That, too, is a given.

Within the given situation of their individual lives, however, both Ann and Franklin are presented with a calling to become who he or she potentially can become. Identity, considered theologically, thus implies calling and intentionality as well as destiny and roots. In the mode of his marriage and occupation, as well as in probably a number of other aspects of his life unknown to us, Franklin had worked out his response to the given situation and calling of his life. His response had involved compromise in the significant relationships of his life: compromise that represented a dialectic between freedom and the full use of his powers, on the one hand, and acceptance of his destiny to remain dependently in someone's shadow, on the other. In a remarkably pointed way the new situation of his parents' retirement presented him with a fresh opportunity to come to grips with the deepest issues of his life. The new situation was thus crucial for him beyond simply the level of creating psychological anxiety.

Second, the Harris family's situation of identity crisis illuminates by making concrete and specific Wolfhart Pannenberg's understanding of sin as the refusal to accept the provisionality of all human constructions of reality. The crisis in the family was precipitated by the unconscious and therefore unexamined perpetuation of old structures of relationship on the part of both Franklin and his parents as much as or more than it was precipitated by the event of the parents' retirement itself. Ann, too, unconsciously was caught in a perpetuation of an old way of resolving the issue of her place in her household. What had been a provisionally operable way of resolving the tensions of living was now being perpetuated into a new future that called for a higher level of maturity, a new structure of family relationships. At the level of implicit faith it might be said that the basis of providential faith exhibited by the Harrises lay in the preservation of the past rather than the promise of God's loving participation in their lives in an open-ended and contingent future. The new events brought a fresh calling from God which the Harrises were having difficulty hearing because of their clinging to the securities of the past. In that, by Pannenberg's definition, the Harrises were caught in the sin of grounding their lives in what was inherently human and temporary.

A third aspect of the Harris family's identity crisis that is brought to the fore through theological reflection has to do with the meaning of the family's apparent inability to confront the rising conflict of the situation directly and forthrightly. One senses in talking with them that all members of the family are aware that there is a problem, but there is a reluctance to bring it out in the open. It is as if something shameful and unseemly must be kept secret and unrevealed. One suspects that both guilt and shame prevent dealing with the situation in a realistic and open way. Negative feelings and perceptions of other family members are being kept under wraps. The problem is taboo because the feelings connected with it are unacceptable. Guilt and obligation increasingly provide the impetus for efforts at relating. This is particularly true in Franklin's relationship to his parents.

The question then comes as to a basis upon which the Harris family can afford to cut through the pretense and guilt-laden behavior in order to bring the identity crisis into the open and restructure their lives to meet the changed situation. On what basis can the risks of truth speaking and new modes of relating be undertaken? Clearly an atmosphere of both forgiveness and liberation must be introduced into what has become a stifling situation. Each of the four adult members of the family needs liberation from old and outworn self-understanding that in subtle but powerful ways dictates behavior in a new situation calling for free and open response. How is this to be accomplished without the undergirding of a theology of hope and liberation—what Jürgen Moltmann calls "the rebirth of a living hope"?[4] A context in which God's promise to come toward the family in its exodus out of a stable and comfortable past into a new and potentially frightening future comes alive for them must undergird any effort to be of help to the family.

Pastoral Care Methodology

Traditional pastoral care approaches to family identity crisis problems such as those of the Harris family have tended to emphasize nondirective listening to one or another of the family members in hope of clarifying feelings and motivations on an individual basis. Sometimes couple counseling has been pursued, in this case for either the elder or younger Harris couple should they present their marriage as the problem or seek pastoral help together in coping with the stress they are experiencing. The expectation has been that if individual identity problems are resolved or at least clarified, the person will be enabled to relate differently in the home situation and thus change the family relationships. This approach has had the advantage of meeting the individual who comes to the pastor for help at the point of his or her individual discomfort and concern, thus providing an interceding, outside source of acceptance and empathic understanding.

Marital counseling can likewise lead to a strengthened marriage bond that facilitates a joint effort at coming to terms with the changed circumstances of the home. Certainly Ann and Franklin Harris could profit from an opportunity to talk through their distorted perceptions of what the other is experiencing and renew the covenant of trust between them. The communication barriers that have grown up between them over the past year can profitably be broken through with the help of a sensitive pastor to assist them in hearing each other's fears and guilts, resentments, and misperceptions of each other's actions and emotional responses.

Having said all that, it yet remains that the identity crisis in the Harris family is a family crisis, related to the way the family has structured itself over the past year as much as or more than it is related to the individual or interpersonal problems of any one family member. Identity is a relational concept; and identity crisis therefore emerges, as we have seen with the Harrises, from the way the relations of the family have consciously and unconsciously been structured. Stated another way, the family covenant of community by which individual and corporate identity styles are governed has become outmoded, its provisionality unrecognized. This suggests that the pastoral methodology needs to take into account the entire family and seek to make possible a restructuring of the family system in such a way as to facilitate rather than hinder the most creative and free development of the powers of each individual to meet the changed situation and respond to the call into the new selfhood the future invites.

With this need for a corporate coming to terms with the changed situation in mind, the pastor may wish to consider setting up one or more family conferences with the entire family. In the case of the Harrises that would include both grandparents, parents, and the two children. This conference or series of conferences would need to be carefully structured and an "agenda" provided by the pastor. An invitation might be given each member of the family, perhaps beginning with the youngest child or the least outspoken of the adults, to share his or her perception of "how things are going" in the family and what he or she sees the problem to be. Others should be asked to listen carefully and openly to what the family member speaking is trying to say. In turn family members may be asked to share what they would like to see changed, both about the way the family lives together (structure) and about the behavior of each individual family member, including themselves (identity). It is to be hoped that out of such a single family conference, or series of conferences, might come several levels of new awareness that might assist the family in breaking out of old and outmoded structures of family relationship and identity:

(1) What has been taboo and secret—the unhappiness with the present family structure—will become an open topic for reconsideration.

(2) The dynamics of power and conservative impulse (the elder Harris' quiet domination of the home and their and Franklin's need to preserve their dominant role) will come out in the open and thus be forced into reconsideration.

(3) The entire family's need for nurture and support as

well as freedom and space will become more openly articulated and the opportunity presented for reaffirmation of family solidarity, albeit in a changed and changing structure of relationship. For this to be possible it will also be necessary, of course, that some opportunity for expression of negative feelings, mutual frustrations, and guilt be provided, though experience with family conferences seems to suggest that a primary focus on negative expressions is counterproductive.

(4) Some new covenants and agreements may be negotiated by which the family is to structure its relationships in the future. Who is to have the use of the kitchen, when, and under what circumstances? How is the family room to be utilized, and who has priority on the television set? What is group space and what is private space? How much and how little do the elder Harrises want to be included in family conversation and activity, and how much do the younger ones want to include them? These and many other family policies and agreements need to be renegotiated to meet the individual and corporate family needs, taking account of both the need for change and the need for continuity.

Family conferences may reveal the need or desire of individual family members for further private pastoral counseling as the enlivened family process stirs awareness of old hang-ups or emerging wishes for personal growth. These opportunities can and should be provided so long as they do not involve the family's scapegoating one or another member as being the one with the problem.

In the case of the Harrises, most likely there will be need for Franklin and Ann to talk through their relationship so that they can in private air their disappointments and fears with each other and renew their efforts together to take charge of their household. The elder Harrises may need help with accepting their aging process. But all of these individual and couple counseling efforts should emerge from a careful consideration of the identity crisis as a family crisis in which the entire family has a stake. From a theological perspective this concretely expresses the priority of a covenant theology of community and a corporate understanding of the salvific process.

Pastors accustomed to confining their pastoral work to one-to-one relationships either in office counseling or in street-corner and living-room pastoral care, will, of course, experience some identity crisis of their own as they thrust themselves into the more open-ended context of family counseling. The counseling situation will feel much more problematic and less controlled. Imaging the pastoral role in these situations as one of mediation, education, and facilitation, rather than the softer images of shepherd or sustainer, will assist in making the transition from the less vulnerable one-to-one counselor role. Often two persons, a pastor and a consultant—a fellow pastor or pastoral counselor or perhaps a mental health professional—can more comfortably join in providing family counseling.

Another image which I have found useful in developing tolerance for the inevitable strain of helping a family open for discussion and reconsideration some of the hidden but very powerful covenants by which they govern their life together is the parental image. Being a male with children of my own this for me is a fathering image. But the image could as well be one of mother if the pastor is female. In a sense, when you suggest a family conference to a troubled family experiencing identity crisis, you invite them to admit you to the inner rooms of their household as a temporary quasi-parent who, by directing one or a series of family conferences, will seek to help them in establishing a new order for their living together. That role implies a certain parenting authority, limited by the agreement to meet a certain number of times, but nevertheless intentional in its offer to act as chairperson, mediator, and guide. Some may prefer to think of themselves as a consultant to the family, but that image fails to communicate the kind of active, participatory stance in which the pastor allows himself or herself to become one of the family, sharing the way in which the family situation appears and affects him or her rather than simply being the neutral or passive reflector. The pastor may want to assign tasks to be undertaken between conferences and make suggestions about new ways of structuring how family decisions are made. He or she will want also, of course, to listen, invite expression of feeling and opinion about the matter under consideration, reflecting what he or she hears in the family interaction. In this way the pastor becomes the temporary leader and model of the good parent for the family while seeking to help the family come to grips with the changed situation in their individual and corporate lives. Several good resource readings in family mediation have been included in the bibliography which will be useful to the pastor in feeling his or her way into what will inevitably feel like a strange role in the beginning.

The identity crisis in the Harris family was precipitated by a common event in the human life cycle, the retirement and decline of health of the aging. Many other common events of all kinds associated with the aging process often bring on identity crisis for individuals and families, sometimes mild and fleeting, often more serious and painful. There are several important passage points in both individual and family life cycles that may be expected to raise identity issues for most people. Among them are the birth of a child, the entry of children into puberty and adolescence, children leaving home, marriage, the passage from the twenties into the thirties and forties, the menopausal period, the time when the last child leaves home, retirement and advanced aging with its necessity for a protective environment. Such transition times as these can well provide a rough rule-of-thumb outline by which a pastor can monitor his or her informal availability to parishioners.

Identity Crisis Precipitated by Social Change

Hovering just in the background of the situation in the Harris family but not, from what we know of them, playing an obviously significant role in shaping the crisis itself lies the process of social change. One can speculate that one of the distant but influential factors that impinge on the Harris family situation is that they live somewhere between the nineteenth-century rural tradition of the extended family and the twentieth-century urban nuclear family. The rural extended family took for granted the sharing of space and household functions by three or more generations. The patriarchal authority of the father figure extended into the time when he became a grandparent. Caring for older family members in the family home until death was likewise taken for granted. But urbanization and a youth-oriented culture have changed all that. Young people quickly want a home of their own away from parental interference. Old people are expected to keep to themselves until and unless they become disabled and then often are institutionalized. The Harrises live between these two cultural worlds, the children loyal to one but wishing for the other and the parents taking one for granted but feeling vaguely that this may make them "the problem."

Viewed in that light, the Harris family's crisis is suggestive of a whole range of human problems that may be understood as involving identity crisis: problems that are either precipitated by or shaped in considerable degree by rapid sociocultural change and pluralism. We have already given some attention to this group of identity crises in our discussion of the impact of changing attitudes about sexuality and abortion in chapter 2. Because pastors are more and more frequently encountering these problems and find themselves often baffled as to how to respond to them, a more detailed scrutiny of their dynamics with particular attention to the pastoral perspective and methodology issues seems warranted.

We have said that identity formation is an interpersonal and social process. Identity is formed out of the interaction between the self and significant others. It is also shaped by the self's appropriation of the cultural options that are presented, particularly during periods of transition in the life cycle. Adolescents are especially aware of changing cultural options since they are in process of identifying themselves as separate from their parents—a process that involves repudiation of some parental values as well as fashioning of fidelity to both affirmed values of the parents and of their own peer group. A dialectic develops between loyalty to heritage and the wish to embrace changing possibilities.[5]

Persons moving through the crisis of the middle years, with its anxious reminder that life is not endless and that the choices one has made have consequences not always foreseen, are likewise subject to heightened awareness of changing possibilities. Their sensitivity to alternative ways of shaping their sense of self is, however, heavily influenced by other dynamic factors such as their own and others' assessment of their relative "success" to this point, the staying power of the values that have sustained their commitments through their lives, and the relative force of the impact of social change on their immediate environment. Middle-aged persons who experience their lives as satisfyingly successful, who have had little reason to change their values and belief system since childhood, and who live in the same community in which they grew up will obviously not be as sensitive to alternative life-styles as will those whose life pattern has been marked by the opposite trends. The conservative impulse sustains them. However, if these persons are transplanted into a radically different social situation they can experience profound cultural shock with accompanying identity crisis.

Here we see the possibility that identity crisis springing from change in the sociocultural living context may be related to two social processes: that of mobility and consequent social dislocation, and pluralism with its consequent presentation of multiple possibilities for self-identification. Pastors will often encounter the first of these in newcomers to a community who have moved from one location to another: rural to urban, urban to suburban, Southern to Northern, family home to retirement community, or home to college, for example. Pastors who have moved from church to church in often very different communities will have experienced something of this kind of identity crisis until they were able to establish themselves with a group of parishioners, fellow pastors, and others who provided an acceptable and accepting reference group. Failure to find such a group of persons with whom to find compatibility and reciprocal affirmation results in identity crisis marked by loneliness, self-doubt, and feelings of alienation from one's surroundings. Urban sprawl with its thrusting of suburban housing developments into outlying rural areas can create such a sense of dislocation for both newcomers and natives alike.

Pluralism, which in this context we will define as the presentation to the self by the social setting of multiple models of selfhood and life-style—models which are expressions of multiple, often contradictory value systems—is a much more complex and subtle force in creating identity crisis in contemporary America. Here the self, rather than shaping and sustaining its identity vis-à-vis a relatively stable and single-minded cultural image of personhood and life-style, is presented with multiple and often confusing options. As we often hear said in pluralistic America, "everything is up for grabs." Many persons no longer have a single unified primary reference group, but are bombarded by different expectations and contradictory standards by which to evaluate their acceptability as a person or guide their choices in forming and maintaining a life-style.

In the pluralistic cultural context a number of powerful dynamic forces come into play which tend to undermine the reciprocal process of self-identity shaping and the self's impact on its social milieu. An atmosphere of uncertainty and tentativeness tends to prevail with an accompanying tendency both to legitimate any identity style that may present itself and to rigidify the need to declare the absolute validity of traditional identity patterns by their adherents. The conservative impulse is thwarted in its ability to facilitate orderly, balanced transition to new identity definitions. The result is an anxiety-laden sense of being up in the air not knowing where to land, or, on the other hand, an equally anxious awareness that what had been taken for granted is no longer embraced by many of one's contemporaries, to say nothing of the next generation.

Fragmentation of personal and group identity is a second result of the impact of pluralism. Self-perceptions tend to vary according to the widely varying social contexts into which some individuals are thrust in an urban society in which one may find one set of values affirmed and acted upon in one's working community (as, for example, the generally conservative and work-oriented business community), another in one's peer group (as, for example, the young singles apartment complex), and yet another in one's family of origin. "When in Rome, do as the Romans" can become a technique of survival that results in a fragmented self without integrity. The following example presented by a young pastoral counselor at a supervision conference is perhaps prototypical:

Ray Gunter is a salesman for a large national corporation. His background is small-town, Bible-belt Protestant and conventionally traditional. He married his high-school sweetheart, and they moved to a metropolitan area where Ray, after college, began his career in sales. The Gunters have two young children, live now in a relatively conservative, middle-class suburb, and attend the Baptist church and Sunday school regularly.

Recently, Ray went to a sales training seminar with his district manager where they roomed together in a motel. After a late training session the district manager returned to the motel room with two women he had picked up in the motel bar, saying to Ray that they both "needed some relaxation after a hard day." Ray, feeling pressured by his boss but also titillated by the possibility of relatively anonymous taboo-breaking, joined in a night of group sex. The next day he felt depressed and anxious, and when he returned home he blurted out to his wife, Sally, a confession of what had happened. Sally was dumbfounded, hurt, and angry. The marriage, once relatively happy and stable, if unexciting and conventional, is now on the skids. Ray confesses to the pastoral counselor after being referred with his wife for marriage counseling that he really doesn't know what happened. Mrs. Gunter, still angry and hurt, is beginning to ask herself if she has been a good wife.

Taken as an incident illustrative of the impact of rapid social change and pluralism, Ray Gunter's identity crisis and the accompanying serious threat to his marriage demonstrates how rapid changes in sexual mores permeate a culture. The identity confusion Ray allowed himself to be trapped into is perhaps typical of the experience of many persons forced to live in several different value worlds in pluralistic America. Because of the pressures he felt to go along with his boss and the more subtle pressure to experience something newly legitimated by segments of his culture, he found himself acting on a value orientation radically different from that of his home and church. Sexual behavior is only one of many areas in which quite contradictory values are expressed in behavior by the same people in the different settings in which they live their lives. The undermining of both traditional values and the cohesiveness of the society is the result. This subtle process serves to create identity crises for increasing numbers of individuals.

Seen in pastoral perspective, the crisis in Ray Gunter's life brings into view some important aspects of the contemporary experience of guilt and shame. In a sense Ray had permitted himself to be shamed into behavior that went radically against his identity as formed by upbringing and basic relationship commitments. He feared being exposed as afraid or too "hung up" to comply with the convention atmosphere of loosened sexual standards. Behind his impulsive conformity to the expectations of that atmosphere lay the shameful fear of contempt on the part of his boss which, at a deeper unconscious level, spells fear of abandonment.[6] Upon returning home next day, however, Ray was flooded with not so much shame as guilt—the guilty awareness of transgression. He had, under the pressure of the shaming experience in the motel, violated the cultural taboos that had been built into his primary identity through identification with his parents and upbringing. When guilt overwhelmed him he attempted to assuage it by blurting out a confession to his wife. Thus exposed to her, however, he was again thrown into shame—exposed as one who had been weak and unfaithful. Guilt and shame were compounded, and Ray's identity was fractured.

Not unexpectedly, the revelation of the incident in the motel set in motion vague and ill-defined feelings of shame and guilt for Sally Gunter as well. Her husband's confession, though it made her scornfully and contemptuously angry, stirred in her other thoughts and feelings related to the shameful possibility that she might somehow be to blame for her husband's transgression. The image of the good wife as one who keeps her husband so satisfied sexually and otherwise that he will not be tempted to stray from home was built solidly into Sally's self-image. Now her feared inadequacy as a wife and sexual partner had been shamefully exposed. Try as she might simply to blame her husband for the threat to their marriage, she could not escape the nagging possibility of her own inadequacy as a wife which now had been forced into the open.

The pastor to whom Sally and Ray Gunter have turned for help with their marriage is presented with a potentially crucial choice that at its core is theological. The logic of adjustment that informs much of the secular crisis intervention literature places high priority simply on restoring the disturbed situation in the marriage to its former balance by allowing the hostility and guilt to be expressed and facilitating the reaffirmation of the strength of the marriage, thus moving as quickly as possible to a closure of the disrupting incident and a return to the prior state of relationship. The impulse to perform a ministry of reconciliation and forgiveness would likewise move the pastor in that direction. To attempt to do more than that is both time-consuming and risky. Encouragement to look more deeply at whether the state of the relationship prior to the crisis incident is, from a normative or moral perspective, what it should or might be may open a veritable Pandora's box of underlying issues and problems. Prudence and economy of effort both seem to dictate a brief, restorative encounter in which both Ray and Sally experience forgiveness and affirmation of the strength of their marriage.

But viewed theologically, in the sense that theology seeks to hold all human behavior under the scrutiny of the gospel and the standard of the Christian vision for human selfhood and relationships, the choice as to what level of ministry *at least as possibility* should be offered the Gunters is not so clear cut as first appears. This is particularly the case if the theological stance taken is from the futuristic perspective of a theology of hope and expectation of the kingdom of God. All human relationships are from this perspective called toward fulfillment of that hope and liberation from the limiting structures of past relationships.

Potentially destructive of both selfhood and marriage relationship as Ray's behavior has been, taken as a whole the identity crisis contains such a creative possibility. A new and potentially liberating future for both self-identity and marriage has been opened. The rather drab and conventional marriage may now be reevaluated. Fractured by the crisis, the relationship between Ray and

Sally may now be reexamined, its failures and disappointments exposed. Likewise, the self-identity of each partner in the marriage is now called into question and potentially opened to the possibility of growth and change.

Stated in more specifically theological language from the perspective of the theologies of hope, the contingent event in the motel, together with what has occurred subsequent to it, has presented Ray and Sally Gunter with God's judgment concerning the provisional quality of their previously taken-for-granted covenant of relationship and the values that informed that relationship. The structure each had assumed to be adequate to support their personhood and marriage has been exposed as human, inadequate, and in need of change. The impossibility of restoring their life to its state prior to the incident that precipitated the identity crisis will become more and more apparent the deeper they get into coming to terms both morally and relationally with what has happened. In this is to be found both a judgment and a call to look toward a new and more hopeful, open-ended future. The creative possibility is that both marital partners may, in coming to grips with the shaming experience, begin the formation of a new identity shaped by increased self-awareness, value clarification, and an enlarged intentionality about the future of their life both individually and together.

Here we see how a theology of God's providence rooted in the contingent rather than the stable, the future rather than the past, and hope for change rather than restoration to a formerly secure state is specifically crucial in determining the stance to be taken and the data to be examined in care of persons in identity crisis. Crisis intervention methods that simply seek to restore the former equilibrium that existed prior to the crisis risk ignoring the word of judgment and call that is implicit in the crisis.

The case of Ray and Sally Gunter reveals the ambiguity

of the experience of shame and guilt in identity crisis. Guilt has to do with acts of transgression that violate an internalized code of conduct or set of taboos. In a rapidly changing and pluralistic culture, however, there is a lessening of the social and relationship supports for a common code of conduct, and the individual is left more frequently caught between an internalized code and the social pressures for conformity to the behaviors newly legitimated by a reference group significant to the individual. Guilt as a control on behavior is thus undermined.

Helen Merrell Lynd, in a provocatively prophetic book published in 1958, proposed that Western society is shifting from a "guilt axis" culture in the direction of a "shame axis" culture.[7] The loosening of behavioral controls by means of taboos has meant that, while guilt remains, as we have seen in Ray Gunter, a dynamic that both creates and judges behavior, there has developed a more powerful dynamic in the pressure upon the individual to be adequate to a complex and changing value situation. Shame, in contrast to guilt, involves a judgment on the total self or an exposure of the "quick of the self, most of all to oneself."[8] It involves exposure as being inadequate or, in the now common phrase, being exposed as "not having it all together."

The ambiguity of the shaming experience lies in its potential as a creative or destructive experience. To be consistently shamed as inadequate, less-than-expected, or unacceptable, not so much in terms of specific behaviors as in terms of one's total personhood, is a devastatingly destructive experience. The victims of racial prejudice and discrimination are many of them tragic examples of what that level of pervasive shaming can do to personhood. To be belittled and made to feel ashamed of one's identity over which one has little control is a dehumanizing experience beyond the imagination of those who have not experienced it firsthand. On another level, the consistent shaming of children or a spouse can lead not only to mistrust of the perpetrator of the shaming experience, but deep distrust of the self.

On the other hand, shame provides a positive dynamic for social control and loyalty to one's supporting community. The cohesiveness of a social group is in great part determined by the necessity that individuals experience to avoid the feeling of being shamed by those whose respect and power to assign evaluative meanings to behavior is needed and recognized. In a society marked by a thoroughgoing pluralism of values, the subtle currents of shame's influence can create contradictions or lacunae in the consistency of an individual's identity expression which bring unexpected and threatening experiences of shame.

Shame likewise plays an important role in the positive appropriation of new insights that enable persons to initiate as well as accommodate to needed changes in established patterns of value and relationship. The continuity of identity entails a quality of homeostatic balance of perception and response between self and world which tends to perpetuate itself. Events and relationships that force confrontation with different ways of perceiving and making sense of reality can, by means of a shaming process, present the self with the necessity to change attitudes, ideas, and behavior.

Figure 14 schematizes the process by which, through a creative shaming experience involving a fracturing of understanding of both self and world, fresh visions of what both self and world might be can come about. In this sense, identity crisis and the shaming experience that goes with it contain the creative possibility of liberation and growth. For there to be a creative outcome to the shaming experience, however, there are several essential ingredients that must be present. There must be a certain openness on the part of the individual to the experience of vulnerability to intruding events and new possibilities in relationships, with an accompanying willingness to avoid protection of the self from exposure through

The Creative Experience of Shame

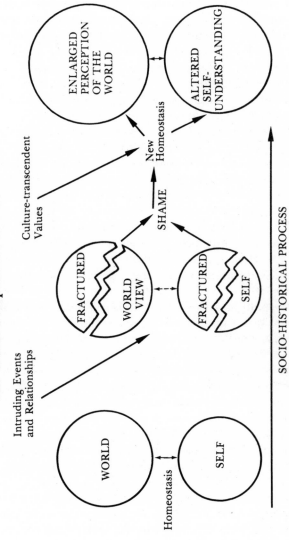

Figure 14

withdrawal, role playing, depersonalization (what Lynd calls "the code of the pose"[9]), or regression to some earlier homeostasis between self and world. Creative shame requires allowing oneself to be taken by surprise and thus have one's provisional construction of self and reality called into question.

For a truly enlarged perception of the world and an altered self-understanding more congruent with that enlarged perception to take shape, the new integration between self and world requires the intrusion into the shaming experience of values that transcend the immediate culture both in terms of the traditions in which the self is embedded and the pluralisms of the immediate cultural situation. Without such an experience of intrusion of overarching values that transcend the pluralism of competing claims upon the self, continued fragmentation and consequent erosion of the sense of clear self-world understanding will result. By culture-transcendent values I mean all that is contained in the normative Christian vision of what self-world relationships should and might be—love, justice, and the empowerment of persons toward freedom and responsibility.

Don S. Browning, in his book *The Moral Context of Pastoral Care*,[10] had underlined the difficulty that all modern persons, including pastors and pastoral counselors, have in reaching for a culture-transcendent vision of the moral good. He points out that the sayings of Jesus "point to a rather non-specific vision of how moral thinking can rise above the customary, inherited code of a particular cultural situation."[11] He goes on to say, however, that "one cannot transcend morality without first having a morality." Western society, with its rapid change and pluralism, has tended to undercut any sense of cultural tradition about rules and patterns of conduct. Therefore our efforts to be what Browning calls "supra-legalists" inevitably tend to take on the character of antinomianism. While I am in agreement with much of what Browning says of the difficulties in grasping a truly culture-transcendent vision, I would nevertheless consider the search for such an enlarged perspective that can intrude into and stand over against the competing claims of the cultural situation to be crucial for a creative outcome to identity crisis in a pluralistic, rapidly changing sociocultural situation. It is precisely the task of Christian ministry to embody and articulate such a perspective.

The Christian pastor will see himself or herself as both participant in and facilitator of the creative shaming process. He or she is participant in that new experiences, one's own and one's parishioners, should open the pastor to the shame of unrecognized involvement in imperfect views of self and world. As facilitator he or she will seek with the person for a creative rather than fragmenting outcome of the experience. While respecting the right and responsibility of the person in identity crisis to choose whether and how he or she is to confront the shaming experience, the pastor's intention will be to facilitate in every way possible that respects that right the liberation of the person from old, outmoded, and constricting modes of maintaining the balance between self and world. Here we encounter one of the facets of the prophetic function of pastoral care ministry. At the same time the pastor will want to work diligently to help persons break through the vicious circles of shame-guilt-shame that characterized Ray Gunter's initial reaction to the precipitous event that threw him into identity crisis. Shame can be a creative, opening experience. It is not a weapon to be used to force persons to identify with the pastor's perspective on the way things ought to be. Rather the pastor's response to shame will be flavored with an attitude of acceptance and forgiveness as well as a hopeful, expectant invitation to look toward some larger vision of what is possible.

CHAPTER VIII

The Generation Gap
and Alienation

Alienation and Pluralism

Our study of identity crisis has revealed that in a rapidly changing and pluralistic society radically different perspectives on reality can exist side by side in the same community, family, or even within the same individual. In that cultural situation the problem of fragmentation and consequent alienation seems fated to become ubiquitous. By referring to this condition as alienation I mean to point to the tendency in the situation of rapid change and pluralism toward estrangement within and among persons which, in turn, makes for separation, loneliness, and an absence of a sense of cohesive unity. In a society of alienation and estrangement there thus is both internal conflict and interpersonal and intergroup conflict. The pastor in his or her role as reconciler and shepherd both of individuals and of various groups within a community of faith that seeks to relate itself to a still larger and more pluralistic world must be prepared to recognize and understand the evidences of alienation as they come into play in every aspect of the life of persons. Furthermore, he or she must know something about the difficulties and pitfalls as well as the opportunities and practical methods of reconciliation.

So pervasive is the problem of alienation in Western society that it is appropriate to ask whether it can be considered a "crisis" in the sense we have been using that term in this study or whether it is not in some larger sense a crisis of culture with spinoffs in terms of continuing conflict at a number of significant interfaces where differing perspectives and values collide. If this is a more or less chronic state of a rapidly changing and pluralistic society, in what sense and under what conditions can it become a crisis state for individuals, families, and groups within the range of concern of the pastor? To this task we turn our attention in this chapter.

Alienation and Contemporary Consciousness

It may be useful to consider the contemporary problem of alienation from the standpoint of the image of modern consciousness with which we began our study of crisis experience: the image of infinite human aspirations encountering finite limitations and boundaries. Seen in this light, conflict at the interfaces of differing perspectives on reality and value reveals itself as evidence of the human penchant for attempting to grasp all of reality and make it both whole and manageable, even controllable, as that penchant encounters human limitations in the inability to see reality and valuing from more than the one limited perspective of a time and place. Said another way, we are all fundamentally persons conditioned by our own experience and that places limitations upon our ability to see things from the perspective of someone with radically or even slightly different experience. Yet we strive for consensus and unity of perspective. In less rapidly changing societies the mechanism of consensus about the way things are and what is and is not valuable functions to provide commonly held views that are understood by all ages and groups in the society and passed along to the rising generations as traditions, rules, and images to be appropriated and preserved. Structures of such societies may indeed be processes of change, but the changes are at a slow enough pace and are appropriated by a wide enough spectrum of persons and groups in the society to make for a minimum of intergenerational or intergroup conflict. A certain sense or way of grasping the whole of things exists in common by most if not all persons in the society. In a time of rapid change and pluralism, the human need and desire for wholeness and consensus persist but sharply and sometimes painfully encounter the limitations of differing perspectives. Striving both for consensus and for difference is the inevitable result.

The Generation Gap as Paradigm of Alienation

Although, as we have suggested, it is probably the case that alienation exists at every level all across contemporary Western society, the upheaval of the sixties and early seventies brought to the forefront of American awareness the alienation that existed between the generations. Though the violent outbreaks of conflict between youth and the dominant adult generation that characterized the Vietnam war period have subsided, the uncomfortable differences in outlook and value affirmation persist. I have therefore chosen what has commonly been termed the generation gap as the paradigm of alienation and estrangement. By making a brief but careful study of the dynamics of generational differences in perspective and valuing, I would hope that a broad range of human conflict brought about by the limits on human perspective can be helpfully illuminated.

We ordinarily think of the generation gap as primarily manifesting itself in the conflicts between parents and their teen-age children. Teen-age runaway, conflict over sexual and other social behavior, authority struggles in the transition from parental control to self-control all are marked by conflicting perspectives and value conflicts that often threaten to throw a family into crisis that takes on the superficial appearance of a conflict of generations. As our study of styles of attachment and separation in an earlier chapter reveals, however, these conflicts may tend to reach crisis proportions in those families where inordinate dependency and struggle over control of behavior has characterized family life from the earliest age of the children. The crisis quality of some parent-teen-ager conflict may then be more closely related to the continuity of a family style of relating into a developmental period in which that style becomes increasingly inappropriate and dysfunctional rather than being a manifestation of the existential structure of the generations as such. This suggests the possible usefulness of a more broadly conceived, multi-faceted approach to understanding the generation gap and through that the larger human problem of alienation between persons and groups in a changing society.

Four Approaches to Understanding the Generation Gap

1. The Generation Gap as a Difference in Direction of Vision.

Common sense, as well as our contemporary way of thinking about the human life cycle, tells us that young people, adults, and the aging tend to differ in the direction of their vision as they look at both present reality and the valuing of things. The direction of vision seems directly related to one's position with reference to the time boundaries of the human life cycle as we developed them in chapter 3. A very simple schematic presentation of those differences is found in Figure 15. The diagram presents a very rough and broad generalization about the way reality is envisioned by what roughly can be termed the five generations that are living at any one time (generations conceived as social groupings rather than as biological children and grandchildren). Children and youth can be expected to have a direction of vision on present reality marked by anticipation. Reality is not considered to be "in their hands," but rather in the hands of the adults who stand ahead of them in the procession of generations. Therefore reality is experienced as imposed upon them by others older who could change it if only they would.

Generational Differences in Direction of Vision

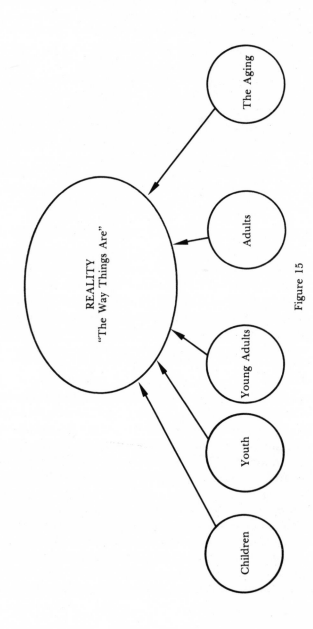

REALITY
"The Way Things Are"

The Aging

Adults

Young Adults

Youth

Children

Figure 15

But reality and final decisions about what is to be valued is out of their hands. Anticipation, for children, then takes on the quality of fantasy or playing at games designed to anticipate the fuller responsibility and freedom of adulthood.[1]

As children enter adolescence this angle of direction of vision becomes sharper and more immediate. Decisions must be made that anticipate the impending status of young adulthood. Options must be considered and tried on for size. The press both for commitment and exercising one's impact on the way things are becomes urgent.

The young adult has a direction of vision marked by both anticipation and the gradual taking on oneself of the fuller responsibility for both how things are and how they will be. Value commitments are being made and consequences experienced. The coming of children brings the angle of vision more clearly toward the perpendicular—the right now of acting to fulfill what has been only anticipated in the past. A sense both of being crowded into adult responsibility and being prevented by vocational superiors and present realities from fulfilling those responsibilities flavor the imaging of one's relationship to reality and what one has now come fully to value.

For the adult generation the direction of vision tends toward preoccupation with the task of carrying the load of present and very real responsibility for the way things are. Whatever is wrong or goes wrong with what happens must be managed, tended, and in some way taken upon oneself. In Harry Truman's famous saying, "the buck stops here." This sense of being responsible for the way things are and the final coping with whatever contingencies occur makes for a vague but definite feeling that those in other generational groups, be they younger or older, cannot fully "understand" how things are or must be.

Older persons who have begun to relinquish vocational

and parental responsibility for how things are and whatever occurs tend to have a direction of vision that is retrospective. "The way things are" is constantly seen in the perspective of "the way things were." This provides older people both with a certain distance from the pressure of decision and responsibility that colors the vision of the adult generation and a certain sense of again becoming, as they were in childhood, subject to the decision of others. This makes for a certain kinship between the old and the young which is not so easily experienced between children and their parents.

The reflections that emerge from Figure 15 suggest that the gap that seems to exist between the generations that makes for a degree of alienation is in part a problem of the differences in perception that come about because of built-in differences in direction of vision. Things simply appear differently when seen from the anticipating angle of vision of the young than they do when viewed from the perpendicular angle of responsibility of their adult parents. Yet there continues to operate the human wish that there could be a consensus or that "others could see things as they look to me from where I stand." Unless these differences in direction of vision can be recognized, negotiated and bridged, and the legitimacy of each accepted, conflict between the generations seems inescapable.

2. A Socio-historical Definition of the Generation Gap.

The social crisis of the sixties produced a number of efforts to understand the dynamics of the radical generation gap crisis of that time from the standpoint of the ongoing process of social and political history. In this view a generation is defined as an age group of people whose collective identity has been shaped by some great historical event or events.[2]

The events that were in the forefront of public attention at the time a given generation was growing through adolescence into young adulthood are seen from this perspective as shaping a stance or quality of

consciousness that becomes the conscious and unconscious model or template by which all subsequent
perceptions and imaging of reality are shaped. Though it
is beyond our purpose to engage in an in-depth analysis
of generational consciousness from this perspective, what
follows is suggestive of the possibilities for understanding
the generation gap as viewed in the light of historical
events.

The older generation. For this generation the dominant
events that shaped consciousness were undoubtedly the
Great Depression and World War II. Many in this
generation, though they have gone on to become the
backbone of American affluence, remember the hardship and hopelessness of the Depression and the limited
job opportunities that were theirs as they entered
adulthood. A certain frugal awareness that another
financial catastrophe could occur pervades their attitudes
about the taken-for-granted abundance of present
middle-class life. World War II was for them a "good"
war in that the enemy was clearly evil and the fight was
one that had to be made for honor and liberty.
Subsequent attitudes about the forces of good and evil in
the world tend for many to remain unambiguous—either
good or evil with less natural openness to the possibility of
evil structures in the hands of good people.

The adult generation. In the seventies these are the
folk who grew up in the years of the post–World War II
boom and the relatively tranquil period of the Eisen-
hower years. America was on the move again, keeping the
peace around the world and building big cities, big
churches, and bigger corporations. The restlessness of
youth with the bland conformity of American middle-
class life was just beginning and for many had not yet
strongly influenced their growing up. A certain success
orientation colors the perceptions and values of this
generation that makes for profound disturbance over the
refusal of their children to join the "rat race."

The young adult generation. These are the young

people, white and black, whose consciousness is forever colored by the devastating awareness of both the poverty and the injustice in America that was thrust upon the nation by the civil rights movement and the terrible, tragic events of the Vietnam War. They know deeply that Americans can be wrong and that there is a profound sickness in our culture. Their lives are marked either by efforts to find personal satisfaction in spite of these recognized evils or by a more or less total rejection of the way of life of their parents. This is the generation of both Kenneth Keniston's *Young Radicals* and *The Uncommitted.*[3] It is also the generation that saw the coming of the new sexual morality and the drug culture into public view. Questioning, protest, and disillusionment tend to influence heavily many of this generation as they view reality.

The youth of the seventies. It is perhaps too early to get a clear perspective on the events that have shaped and are shaping this generation. Certainly their view of things is influenced by the turn toward privatism and the turning inward that the seventies have brought to American society. The cults of self-actualization and what has been called the new narcissism certainly color their view of themselves and their place in society, as does the rise of the new conservatism for some. Watergate confirmed for them the same awareness as their older brothers and sisters had of the problems and injustices of American social structures. They seem, however, to have less hope for useful and significant change and to have turned toward self-realization as a compromised but meaningful purpose in life.

Even so brief and sketchy a characterization as we have here undertaken reveals how marked the gap in generational consciousness can be when seen through the lens of historic events that shape the cultural mood of a time and place. Generational perspectives, seen in this broad perspective, seem not only to differ radically but to have about them a certain rhythm of action or stance and reaction or contrast. Thus we can see the possibility that there may tend to be conflict between contiguous generations based upon the effort to come to terms with the negative experience of the previous generation by their successors. Repudiation and correction seem consistently to flavor the shift of experience from one generation to another.

3. Adolescent Coping Styles and the Generation Gap.

The strident intergenerational conflict of the sixties prompted a number of important social scientific studies of the youth of that time, two of which have already been cited in the work of Kenneth Keniston. For our purposes the studies of adolescence of Erik Erikson remain, however, foundational because of Erikson's ability to draw together the biological, psychological, and socio-cultural factors in the adolescent transition from childhood to adulthood in his concept of identity formation. The firming up of a positive identity that somehow combines loyalty to the values and style of living learned in the family with fidelity to new commitments shaped by enlarged personal experience and relation-ships with peers is for Erikson the central task of adolescence. Here is where the transition from one generation to another primarily takes place.[4] Failing that task the adolescent risks falling into what Erikson calls identity diffusion: the self that does not know itself, is splintered in its loyalties and at war with the passage of time in the human life cycle.

Out of his studies of dissenting youth in the 1960s, Erikson altered his formulation of the adolescent transition somewhat to acknowledge that a period of identity diffusion may be necessary for the young person to accomplish the goal of leaving behind the world of childhood loyalty to familial values and style of living and forging a vision of life and selfhood of his or her own. Here in a crucial way both continuity and change must be brought together in a new synthesis.[5] The generation gap thus for Erikson is one that young people must leap, and it contains both the old and the new, both continuity and change. The identity confusion that sometimes results from difficulty in making that leap produces persons who are neither able to adapt to the changing times that are emerging with their generation nor to remain fully children of their parental generation. Such identity confusion becomes marked by inauthentic behavior that wears the guise of acting purposefully, but is actually quite confused and meaningless.

Working out of this background of Eriksonian identity theory, we begin to see the apparent alienation in the generation gap as much more involved than the simple idea that parents and young people have difficulty communicating because they see things very differently and have very different values. Once more we encounter the complex dialectic of continuity and change within the same persons.

Of the several empirical studies of intergenerational transition that have been done in recent years, one of the more useful, particularly for pastors, is found in the latest of a series of reports emerging from a longitudinal study of a group of children at the Menninger Foundation, Topeka, Kansas.[6] These fifty-four Midwestern children, unfortunately all white Caucasians, have been followed closely by an interdisciplinary staff since birth with periodic psychological testing, interviews with both subjects and parents, and other observational tools. At the time of preparation of the volume in which we are particularly interested, the subjects were all in late adolescence. The theoretical undergirding for the report of the study is essentially Eriksonian identity theory, though the authors are careful to point up their shift, along with Erikson, away from Erikson's first formulation of adolescent theory toward acknowledgment of adolescent need for a period of diffusion followed by a revisioning of reality and value.[7] The word the authors prefer in pointing to this process is the word "coping."[8]

The Menninger adolescent study proceeds to sort out

the coping styles of their adolescent subjects first into two broad groupings they refer to as the "censors" and the "sensors" and later into four subgroupings: obedient traditionalists, ideological conservatives, cautious modifiers, and passionate renewers. These groups thus span a spectrum from "those holding on to established values whether unquestioningly or passionately, to those seeking renewal, whether cautiously or with abandon."[9] Censors, representing 28 percent of the total, tend to limit their trust in and testing of their own sensory experience of reality. Obedient traditionalists filter all their perceptions through a screen made up of what they have come to believe is sanctioned and expected in their traditional culture. Ideological conservatives, while relatively more free to utilize their own sensory perceptual data, yet remain constricted in their ability to trust their own exploration, setting firm ideological limits guided by their convictions. What they do sense on their own thus is used largely to verify the values they have adopted from their upbringing.

The "sensors," on the other hand allow themselves considerably more freedom to utilize their own senses in testing and ultimately modifying the structures of reality and values they have inherited. Forty-six percent of the total sample were found to be cautious modifiers, allowing their values and opinions to be changed on the basis of their own testing and experimentation. Passionate renewers (26 percent of the total sample) "constantly seek new input from their senses and frequently use this input to question or modify any and all of their views as well as their overt behavior."[10]

In the Menninger study we are presented with a small but significant body of data that suggests that the so-called generation gap is better understood as a range of styles of coping with both the necessity young people experience to begin relying on their own perceptions of things rather than their parents' perceptions and the necessity to make decisions about rapidly changing social values. The degree of alienation between parents and children seemed to vary considerably and, as might be expected, was related to the degree to which the young person was a sensor rather than a censor. While the passionate renewers tended to have more liberal parents,[11] many of the sensors had very traditional, even conservative parents.

Drs. Moriarty and Toussieng, in the conclusions they draw from their data, come down strongly favoring the sensors over the censors in terms of their developing ability to cope in a rapidly changing and pluralistic society. While they affirm that there are many relatively happy and well-adjusted young people in the censor group, they point sharply to the price these youth pay in a much more constricted ability to live in the full sense of experiencing life for themselves. "In our censors we may observe the result of not having achieved a full identity in Erikson's new sense. They are impeded in coming to a total vision of life. Rather they tend to retrogress to a preadolescent mode of coping with a world they for one reason or another can or will not allow themselves to perceive fully."[12]

Sensors, on the other hand, have a much less smooth and predictable development with more chance for error, a greater possibility for conflict with parents and established rules. Much time must be spent on figuring out what life, other people, and the world are all about. With tradition de-authorized they must live with many more open questions and a greater degree of uncertainty. The gap they must leap in envisioning their future is wider and more risky than that of their censor contemporaries.

Though they clearly favor the sensors as better able to cope with a changing world, Moriarty and Toussieng attempt to avoid an absolute value judgment by pointing out that it is the censors who preserve the wisdom of the past that can be applied in a new way in a new world.

Their presence in the society assures continuity with the past.[13]

It may be well for us to pause at this point for some brief reflection on the possible implications of these interesting empirical data for a pastoral stance based upon a theology of hope and futurity. At first glance the data seem clearly to support Wolfhart Pannenberg's view that the perpetuation of human structuring of reality arbitrarily out of the past into an ever-changing future is constricting of life and blocks the fuller appropriation of that enlarged vision of possibilities of the future that God is presenting to humankind as he draws us toward his kingdom. Wooden adoption of styles of perception and rules for living from the past so that these human constructions of reality become screens that prevent us from the possibility of seeing the new reality do indeed stifle and hinder new life from coming into experienced reality. A theology for life must do more than perpetuate the past.

But the Menninger data also point to the risks involved in simply building a world on the platform of our own senses. It risks ever more radical discontinuity and alienation as well as the possibility of simply being swept along with the tide of the times. The question as to whether an individual simply on his or her own powers of perception can transcend the powerful forces of cultural movement remains before us. Once more we encounter the necessity of a theological judgment as to whether the full weight for building a structure for the perceived world is finally up to each individual. Is not a larger, ultimately transcendent vision of both the good and the possible needed in which the individual can finally place his or her trust? Is it not possible that we are here presented with not only the need for a renewal of the sense of God's providence in the futuristic sense we have considered earlier, but also with the need for a renewed understanding of the church as an ongoing community of search and interpretation? Would not a renewed understanding of the Holy Spirit as the spirit of truth leading us toward that vision of the kingdom of God be an important corrective to the loneliness of purely individual sensor styles of coping? The Menninger researchers conclude their study by placing their trust in the openness of the individual to new realities as presented and evaluated by the senses. Does that not risk distortion of a different but equally serious order as the distortion of censorship by the filter of tradition? More of these questions later.

4. A Cross-sectional Study of Intergenerational Conflict in a Family.

We turn now from the longitudinal study of intergenerational transition to looking at the same phenomena from the aspect of a cross-sectional study of the appearance of intergenerational value conflicts in a single family. Our effort will be to uncover ways in which generational values produce gaps in the valuing process in both individuals in the family and within the family as a whole.

The family chosen for consideration is in many ways typical of American middle-class and upper-middle-class families found in most white and some black main-line churches in America today. They are affluent, having been strongly upwardly mobile during particularly the parents' generation, and exhibit on outward appearance many of the value conflicts associated with the popular conception of the generation gap. Work with this family took the form of a pastoral counseling relationship involving primarily the mother and father, but with a number of counseling sessions with the parents and one or more of the children. We will call the family the Daltons.

Mrs. Dalton was the member of the family first referred to me for counseling by her pastor. Over the course of several months of casual observation of the family at church activities the pastor had become aware that Mrs. Dalton seemed unduly depressed and listless. A pastoral call confirmed this impression and resulted in the referral. After two conversations with Mrs. Dalton and upon my insistence, Mr. Dalton joined us and continued to come for most, though not all of our counseling sessions thereafter.

Mrs. Dalton was a rather attractive woman of forty-two, the daughter of a rural lay pastor in one of the smaller sect groups of the Wesleyan tradition and his equally strictly religious wife. Mrs. Dalton was the second oldest child in a family of five, the oldest being a boy who had also become a pastor in his father's denomination. Mrs. Dalton's parents, retired at the time of my involvement with the family, came to visit in the Dalton home quite frequently, sometimes staying for several weeks at a time.

The Daltons lived in an affluent section of the city in a large, well furnished home. Mr. Dalton was a highly successful corporation executive in a company he had helped found and develop. He was considered a highly qualified expert in solving technical and organizational problems in his company. He also was an officer in his church, one of the liberal churches in the community, and was considered a leader in community affairs.

I learned all of the above about Mr. Dalton from his wife in the first interview with her, the information coming at the point in our conversation at which I had suggested that Mr. Dalton be asked to join us. From him I learned further that he was experiencing some restlessness in his work and that he had even considered an early retirement in the not too distant future "in order that I can pursue something a little more altruistic."

Mrs. Dalton left her parental home after high school, in part to get away from the strictness of parental control and in part on the encouragement of her maternal grandmother who instilled in her the desire to move out into the world on her own. She completed training as a medical technician and subsequently worked her way through college. Not long after entering college she met Mr. Dalton, and they were married after her graduation.

She then worked to support them while he completed a graduate degree in engineering.

Soon after completion of Mr. Dalton's graduate work the Daltons' first child was born, a boy, followed in regular succession every two years by two other children, a boy and a girl. The Daltons' third son, six years younger than his sister, was twelve at the time of my work with the family. The oldest son is married to a woman not fully accepted by Mrs. Dalton because of her lack of interest in "womanly things"; she is amiably tolerated by Mr. Dalton. The oldest is also a college drop-out, having decided after one year at the state university to quit school and get a job "because he couldn't see getting any deeper into the same rat race that his father was in." He has since held several jobs, is still partially dependent upon his father financially, and appears to the Daltons to be floundering hopelessly "like so many young people his age."

Mrs. Dalton's depression took the form of overpowering feelings of uselessness and futility accompanied by much self-flagellation often expressed in pietistic religious language because she "can't seem to find anything she wants to do that does for me what the business seems to do for my husband." She often spoke of not being considered or appreciated by her family, of wanting to "do something new with my house," and of wanting to do something outside the family "on my own." Numerous efforts to do volunteer work no longer seemed satisfying. She both dreaded and looked forward to her parents' visits, confessing that they made her feel strangely guilty for having such a big house and so many material things. She and her parents often talked about the Bible on their visits and occasionally argued over the parents' literal interpretation of scriptural passages.

Mr. Dalton came quite willingly for the interview to which his wife reluctantly invited him, though he quickly let me know that his presence was for his wife's sake rather than because he felt any need for pastoral counseling himself. After several sessions I suggested that there might be some connection between his own "success" and his wife's very apparent despair. At first this puzzled him, but he took the challenge and began to share with me his impatience with her for being so weak and dependent on him and so unable to "manage better with the children." He had learned in management that one had to tolerate all kinds of people and be firm with them only when company policy was at stake. He expressed his frustration with his wife both for not being more lenient with the children and not being able to be firm with them when firmness was needed. I had the impression that Mr. Dalton maintained only a rather distant relationship with his two older sons and that they challenged their mother's judgment in imitation of their father as well as to avoid a more difficult confrontation with their father.

One of the focuses of contention in the Dalton home was Sunday. The older boys had long since quit going to church with the family. They had other, more enjoyable things to do—tennis, a motor bike, and sleeping off what was suspected by the mother to be a Saturday night pot party with teen-age friends. This latter practice the second boy seemed to have adopted from his older brother now away from home, while the daughter seemed not to participate, remaining more nearly true to her mother's ideas about the rights and wrongs of teen-age behavior. Sunday family church attendance may have been compromised in the Dalton home, but Sunday dinner was an institution Mrs. Dalton struggled valiantly to keep alive. She liked to cook for her family, usually invited the oldest son and his wife to come, and did her best to maintain the formal family dinner tradition. The boys came, though often late, ate mother's food and, without comment or offer to help with the dishes, left again to spend the afternoon with their friends and outside activities. Mrs. Dalton, angry and depressed, but not knowing exactly why, was left to do the dishes by herself while Mr. Dalton went off to his study to bury his nose in a technical journal. Only the daughter remained at times loyal to her mother, though she, too, complained about "hating work in the kitchen."

These were the Daltons as I first met them and as they appeared for several months thereafter. Mrs. Dalton was the focus of concern (what family therapists refer to as the designated patient) as she struggled with her shame over not being able to live up to her husband's expectations and her nagging guilt over the conflict she experienced between the values her family's life expressed and the more Spartan piety of her upbringing. Her resentment of her husband's success and her children's increasing separation from her became more apparent to her, but still she continued to carry the burden of family conflict. Mr. Dalton was the puzzled, somewhat impatient, but self-confident helper who in our sessions together encouraged, cajoled, and subtly demanded that his wife "snap out of it" and find something to utilize her energies now that the children didn't need her full attention any longer.

But slowly, and only after much pressing of the issue on my part, Mr. Dalton began to talk about his own doubts about himself, particularly those he had experienced in the early years of his adult life when he had been struggling to leave behind an equally sheltered if not as rigidly pietistic home as that of his wife. His loneliness as one of the leaders in a business that had to keep expanding to keep ahead of inflationary costs and a growing market became more shareable. Responding to this new sense of openness to shared pain on her husband's part, Mrs. Dalton became more able to take the risk of sharing her feelings of neglect by her husband and her fear of what would happen if he ever experienced any of the failure she lived with daily. Mr. Dalton's need to be always competent to handle any eventuality surfaced as did his growing misgivings about the worthwhileness of his success. The husband's emotional absence from his home and the perfectionism that he inflicted on his three sons became visible, accompanied by a growing recognition that Mrs. Dalton had been carrying a burden of value conflict and fear of inadequacy for him as well as herself.

At this point in my relationship with Mr. and Mrs. Dalton, I began to suggest that the children be brought into our conferences so that they could share their perspective on the family problem. This was accomplished only after much discussion and anxious wondering if the children would understand that their parents were having difficulty. The parents were not, in fact, ever able to bring more than one of the children to a counseling session at a time, but the several sessions to which one or another of the younger children were invited proved valuable. It became apparent that the children were quite aware not only of the mother's unhappiness, but also of the father's isolation and perfectionistic dominance of the home. The second son in particular was able to confront his father with his unavailability and relate the seeming rebellion on his and his brother's part to their struggle with their father and his imposed values with which they had difficulty identifying. The family conflict over rules and expectations; the relative value of work and pleasure; the importance, even tyranny, of the parents' success orientation and their children's quiet or more overt resistance to that all began to come into open discussion. The mother began to be less the patient and more the participant in the increasingly lively exchange of confrontation, reflection on family life, and search for new directions together.

Much more could, of course, be said about the details of the pastoral counseling process with the Dalton family. For the purpose of our study of intergenerational conflict, however, we will shift now to an examination of the way in which the values of at least three generations came together to determine in part the shape of the individual and family conflict the Daltons were experiencing.

The underlying matrix of the value conflict in the Dalton home came quite apparently from the generation of Mr. and Mrs. Dalton's parents, in this case most particularly the parental home of Mrs. Dalton. This was a home in many ways typical of the Southern Bible Belt—a home preoccupied with prescriptions and proscriptions concerning right and wrong behavior. Obedience to parents and obedience to God were seen as virtually synonymous.

Mrs. Dalton seemed quite unable to bridge the gap between her own and her parents' generations. She had equal difficulty in recognizing and accepting the gap between her generation and her children's. Thus her perceptions of her own and her children's behavior stood constantly under the judgment of her parents' values. Mrs. Dalton's agonizing descriptions of her parents' visits reveal that these structures of reality and value continue to dominate much of her understanding of both how life is and how it ought to be. Her preoccupation with not doing what she ought to be doing, her tight control on her anger and frustration, her vision of what home life should be, symbolized in her worries about what was happening to Sunday—in short, all the internal conflicts growing out of a strict pietistic view of the world and the Christian life were central to her identity conflict. In a radically changed social situation she now felt alienated from her parents, her children, and her own childhood commitments. It is important to note, however, that we can see in Mrs. Dalton glimpses of the strengths of her parents' generation as well. Her earnestness, her willingness to suffer and struggle to find a solution to her identity problem, and her acceptance of the problem as hers to be overcome all spoke of the sturdy sense of individual responsibility that characterized that generation.

One can also see some evidence of the reality structure

and values of the grandparent generation in Mr. Dalton. He was a perfectionist who must never make a mistake; the disciplined life provided a major structure of security for his coping with both his business and his home life. He was impatient with weakness and, like his wife, exercised tight control over his emotions. But the social roles that had opened to him in business, church, and civic affairs had made possible for him, as they had not for his wife, the fuller appropriation of the common values and views of reality of his own generation. He became a leader in a generation of upward mobility.

In the Daltons we see the values and conflicts of their own generation primarily in two forms: the overweening burden of their success-oriented life and their bafflement over the results of their permissiveness with their children. Mr. Dalton revealed himself as a man driven by his need to succeed and be competent for all contingencies. Having climbed to the top of the heap in his work he was lonely—more lonely than even he realized. His sons were not interested in following in his footsteps and he wondered vaguely if he really wanted to be president of the corporation after all. Having arrived at where he had been going, he now wondered out loud if it was where he wanted to be.

Mrs. Dalton seemed caught in that time of life when what she had given herself to so fully and devotedly—the raising of her children in the style so characteristic of her generation—was no longer needed or valued by the very ones to whom she had devoted everything. Mistaking that as evidence of failure, she saw herself as unsuccessful both as a mother and as a woman who, according to the magazines she read, must have something outside the home to be fulfilled. The child-centered values of her generation had trapped her into becoming the scapegoat for the family value conflicts.

If the Daltons exhibited the value tyrannies of their generation, they also possessed the strengths that come with those values. They worked hard and productively in the counseling relationship and evidenced determination to succeed at reordering their lives. Once Mrs. Dalton began to break through her despair, they became more and more able to direct their obvious strengths toward reevaluating their style of family life, seeking new ways of enjoying a less pressured, more relaxed life together. The earnestness of their parents' generation began to combine with the strength to succeed of their own generation in ways that were productive of some genuinely new and creative value commitments.

The situation in the Dalton family is likewise overlaid with the style of reality structuring and valuing of the generation of their adolescent children. Not only are the children less goal oriented and less restricted by rules and behavioral prescriptions than their parents and grand-parents, they also seemed so bent on seeking the pleasure of the present as to be dominated by a certain aimlessness and diffusion. Clearly for these young people that past had been de-authorized to a degree only at times wished for by their parents, who must still justify their departures from the life-style of the grandparent generation. Yet there was in these young people a deep commitment to honesty and fairness in which echoes of the deeper intergenerational values of the family can be recognized. Theirs is a generation that values truth-telling to the point not only of "telling it like it is" with their parents, but also of asking their parents openly and honestly whether life really needs to be such a heavy burden of success-seeking and self-examination as their parents embody.

Cultural Process and Generational Loyalty

Here then is the so-called generation gap as seen from four somewhat different but related aspects. Taken together they reveal a rapidly changing culture, but one that is still in process of revising and reappropriating the style of reality structuring and valuing of at least three generations. This is a process that involves each succeeding generation in a continuing dialectic between continuity and change—visible and invisible loyalty to ancestral modes of perceiving and valuing and the need to correct and modify those styles of constructing life. It is evident from all four aspects of our study that alienation exists between the generations, but it exists within a matrix of intergenerational loyalty. Thus there seems to be in each generation an authentic pull toward both past and future, the way things have been seen and the way things must now be seen in the light of the errors and distortions of the past and the new views of reality and value that are coming out of the visions of the future presented by the kaleidoscope of a changing culture.

The Menninger studies, as well as our cross-sectional analysis of value conflicts in the Dalton family, offers the possibility that individuals will develop unique styles of resolving the dialectic of the generation gap for themselves. Some will tend to be obedient traditionalists and others passionate renewers. The Dalton family offers the possibility that family conflict may be heightened when one spouse tends strongly in one direction while the other moves toward developing an opposite style. Mrs. Dalton was an obedient traditionalist married to a man who was probably more nearly a cautious modifier, if not a passionate renewer. She demonstrates the Menninger study thesis that obedient traditionalists will have less well developed identities and be more vulnerable to the conflicts created by rapid cultural change. On the other hand, Mr. Dalton's repression of his own traditional loyalties presses him toward a perfectionism of which he is only vaguely aware and makes him less available to his children than is Mrs. Dalton.

The generation gap and its varied resolution is thus revealed as a powerful dynamic in family conflict, but a much more complex one than the simplistic popular notion that parents and their children tend to disagree about values and see things differently. The double pull toward tradition and innovation is a gap each generation must resolve for itself, and individuals within generations vary enormously in how they come to grips with that task. Rapid cultural change accelerates that process to the extent that some families and individuals will experience the crisis of fragmented identity found in the Dalton family. How that crisis will be manifested will depend upon such factors as who in the family most acutely experiences the rupture in continuity of reality perception and valuing, how rigidly traditional values are adhered to in the structuring of family life, the degree of renewal and change embraced by the rising generation of adolescents in the family, and the like. Most families will perhaps experience intergenerational conflict only as one aspect of the painful but necessary process of separation as adolescents grow away from parents and separate themselves from the family. For some, however, the issue of changing styles of perception and valuing will become more crucial.

A Theological Perspective

Seen in theological perspective the data we have reviewed concerning the generation gap reveal in concrete detail the problem involved in human appropriation of both tradition and hope, memory and expectation. A dialectic between loyalty to the models of perception and valuing of the past and the trusting of one's own experience corroborated by one's contemporaries is set up, threatening alienation within the self and between persons of preceding and succeeding generations. Just as human traditions tend to become oppressive and constricting, human hopes and expectations tend to become reactive and in their effort at liberation form the basis for new structures of oppression and distortion. The need for a larger view of both history and future, tradition and expectation is revealed if persons are to avoid either being trapped in the patterns of perception and valuing of their own generation or, like Mrs. Dalton, being caught with a weak identity between the generations. A critical principle must be found that holds together past and future, tradition and expectation.

For the Christian community, particularly as viewed through the lens of the theologies of hope, this larger vision and critical principle are found in the linking of the Judeo-Christian tradition and that tradition's hope for the fulfillment of God's promise concerning the kingdom of God. The Judeo-Christian story of human history is a story of a pilgrim people on the way toward fulfillment of what has been and is now glimpsed only in fragments and provisionally. The fulcrum of that story is found in the gospel as embodied in Jesus, the Christ, who was himself the preliminary fulfillment of that promise.

Life "in accordance with the gospel" is life in recognized and accepted personal individuality, but an individuality that is charismatically alive, a personality that is lived in and for the community, and an independence that does not suppress originality but sets it free and develops it in relationship to forefathers and contemporaries. A life "in accordance with the gospel of Christ" seeks the individual and common messianic way of life. It cannot have anything to do with legalism or lawlessness, for it looks for forms of the liberated life in experience and forms of life's liberation in practice. The messianic gospel liberates oppressed life. It gives it bearings and meaning. It gives its stamp of life in the Spirit.[14]

Here a theological norm comes into view that stands over against all the oppressive ways in which generational styles of perception and value tend to impose themselves on individuals, whether contemporaries or offspring. But it is also a norm that stands against the lawlessness of any simple libertinism that ignores either tradition or responsible community. It is a messianic norm in that it seeks to anticipate and fulfill that final consummation of things that will make all things new and whole; it is a liberating norm in that it "looks for forms of the liberated life in experience and forms of life's liberation in practice."

Clearly the church that is fulfilling a ministry of liberation and messianic anticipation will seek to provide a context within which intergenerational alienation can find reconciliation, whether that alienation is found within the individual self, the family, or a community that is in conflict between traditional and avant-garde values. But the church, too, tends to be caught in the cultural process of continuity and change. So a tension is set between the church embedded in that cultural process and the church called to be a liberating and messianic fellowship. An atmosphere of inquiry and reflection, truth-telling in the sharing of different generational perspectives, and critical evaluation as all structures of human perception and value are held up to the light of the gospel needs to be created. Only in such an atmosphere can reconciliation that liberates persons for participation in the in-breaking of God's kingdom take place. To fulfill that ministry, theology must be brought directly and concretely into contact with both the alienation of differing perspectives and the dilemmas of living the liberated life in the here and now of a changing social context.

Here the infusion of an atmosphere of hopefulness and expectation of transformation becomes a crucial element in the style of both the ministry of pastoral care and of pastoral leadership. Any congregation, when scrutinized in terms of the generational gaps that exist, will reveal such a tangle of value conflicts and perceptual differences as to appear hopeless of ever achieving reconciliation. Only as a theology of hope and liberation is translated into the atmosphere of a congregation's life together can some of these conflicts and differences begin to emerge in ways that open them to the possibility of transformation. Here the dialectic of hope and hopelessness will become very real and concrete for the sensitive, perceptive pastor. The pastor who enters actively into a ministry of reconciliation will need not only to sharpen and develop his or her skills as a facilitator of reconciliation, but also deepen and confirm repeatedly his or her lively faith in the hopefulness of the gospel. Keeping central the concern for persons who, like Mr. and Mrs. Dalton, are caught in the "gap" of conflicting generational perspectives will provide the pastor with something of the compassion as well as the objectivity that are needed to keep his or her reconciling work in perspective.

Strategies for a Ministry of Reconciliation

If the church is to fulfill its role as the context where an enlarged theological perspective may be brought into direct contact with the alienation of the generation gap and the dilemmas of living the liberated life, some purposeful strategies of reconciliation ministry must be developed. These strategies need to be brought to bear on a broad range of activities and relationships within the community of faith so that they function at one or more of the following three levels: (1) prevention or liberating consciousness raising, (2) crisis intervention, and (3) search for the liberated life in accordance with the gospel. Strategies for a ministry of reconciliation should thus include much more than what has traditionally been thought of as pastoral care.

1. The Liberation of Consciousness Raising.

The movements for the liberation of minority groups and women have taught us a great deal about the value of simply creating occasions where persons have their consciousness raised about the oppressive structures of race, class, and sex that prevent persons from exercising their full creative powers in an open and free society. Getting persons together of widely differing backgrounds for serious conversation about the commonalities and differences in their heritages has in many churches and communities provided a healthy leavening effect on the larger process of human liberation. In this kind of person-to-person contact many of the myths of difference and separation can be broken through and larger common loyalties and aspirations shared.

Similar occasions for intergenerational conversation will often open up for examination in a context of acceptance the issues that separate and unite the generations. I recall one such evening of animated discussion in a middle-sized congregation in a county-seat town church attended by some thirty members of three generations that went something like this:

Mrs. Brown (mother of two teen-agers present): My problem is that I can't keep up with these young people in the way they are trying to get all the rules changed. I think they gang up on parents and make us believe that "everybody's doing it" when really none of the other parents are any happier than I am with giving them so many privileges.

Male senior citizen: If parents would just teach their children the difference between right and wrong and stick to it we wouldn't have all these problems with drugs and sex that we have.

High-school teen-ager: Who knows what's right and wrong any more? Things have changed. They aren't like they were when you were kids. I have to decide for myself what I want to do.

Senior citizen: When you lose track of what's right and wrong, the difference between good and evil, you're in trouble. I've always done what's right, and that solves a lot of problems.

College youth: The problem, Mr. Jones, is that your generation and my parent's generation thought they were doing right, and a lot of people were getting trampled on. We've learned that it isn't just a matter of right and wrong. The choices are all between shades of gray. You thought you were doing right when really your generation could have done a lot better.

Mrs. Smith (a second senior citizen): I agree with Mr. Jones. There's right and there's wrong, and everybody ought to know the difference.

Mrs. Brown: I wish I knew what was the right thing to do with my kids. I don't want to be rigid with them like my parents were, but . . .

Leader: Have we possibly bumped into a generational difference here? Mr. Jones and Mrs. Smith see things as either good or bad. Mrs. Brown confesses she's not as sure about that as she once was. The young people tend not to see things that way, but as much less either-or—good and better, less good and worse, a kind of continuum in which you have to choose. The different generations seem to see good and evil differently.

There followed a vigorous discussion in which the different generational experiences with the whole matter of good and evil were recognized around such issues as poverty, the Vietnam war, different styles of parenting, and honesty in human relationships. Though none of these issues were "settled" in the sense of a complete consensus, an atmosphere of open acceptance of difference and sincerity of purpose developed that began to make possible more open discussion of differences and a common search for new solutions.

Another potentially fruitful pastoral approach to raising consciousness of generation gap issues is the family life conference that can be approached on either a group or single-family basis. Here the purpose is to provide families, particularly those with teen-age children, the opportunity to reflect on the values that shape their life together, uncover the sources of those values, and consider whether in the light of the family's commitment to "life in accordance with the gospel" any of these value commitments need to be changed. One approach to this kind of family value assessment is to suggest that the family put together an intergenerational-value family tree similar to the analysis done earlier of the Dalton family. Surfacing the inherited value perspectives and differences between contemporary generational values of the parents and young people may bring into sharper focus the issues of perception and valuing that underlie the conflicts a family may be experiencing in the transition of adolescent separation from parents. With these issues sharpened, it may be possible to move toward consideration of the implications of a gospel of liberation for the members of a particular family as they confront the specifics of perceiving their situation and value choices. The theological purpose of the family life conference is thus to engender in the family what Moltmann has called "the messianic life style."[15]

2. Crisis Intervention.

The Dalton family illustrates that intergenerational crisis in families will not always be readily identified as such and that intergenerational conflict may be only in part responsible for the etiology of the crisis being experienced by one or more family members. The pastor is therefore always presented with the necessity of making a judgment whether a family or individual crisis situation that comes to his or her attention should be treated as generation gap crisis or within some other frame of reference. In the case of Mrs. Dalton it proved useful to consider and respond to her situation within that framework rather than simply as her depression and despair. The judgment is a pragmatic one based upon such factors as (1) the degree to which the person presenting the crisis seems caught in issues of value and differing generational styles of self and world perception, (2) the degree to which the crisis is presented as a conflict between the generations in a family or other social grouping or evidences the breakdown of generational boundaries by either inordinate control or reactive, rebellious behavior, and (3) the degree of hope for resolution of the crisis if it should be approached from this frame of reference. Not all persons, families, or groups will seem open to intergenerational conflict resolution, and in these cases a more individual or interpersonal approach to uncovering emotional blockages, conflicted feeling relationships, and the like may be necessary. Following work at that level centered more on feelings and relationships the approach we are considering here may prove useful at a particular stage in the counseling process.

In those cases in which the pastor has determined that an approach in the framework of the generation gap and intergenerational conflict seems to offer hopeful possibilities, one or more of a number of strategies may prove useful.[16]

(a) Clarifying generational boundaries. Particularly in families in which intergenerational conflict has developed to crisis proportions, but also on occasion in groups where conflicts between young persons and adult leaders have developed into group crisis, one strategy that often proves helpful is that of clarifying and affirming generational boundaries. Just what "business" is appropriately the prerogative of one generation or the other is the point at issue here. What questions should parents decide and what questions must ultimately be left to young persons themselves often needs clarification. The generations in conflicted families tend to encroach on each other in this regard, and the pastor may need to assert his or her authority in affirming the "rights" of one generation or the other to the prerogatives appropriate to that generation. Here the pastor will, of course, need to come to terms with his or her own tendency to identify with one or another generation. The narrow path that needs to be followed will most often be one that balances support of the parents' right and responsibility for determining basic behavioral parameters for the family while yet supporting the adolescent's right and responsibility to develop increasing autonomy in making decisions. Weak and indecisive parents will need support to set appropriate boundaries that give security to their children as they meet the conflicting value claims of budding adulthood and something to push against as they assert their growing independence. Rigid and encroaching parents need support to give more re-

alistic and flexible control that respects generational differences.[17]

(b) Siding. A ministry of reconciliation will always give attention to issues of oppression and victimization. It is of the nature of generation gap crises, whether they are individual, family, or group in their manifestation, that the values and perceptual structure of one generation or another symbolically if not directly tends to dominate while the other is suppressed and devalued. As a representative of the liberating gospel the pastor will give attention to the need for an advocate of the weak or devalued side of a conflict, though his or her advocacy will always be with the purpose of assisting the weak side to be heard and the hidden weakness of the strong to be acknowledged.

Taking sides is, of course, always a risky and potentially dangerous act. It invites "choosing up sides" and reducing the conflict to a simple struggle for power. This means that the pastor as reconciler must always take a siding stance responsibly and with a view toward ultimate recognition of the imbalance of power and the need for a more creative solution that balances the rights and perspectives of all concerned. Siding should always be done at the pastor's own initiative and not on the invitation of one or another of the alienated to join them in order to overcome the opposing view. The reconciler will not remain long as the advocate of one side over against another, but will move quickly to support the value that is being overlooked, the person who is being pushed down, the perspective that has not been recognized. In this way he or she functions to assist the alienated in breaking out of stereotyped, locked-in modes of managing value and reality perception conflicts and actively works to open up the fresh and new possibility more in tune with the gospel of liberation.[18]

(c) The pastor as go-between. Occasionally the pastor will encounter generation gap crises that have become so acute and the alienation so intense as to become

explosive. Communication has broken down completely. Feelings of anger and hurt, distrust and fear of misunderstanding have become so strong that the persons involved can scarcely stand to be in the same room together. The positive feelings and ties that bind persons together have been covered over by negative feelings, accusation, and counter-accusation. This is frequently the case in situations of teen-age runaways, for example.

In situations of this kind the pastor will often find himself or herself drawn into the position of being the go-between to whom persons on either side of the gap can talk while they are yet unable to communicate usefully with each other. This is, of course, a difficult position to be in, in that it requires great skill if one is not to be drawn toward inappropriate collaboration with one side or the other. Pastors frequently receive such invitations from either teen-age parishioners or their parents. But the position of go-between, if it is temporary, is a potentially useful role of reconciliation. It involves listening carefully and with acceptance to persons on both sides of the gap and searching with them for some basis upon which communication can be restored. The goal should always be to move as quickly as possible to getting the estranged persons back into conversation, with the pastor serving as mediator, clarifier, and authoritative control to prevent the degeneration of the relationship again into accusation and blame placing. Sometimes ground rules for discussion need to be established and enforced. The task can be seen as one of providing a safe context in which the negativities of the estranged relationship will not be allowed to overpower the often feeble desire for reconciliation until such time as that hidden side of the relationship can be expressed and a new basis for negotiation of a relationship covenant be found. In some cases the pastor may want to consider making a referral to one of the family crisis centers that have now been established in most metropolitan areas. This, of course, should not mean that the pastor will abandon his or her role as reconciler; that role continues as support and encouragement are offered to help the persons involved sustain their efforts at reconciliation through what is inevitably a painful process.

(d) Negotiating family or group "policy." Alienated families or other intergenerational groups often need help in renegotiating the rules and policies by which their relationships are to be governed as they seek a new, reconciled life together. Such things as the rights and privileges of individuals as distinguished from what must be considered corporately, what individuals may expect of one another, and what rules are to govern relationships with the outside world must all be reconsidered. Often it is around the renegotiation of such rules and policies as these that a new and more liberated relationship covenant can be established. If attention is not given to these structural aspects of the family or group relationships, new controversies and issues around which alienation can again develop will almost inevitably follow. Clarification of positive and negative feelings is vitally important in a ministry of reconciliation; by itself clarification of feelings cannot sustain liberated new life for the family or group.

The pastoral role in assisting people to renegotiate the policies that govern their relationship covenants is most often an active one. Areas where policies need to be established or reconsidered need to be pointed up and opinions invited. Inequities or areas of generational encroachment and dominance need to be confronted. The larger value issues need to be lifted up so that policy decisions can reflect the value commitments that have been affirmed or are emerging. New intentions and hopes for the future must be elicited and their implications for family or group structuring explored. In all this process the pastor can serve as temporary leader, referee, and mediator.

3. The Search for the Liberated Life.

A ministry of reconciliation with persons experiencing generational conflicts is not complete simply with the resolution of the acute crisis and the restructuring of a covenant of relationship on the basis of which the generations can for the present live comfortably together. This is true because, hidden in the tangle of conflicting views of reality and conflicting values, lies the call of the gospel for the truly liberated life—a life which can only be provisionally and fleetingly achieved by the best of human negotiation and struggle. Once those in conflict have been set free from the tangled web of confused perceptions and conflicting values, there yet remains the continuing task of search for the full meaning of the liberated life in the future.[19] The new structures for living together hammered out in coming to grips with the crisis will themselves become obsolete and constricting unless the process of liberation to an ever new future is kept open. Life together must continually be liberated.

As I write this I am reminded that one of the most satisfying and stimulating times in my work with the Dalton family came after the heaviness of Mrs. Dalton's depression had lifted and Mr. Dalton had begun to acknowledge his own participation in the family problem. Through the tangled web of conflicting emotions, generational loyalties, and confused values began to emerge a new shared intentionality. The Daltons began to experiment with new ways of being together, raised questions with each other about the style of material success and heavy social entertainment involvement of their upper-middle-class life, and generally explored what a more liberated life together might entail. The hopeless tangle of conflicting loyalties was more and more transformed into an exciting shared quest for transformation in their life together. A loosening of the value and interpersonal conflicts took place that opened the way to a more "questing" attitude toward their future

271

together. Hope began to replace the despair and frustration that had dominated our earlier conversations.

It is at this point that the work of the pastor and the life of the Christian community in helping individuals, families, and generational groups to experience their struggle for liberation within the larger context of the history of God's liberation of human life becomes crucial. To struggle for reconciliation within oneself or with persons from whom one has been estranged is painful, suffering work; to experience that struggle as the personally relevant meaning of God's liberation of one's life and the life of those to whom one is attached from bondage into freedom and hope is to experience new birth.

This larger context within which the inevitable tensions of human perception and valuing may be experienced is what Jürgen Moltmann reaches for in his concept of the messianic life-style. He speaks of that life-style as a life that values both its memories and its hopes, a life that accepts the necessity of living always in creative tension, a life that joins solidarity with a continuing search for transcendence. It accepts the judgment that no one human perspective on reality or value, be that of an individual or a generation, is adequate to exhaust the possibilities of that Kingdom which is the eschatological ground of our hope. So Christian life together is a life of search and expectancy. It is life in the Spirit.[20]

CHAPTER IX

Marriage Crisis
and Broken Relationships

Our exploration of the common crisis experiences of modern life would not be complete without attention being given to marriage crisis. Indeed, if we want to point to the one most common pressure point at which the conflicts and dilemmas of life in a rapidly changing and pluralistic society seem to converge, it would be at the point of marital conflict. Though statistical reports vary, it is generally recognized that at least one in three marriages may be expected to end in divorce. Many other marriages undergo multiple crises as the stresses upon the marital relationship ebb and flow through the family life cycle. Parish pastors who engage in any extensive counseling may expect that a large proportion of their formal counseling time will be spent in work with individuals and couples whose presenting problem is a crisis in their marriage.

Just why there has been such a dramatic increase in marital crisis in our society over the last thirty years is, of course, subject to much speculation and even controversy; the fact of the increase is, however, undisputed. In this chapter we will consider from both a sociopsychological and a theological perspective some of the possible causative factors in the dramatic rise in marriage crisis and suggest in broad outline a pastoral approach to marriage crisis counseling. For a more detailed exposition of marriage counseling theory and technique the reader is referred to the resources listed in the bibliography.

Marriage Crisis and
Contemporary Human Vulnerability

In the beginning of our study of crisis experience it was proposed that the image that best captures contemporary consciousness in Western society is the image of human life caught between infinite aspirations, on the one hand, and finite possibilities, on the other. Caught in that tension between aspirations and boundaries, contemporary persons feel profoundly vulnerable to life's contingent possibilities and look for a source of ultimate security. But the modern consciousness is further made vulnerable by the erosion of a genuine, potent sense of divine providence. (Minus that security in God's providential activity, persons are thrown for their security back upon themselves and the immediate interpersonal and structural relationships of their lives.) These relationships are no longer experienced by many as the instruments through which God exercises his providence so much as they are the relationships which in themselves must secure human aspiration and hope. Given the depersonalization and bureaucratization of many of the relationship structures of vocation, government, and community in urban society particularly, the weight of human need for security is finally thrown back upon the tight network of personal relationships and, most particularly for many, the marriage relationship. The question then presents itself whether the marriage relationship, even if strong and healthy, can bear the weight of expectation of ultimate security placed upon it. Insofar as it is pressed to bear that weight, as we have already seen in our study of bereavement, it becomes idolatrous.

It is a useful exercise to consider the subtle ways in which the Western romantic image of marriage has evolved into an icon of ultimate human relationship hopes—an icon with built-in disappointment and virtually inevitable failure. Consider, for example, the way in which the marital relationship has come to be the primary, if not the sole bearer of the human expectation

274

of relationship continuity. Mobility may break the continuity of other relationships. Jobs may change and loyalty ties to co-workers be broken. Neighbors move away. Children grow up and move across town or across the country. (But through all relationship changes the marriage relationship is expected to remain not only there but there in the way it has always been.) The expectation that marriage is to last " 'til death us do part" has always been there, but the relative weight of expectation of continuity as compared with other relationships has increased enormously for many persons caught up in societal mobility. To be sure, there are some signs that the expectation of temporariness has crept into some marriage relationships. The number of couples living together without formal marriage contract has increased. The number of people whose marital life is made up of a series of two, three, or even four more or less temporary relationships has increased to the point at which it can be called a de facto established pattern. These signs can perhaps themselves be seen as evidence that the weight of continuity expectation has for many marriages become too heavy to bear. But for the majority the relationship that alone carries the expectation of lifelong continuity is that with the marital partner.

Or consider the manner in which marriage has come for many people to be the primary, if not the sole source of intimacy. In a highly organized, structured society most relationships tend to become instrumental—circumscribed by the function they fulfill in the more or less objective carrying out of the work of the world. With instrumental function setting the boundaries on these relationships, there are sharp limits placed on the degree of personal involvement admissible to them. This means that for most people the need for the personal—the relationship for its own sake—must be fulfilled in marriage. If one reads the popular literature concerning marital intimacy, one cannot help being struck with the almost mystical quality with which intimate union between marriage partners is being sought. Here is the relationship in which, above all else, one is expected to give and receive pleasure. The instrumental functions of marriage must not be allowed to interfere with the primacy of the fulfillment of intimacy needs. It is as if in a secularized society where the hope for both the intimate community of care from our fellow humans and of mystical union with God has eroded, the burden of providing for the human need for mystical union has come to rest squarely on the shoulders of the marriage relationship. Few marriages can consistently carry such a burden.

William Kilpatrick, in his cogent critique of the cult of self-actualization, *Identity and Intimacy,* makes the point that what is lacking in many marriages patterned after the image of intimate love in Western society is what he calls serious commitment.[1] His argument is with temporariness and fluidity in identity and relationship. It is a sound argument, but it perhaps does not penetrate fully to the heart of the matter. What prevents that level of commitment for many persons may be the idolatrous expectation that the marriage should by itself fulfill the human need for continuity and intimate union that cannot be broken. A quality of ultimate expectation has crept into what is by its nature a finite, human relationship.

[margin handwritten note: expecting too much of marriage]

Many of the therapeutic modalities that have emerged over the last decade in response to the increase in marital crises can be described as efforts to increase the "competence" level of the marriage relationship. Marriage enrichment workshops, communication labs, and sex therapy designed to break through sexual hang-ups and increase competent performance in love-making all aim at helping marital partners become more able to relate with openness and skill. In that sense they are directed toward an instrumental purpose for the marriage. Undoubtedly these therapies have been helpful to many couples. But the more fundamental

276

question as to just what a marriage relationship may legitimately be expected to provide is often left to the marriage partners to negotiate as if in a vacuum. Most often only casual attention is given to the possibility that inordinate expectations are being brought to the marriage because of the absence of larger value and faith commitments within which ultimate needs for hope and security can be met. Certainly the marriage relationship with its commitment "to have and to hold from this day forward, for better or worse, to love and to cherish 'til death us do part" is meant to be the most intimate and unconditional human relationship we know. That it can by itself secure the marital partners against the vulnerability of finite life is highly questionable. Yet that is the direction in which the romantic image of marriage in a secularized world has evolved.

A Developmental Approach to Understanding Marriage Relationships

Consistent with our earlier efforts to understand how crisis experience is shaped by an intertwining of social and individual identity dynamics, we turn now to an exploration of the way in which marriages take shape out of individual efforts to resolve identity issues in and through a social relationship that leads to marriage. This is most clearly the case when commitments to marriage are made in the late teens or early twenties, when movement from adolescence to young adulthood requires the resolution of adolescent identity conflicts. In my experience, however, even with adults in their middle years the primary psychological dynamics in the decision to marry or remarry have to do with resolution of identity issues.

Two incidents in my own ministry are illustrative. Both have been chosen because they dramatize what is often more subtly the case in the formation of marriages:

277

CRISIS EXPERIENCE IN MODERN LIFE

Ellen was a student nurse in the large medical center where I was chaplain. I knew her only slightly from having encountered her on the hospital floors and from her occasional attendance at services in the chapel, so her request that I perform her marriage vows came somewhat as a surprise. A slight, wispy sort of girl of 19, she rather shyly made her request, saying that she preferred being married at the hospital to being married at her home church "because I'm grown up now and want to avoid as much of the hassle with my parents as I can."

A problem arose when it came time to set the wedding date. Ellen literally was unable in two conferences to set an exact time for the wedding. The reasons for the indecision, however, were vague and unspecific. A conference with Ellen and Jack, her husband-to-be, produced a tentative date for the wedding that still had to be checked out with both of Ellen's divorced parents before being confirmed. Indecision and a great need to please everyone concerned were the blatant identity issues that were impressed upon me by Ellen's participation in these conversations. She spoke at length of her admiration of Jack for his ability to make decisions, his self-confidence, and driving ambition.

Superficially, Jack presented himself as the embodiment of Ellen's wishes. He introduced himself with all the aggressiveness of a traveling salesman, spoke confidently of his work as a radio announcer, and declared his intention to make Ellen happy and bolster her self-confidence. The immediate impression I received was of an interesting study in contrasts and complementarity.

Further premarital counseling revealed that not only were Ellen's parents separated, but that she had a long history of being caught between them in their endless arguments, during which she had attempted to be the peacemaker. Jack, on the other hand, had been an only child and until very recently had lived at home. He made much of his recent move away from his parents and his highly valued autonomy.

When time for the wedding came I was interested in meeting and talking briefly with both sets of parents. Somewhat to my surprise I found Ellen's mother to be a rather large and strong-willed woman who took charge of the wedding rehearsal, telling the participants how to stand and communicating fairly directly to me her expectations concerning the ceremony. Ellen's father stayed in the background, seemed as shy as his daughter, and generally looked uncomfortable.

Jack's mother and father also stayed in the background during the rehearsal and prior to the wedding, though their open-hearted and indulgent attitude toward their son was readily apparent. The surprise in my impressions of Jack's parents came when, during the reception, the mother confided in me her somewhat anxious pleasure in the marriage of her son. "I do hope Ellen can give Jack some stability and security in his life. He has until recently been much too dependent on us and has been floundering in getting on his own." My first impression of complementarity in the prospective marriage relationship had to be revised. There was a hidden side to the dynamics that drew Ellen and Jack together. I found myself wondering if Ellen could underneath her shy exterior be more like her mother than was at first apparent. And what of Jack? If I was to believe his mother his presentation of himself as self-confident and ambitious had a hidden side as well. I found myself wondering how this marriage relationship, with its (unresolved identity issue ingredients brought by each marital partner, would work itself out. Just where would the critical issues arise? Could this marriage be expected to avoid eventually coming to crisis?

The case of Ellen and Jack illustrates with some specificity the way in which the search for resolution of identity issues and mate selection are tightly intertwined. Superficially, from the standpoint of conscious intent, Ellen is looking for someone to complement her shyness and indecisiveness. She admires and needs Jack's outward self-assurance, his ability to meet people easily and get things done. She is attracted to his outward strength. She is an "admirer"; he needs admiration. On Jack's part, he seems to be looking for someone with whom he can feel strong and protective—one who will support his leadership in the marriage. A "contract" is emerging in which each seems to have accepted the role that complements the other's needs.

My wedding day observations and conversation with Ellen and Jack's parents, however, reveal glimpses of what may be complicating if not conflicting dynamic forces at work less accessible to awareness on the part of both marriage partners. The model of wife and mother Ellen has grown up with is predominantly dominant and assertive, whereas the husband-father image of her childhood was, insofar as I was able to observe, much more passive and less able to provide assertive leadership. It was also apparent that, despite her indecision, Ellen was the one who would in the end decide on the plans for the wedding.

Jack is revealed by his mother's expression of hope for the marriage and her brief report of her perspective on Jack's history as one who has had a struggle asserting his independence and strength to live on his own. We can speculate that his desire for Ellen's admiration and dependency on him for strength harbors his own deep need for the support and encouragement he apparently has always received from his parents. Thus both Ellen and Jack seem to be presenting the marriage with a two-sided set of conflicting needs that may or may not find complementarity in the marriage relationship. What superficially appears to complement may turn out later as a deeper conflict.

My second illustration likewise grew out of a request for the performance of a wedding:

Brett and Nan had both been married before. Brett's first wife, after giving birth to their only child, had suffered a severe mental illness requiring hospitalization and long-term psychiatric care. Brett had remained faithful to his wife until she was somewhat back on her feet and then divorced her, though he still financially supported her and the child as well as paid for her continuing treatment. He was in business for himself and had a substantial income. His early history was relatively uneventful except for the death of his father while Brett was in his early teens—an event that threw him and his mother very close as they mutually supported each other in their bereavement.

Nan was 27, ten years younger than Brett. She was a talented and beautiful woman, though somewhat insecure and lonely. She had married in late adolescence to get away from a domineering mother upon whom she was deeply and angrily dependent. The marriage had been a short-lived affair ending in divorce after which Nan had alternately lived with her mother and by herself in a larger city near her home. She hated living alone, needed the security of knowing she would be cared for, but feared making commitments.

Brett and Nan met shortly after Brett's divorce, and their relationship fairly quickly became a sexual liaison that only with some reluctance and ambivalence on both their parts moved toward marriage. Both spoke of their fears of repeating past failure and loss of independence. Finally the decision was made to marry, largely because both wanted children and the security of a long-term relationship. Because I had known both of them through previous counseling relationships, I was asked to perform the ceremony.

Just prior to the scheduled wedding date a minor crisis arose when Brett announced that he had asked his lawyer to draw up a formal contract to be signed before the wedding, the major purpose of which was to make legal Nan's renunciation of any claim on Brett's assets acquired prior to the marriage. "I've never been able to get free of any commitments to women before, and I want to give myself some breathing room in this relationship." Nan was at first dumbfounded and angry; her need for security in the relationship was severely threatened. Eventually she agreed and the contract was signed; the ceremony took place.

Though the dynamics of complementarity and conflict take somewhat different form for Brett and Nan from those of Jack and Ellen, they too reveal a search for resolution to identity conflict in the selection of a mate. Brett seems outwardly to be attempting to hedge against the errors of his first marriage to a mate who had proved to be weak and unable to cope with the demands of marriage and motherhood. His insistence on a limiting legal contract seems clearly to be an attempt to structure the new marriage so that Nan's needs and his difficulty with setting limits on obligation can be managed. But he has unconsciously chosen another mate with deep security needs and conflict over self-sufficiency versus dependency on others. The issue of his first marriage will continue to be played out in his second. At a deeper level Brett is still working out his solution to the identity dilemma first presented to him by his father's death. That event came just at the time in his own development when as a budding adolescent he both needed his father as a masculine model and needed to develop freedom from his mother. Instead he had been drawn into a relationship with his mother in which her needs for care became primary.

As for Nan, the search seems to be for a mate who will provide her with the security she had in her family of origin without the stifling control of her autonomy that home had demanded. Brett seems to offer that relationship. His demand for a binding legal contract, however, cuts across the grain of both these identity needs of Nan's. Will his need for clear limits allow her enough of the sense of freedom and autonomy she seeks?

In summary, what emerges from these two case vignettes of the formation of marriage is that mate selection and identity formation or maintainance are integrally related. It is as if the issues that form the identity configuration of each individual provide an agenda of issues and needs that must be accounted for in the selection of a mate and the negotiation of a working covenant for the marriage. The seeds of both marital conflict and fulfillment are found in these complementary and conflicting agendas brought to the marriage by the two partners. From this generalization concerning identity and mate selection several principles or rough rules of thumb emerge:

1. All marriage partner selection processes contain to some degree the transference of attitudes and expectations that were present in the individual's relationship with parents. These transference phenomena function at all levels of both awareness and dynamic power, from

repressed unconscious wishes and fears to role models and perceptions of the self in intimate relationships. Stated another way, there is in every entrance into a marital partnership both the expectation that the history of the individual's relationship with parents will be in some way repeated in this new relationship and the intention that the relationship should in some way resolve or work out differently the relationship the individual had in his or her family of origin. Here we see a specific way in which the dynamic of continuity and change plays a significant role in the intimate relationships of marriage and family life.

2. Identity issues as they are brought into mate selection most often contain some fundamental ambivalences that have shaped and continue to shape the individual identity formation process of the marriage partners. This means that a rough rule of thumb of opposites may be applied in evaluating the motivations for marriage of marital partners. Such pairings as autonomy versus dependence, narcissism versus relatedness, wishes versus fears, active versus passive, to name but a few are usually found together, the one conscious and intended, the other covert and unrecognized. Strongly expressed desires for dependency in the marital relationship such as Ellen's, for example, may be expected to have their more unconscious and therefore less well articulated counterpoint in a desire to be dominant and determinative in making decisions that control the direction the marital relationship will take. The polarities of identity become the polarities of marriage relationship expectation and resistance.

3. The usual process of mate selection involves the bringing together of some identity characteristics that complement those of the marriage partner and others that conflict. Marriage and family life can therefore be understood as a process of working out a set of spoken or unspoken "agreements" as to how these complementary and conflicting identity needs will be accounted for in the

relationship. These "agreements" function at several levels of awareness and conscious control of the participants and with varying degrees of congruence in relation to the two individual sets of expectations of the marriage.

Authorities in the marriage counseling field have proposed various ways of constructing a working theory concerning what are commonly called marriage "contracts." One of the more useful set of constructs is that of Clifford J. Sager.[2] He proposes that each marriage tends to embody essentially four working contracts, the first two of which contain the individual expectations and desires of each marital partner which may be quite different in many respects. These expectations and desires function at three levels of awareness: conscious and verbalized, conscious but unspoken, and beyond awareness. These two individual contracts may be expected to be congruent in many respects, complementary in some respects, and conflicting in others.[3] Another functioning contract Sager proposes to call the interactional contract. This is the operational basis on which the coupling relationship begins to take on a life of its own and develop rules, strategies, and tactics by which "the two mates are trying to achieve the needs expressed in their separate contracts."[4] The interactional contract tends also to have both positive and negative elements.

The fourth contract Sager sees as the one which only slowly and partially develops out of healthy growth and maturation in the marriage, often requiring outside intervention to achieve. This is the "single" contract which the marital system develops that takes into account the individual expectations, desires, and needs of each partner as well as the changing tasks and emerging goals of the marriage. Sager proposes that in healthy marriages the maintenance and renegotiation of this single contract become a lifelong process of negotiation and change in which higher levels of congruence and complementarity are achieved.[5]

How useful theories of marriage contracts will be to the pastor is an interesting question, the answer to which will depend a great deal on the level of both counseling and theological sophistication with which he or she makes use of the theory. The choice of the term "contract" seems to me unfortunate in some respects. It implies a certain quid pro quo that seems to invite marital partners to negotiate their contracts to the best advantage possible for each partner and speaks of the marketplace rather than the sacred territory of a profoundly intimate and mysterious relationship. If a satisfactory contract to meet individual needs cannot be worked out it seems to legitimate the breaking of the contract in order to seek a more advantageous one. Yet contract theories are useful descriptions of what tends to take place in many if not most marriages.

A somewhat different image of marriage as a relationship that may begin as two sets of congruent, complementary, and conflicting expectations, and only gradually—with much hard work as well as no small amount of grace—move toward a deeply binding covenant of mutual care and concern, seems both an accurate description and a normative statement concerning marriage. That many marriages remain at the level of simple quid pro quo interactional contracts is both descriptively accurate and expressive of the tragic human failure to fulfill the biblical image of marriage as the most profound of all mysteries in human relationships. So long as the pastor keeps that norm for marriage clearly in the forefront of his or her hope and intention for marriage counseling, contract theories will be useful in sorting out all the developmental factors that make for marital difficulty.

Developmental Crises in Marriage

A developmental approach to understanding marriage relationships elucidates the reality that some degree of crisis is to be expected from time to time in most if not all marriages. The "pure" marriage in which there are no conflicting elements and in which a covenant of mutual care and concern can be maintained at all times probably does not exist. Rather crisis times in the sense of critical points of transition and tension over changing expectations are integral to the growth of a marriage and the deepening of the marital commitment. In this sense marriage crisis may be understood as involving both creative and destructive possibility—the deepening and enriching of the life of the marriage or its regression and movement toward brokenness and death.

Having said that, it is nevertheless important that we press further our phenomenological and developmental analysis of marriage crisis to delineate those most common circumstances in which serious marital crisis may be expected. Recognizing the infinite variety to be found in marriage relationships and their accompanying crisis variations, I would therefore propose the following as the most common relationship situations that may be expected to produce more or less serious marriage crisis:

1. Crisis tends to come early in the marriage when the unspoken expectations and desires brought into the marriage on the part of one or both spouses are so conflicting with those of the partner as to preclude the formation of a covenant of mutual care and concern in the marriage.

These are the couples about whom marriage counselors are inclined to say, "They never really had a marriage." By that is meant that the motivation for marriage is so strongly colored by unrecognized search for self that the relationship as such is quite secondary. It has little value for the person except as a means for getting unspoken individual needs met. If those needs are complemented by a spoken or unspoken desire on the part of the marital partner to fulfill such a deficit, the marriage may yet survive long enough for a more mutual covenant of care to come into being. But if the need on the part of one partner meets the same deficit on the part of the other, or if fulfilling that need cuts across the grain of intentions for the marriage on the part of the less needy partner, conflict of crisis proportions will not long be delayed. For example, if one partner comes into the marriage with deep and unrecognized needs for affection, nurture, and support while the other enters with fear of closeness and need for distance and affirmation of self-sufficiency, conflict is inevitable and early crisis likely.

Loretta and Manfred Austin were such a couple. Their relationship began at a large state university where they were students together. The relationship began as a fairly typical fraternity-sorority romance and moved quickly to a level of casual but satisfying sexual activity. By the time they were college seniors they were living together without the knowledge of their parents. Manfred came from a small town, and though he wore the long hair and ragged jeans that were the uniform of the early seventies, he had secret ambitions to succeed in the business world and move to the city. Loretta was an upper-class child of divorced parents whose childhood had been marked by emotional deprivation from her father and much unhappiness and conflict in her home. As an adolescent she had acted out some of the family conflict through behavior problems at school, a teen-age pregnancy and abortion, and considerable conflict with her mother. A bright girl, she always did well academically but lacked purpose for her life, needed affection which she usually sought sexually, and harbored deep anger and disappointment toward her father, whom she described as a "phony." Her chief desire was to escape the life she had known as a "privileged" but unhappy girl.

At the end of college Loretta and Manfred were married and moved to Loretta's home city, where Manfred with the help of business friends of Loretta's father obtained a job with a large national accounting firm. Manfred soon became heavily involved in his work, joined a young businessmen's tennis club, and began to develop his career. Meanwhile Loretta, bored with apartment life, went to work at the first of a series of secretarial and receptionist jobs, none of which challenged her intellectual capacities. She soon became more and more lonely and bored, began seeing old boy friends, and occasionally went alone to a singles' bar. She soon was involved in the first of a series of casual affairs. Her husband knew of her extramarital activities but was too preoccupied with his own budding business career to allow a problem with his marriage to get in his way and, besides, he "believed in open marriage."

Marriage counseling came after Loretta one day impulsively quit her job and went to see her mother to whom she expressed her dissatisfaction with the deterioration of her sexual relationship with her husband and her sense of not really being ready for marriage. The mother suggested she call me for an appointment. The counseling, however, never really got off the ground. Manfred came with his wife a few times but was clearly not motivated to undertake any significant changes in the marriage or himself. After a few weeks Loretta decided she really wasn't ready to give up her extramarital activities, and the counseling relationship came to an end.

Here we see two young people each of whom brought an unspoken agenda of identity issues to the marriage which, when juxtaposed in the marriage, were probably incompatible from the beginning. Loretta was still struggling with her affectional deprivations and deeply needed as well as feared a close, nurturing relationship. The intimacy of sex had for some time been for her an acceptable substitute for the more childlike affection she unconsciously craved. Angry at her husband for his distance and marriage to his career, she began in her marriage repeating the pattern of her adolescent acting out.

Manfred, on the other hand, seemed more self-sufficient, even narcissistic in his orientation to human relationships. He liked beautiful women in the same way he liked beautiful sports cars. His ambition was the primary engine that drove his life. I was tempted to suspect that his wife's upper-class background had played a major role in his original attraction to Loretta, though there was no concrete evidence in my conversations with him to confirm that suspicion. At any rate, his self-contained, cool distance was in stark contrast to his wife's need for nurturing intimacy. There was little complementarity or congruence in what the Austins had brought to their marriage. Such a marriage is likely to experience early crisis and has a high probability of ending in divorce.

The trend toward prolongation of adolescence into the twenties in our culture has no doubt played a significant role in the dramatic increase of early marital crisis and mounting divorce rates among younger couples. This trend has increased the number of persons who, though their chronological age may indicate that the time for marital commitment has arrived, are not yet far enough along with resolution of adolescent identity issues to be genuinely ready for marriage. This suggests that the decision of increasing numbers of young people to delay marriage until the late twenties or even early thirties may be a reasonable response to a changing cultural situation. Trial marriages, tentative "arrangements," and difficulties experienced by many young persons in making the decision to marry may likewise be seen as struggles in coping with the changed cultural pattern of delayed adolescence and postponed adulthood. The marriage that comes at the point at which adolescent identity issues have been worked through and the persons involved are more genuinely ready for a covenant of adult mutual care will have a far greater chance of succeeding in weathering the inevitable critical transitions that must be made when "two become as one flesh."

2. Crisis tends to come when unresolved or unsatisfactorily resolved childhood strivings emerge in the marriage in such a way that one or both spouses have

become predominantly imaged as parent or parent substitute. The development or maintenance of a covenant of mutual care and concern is blocked by transferred feelings and attitudinal projections.

This was, of course, a strongly complicating feature of the Austin's marriage conflict. Loretta had never experienced a satisfactory relationship with her father, though she longed for some expression of affection and concern from him. When her new husband became increasingly invested in his business career Loretta strongly suspected a repetition of the desertion she had experienced with her father. Manfred became increasingly a parental figure who not only withheld affection but might also be expected to desert her.

Many marriages, of course, survive and even from outward appearances seem to flourish with strong parenting components in the marriage covenant. Many complementarities in marital relationships are colored by transference of parent-child relationship expectations. The relationship in which one partner is dominant and the other submissive is, for example, often a reproduction of a dominant parent–submissive child pattern of development. Generally speaking, where the transferred attitudes are by and large positive and complemented by a desire for a parenting relationship by the partner, the marriage may stabilize for years at this level without serious crisis. Where transferred feelings and attitudinal projections are overtly or covertly predominantly negative in the sense of projected rejection, anger, guilt, and the like, the marriage is much more apt to be stormy and full of crisis-precipitating conflict. Here again the rule of thumb of opposites often applies. Parenting transferences in marriage relationships are usually highly ambivalent so that what is expected and accepted consciously may be unconsciously resisted and countered and vice versa. Such marriages are therefore prone to unresolved conflicts that become intensified when changing circumstances bring stress to the marriage.

Of all the changed circumstances that can precipitate crisis in marriages involving parental transference, by far the most common are those related to the coming of children into the home. Many a marriage that as a complementary pairing has been relatively tranquil flounders when children appear and competition between parent and child for the attention and affection of one parent emerges. In my experience there are at least two crucial times when these marriages tend to experience crisis, the first during the infancy and early childhood of the offspring and the second when children enter early adolescence. Both critical family periods seem to require two parents, both of whom are able to relate to all family members in the parenting mode untainted by covert need for parenting care of their own. Few marriage relationships meet that standard consistently, which is perhaps one reason why marital crisis and family conflict are often interrelated.

3. Crisis tends to come when role concepts become confused or when the circumstances of the marriage shift so as to cause new role expectations to cut across the grain of established role patterns in the marriage.

It is common knowledge that role patterns in marriage have been undergoing marked changes in response to the rapid social change brought by the development of an urbanized and technocratic society. The traditional role division between husband-breadwinner and wife-homemaker has itself been altered considerably by the increased number of women who have entered the job market requiring that adjustments be made to take account of the wife's diminished availability in the home. Two-career families are no longer an unusual exception to the traditional pattern.[6] The appearance of day care centers in virtually every lower- and middle-class neighborhood witnesses to the rapid rise in two-breadwinner marriages.

Shifts from traditional role patterns require that many role responsibilities heretofore taken for granted in marriage and family life be renegotiated to the satisfaction of both partners involved. Traditional patterns generally assume that only one spouse will have a career outside the home and therefore will have obligations as to time commitments, mobility, and vocational priority to which the other spouse, usually the wife, must accommodate. Most occupations still assume this pattern and remain relatively inflexible in their expectations vis à vis the role of the person in his or her family. Changes in these roles therefore must be negotiated not only between the two marriage partners but with an often rigid structure of employment by one or both spouses. Stresses and strains are inevitable in such a situation. If the renegotiation of role expectations is not done openly and with flexibility in relation to the tension between continuance of traditional patterns and drastically altered roles, marital conflict of crisis proportions can result.

Not infrequently the circumstances of a marriage can shift in such a way as to force alteration of roles in ways not consciously chosen by either or both partners. Health failure of one or the other partner, job loss, the inflation of the economy, and other events and social processes can bring about forced changes in role patterns which must then be accommodated in the relationship. I have encountered in my marriage counseling experience several such stressed marriages in which the crisis seemed to have been precipitated by such things as a wife's entrance into active participation in a family business for economic reasons, a move from a family farm to an urban context that required the husband to moonlight at a second job, or the sudden necessity to move to a new locality because of one spouse's employment that required a disadvantageous job change for the other spouse. When changes like these are made suddenly and at the emotional expense of one or the other spouse, marital conflict often follows.

4. Crisis tends to come when for a variety of reasons

communication between marriage partners becomes blocked by unrecognized or more openly expressed negative feelings and guilt.

The onset of most marriage crises is signaled by the breakdown of communication between the marital partners. So long as communication remains open and direct with each partner able to hear what the other is saying and to respond in ways that invite further communication, marriage partners are usually able to work their way through most stresses that even the best of marriages encounter. Good communication will not always be positive. Disagreements, negative feelings, and conflicting viewpoints must be aired. Differences in perspective are of the basic stuff of human relationships and provide the occasion for much of human communication. So long as the relationship is undergirded by a solid base of positive regard and mutual respect, differences in feeling and perspective can not only be tolerated but can provide the spice of lively interchange and mutual search for meaning and purpose in the marriage.

Breakdown in marriage communication can occur in a great variety of ways, some more destructive to the relationship than others. In my experience communication breakdowns tend to occur under some combination of the following conditions:

(a) When the style of communication begins to take on the qualities of blame placing, accusation, and, concomitantly, guilt, apology, and counter accusation. Marriages can only stand so much moralizing and blame placing before they will begin to build barriers to communication and break down into hostility and guilty avoidance of confrontation. The partnership degenerates into a relationship between the accuser and the accused. Protective walls must be erected against the spouse, who has in some fashion become "the enemy."

(b) When unrecognized guilt and hostility begin to creep covertly into marital communication so that the problem at hand cannot be dealt with openly on its own merit. (Defensiveness, denial, projection, and displacement of feelings that relate to old grievances begin to creep into communication so that confusion, misunderstanding, and outright inability to hear what is being said blocks communication.)

(c) (When stresses outside the marriage relationship itself are brought into the marriage so that communication lines become overloaded with meanings and emotions that have been generated elsewhere.) Typically this kind of communication breakdown occurs when one or the other spouse is experiencing stress in relationships at work or with children and efforts to cope with that stress are frustrated in the context in which the stress is generated. The husband is in sharp disagreement with company policies being enforced by his boss but feels impotent to change them and must "go along." He brings that frustration home and begins to assert himself inappropriately in the marriage. The wife is having difficulty coping with the demands of her children but feels she must be the "good mother." Her resistance to the children's demands is displaced to the relationship with her husband and he begins to feel her refusal to "give" in the relationship.

(d) Communication breakdowns sometimes occur (when for a variety of reasons one or both partners begin to relate primarily to an aspect of the selfhood of the spouse that is unacceptable to the spouse's own self-understanding.) It is as if the partner has found the self's Achilles' heel and is for the time being insisting on relating to that flaw in selfhood as if it were the whole self. Guilt, anger, and shame soon begin to block communication in these situations.

5. Crisis tends to come when the total life situation in which the couple finds itself causes the marriage to have to bear more self-fulfillment and security weight than the marriage can sustain.

This is a reiteration of the major point of the first

section of this chapter. In a social situation that has become highly depersonalized and objectified, there are increasing numbers of people who look to their marriage as the primary or even virtually sole source of self-fulfillment and security. That this brings inordinate stress to the marital relationship generally has already been demonstrated. But there are situations that occur from time to time in many marriages in which this variety of stress becomes acute. A husband's job has required that the family move their residence four times in five years so that the family has had little opportunity to form sustained relationships outside the home. Another husband's work requires that he leave home early Monday morning and return Friday evening so that not only must the wife cope with all the family problems alone during the week, but the weekend is filled with children's activities, yard work, and resting up for the next week's burdens. Both partners can begin to feel overworked, deprived of nurturance, and lonely. The little time that they have together does not seem to provide enough opportunity for the leisurely talk and shared companionship most marriages need to be experienced as fulfilling. The time and role structures of the marriage cannot sustain the fulfillment and security expectations one or both partners bring to it. Frequently one or the other begins to feel abandoned. Distance comes between them, and the marriage moves toward a crisis of separation.

Not infrequently a pattern develops in which one partner has considerably higher expectations of the marriage than does the other. One may be satisfied with what Clifford Sager calls a parallel partnership.[7] This is a relationship of independence and relative distance such as that of Manfred Austin. The other brings more need for security and fulfillment to the relationship. The marriage, particularly if the circumstances require considerable absence from the home by the parallel partner, cannot sustain what both partners want from it.

Again the pattern tends to develop of interpersonal distance, feelings of abandonment and separation. The acute crisis comes most often when the abandoned partner can no longer tolerate the deprivation inherent in the structure of the marriage. Not infrequently these marriages come to separation when one or the other partner develops an extramarital relationship.

An Example of Marriage Crisis Counseling

Having outlined separately the developmental and situational elements that tend to create breaks in marriage relationships, we now need to consider how these elements are most often intermixed in marriages in crisis. A concrete example such as the following will demonstrate (the complex ways in which multiple causative elements blend together to generate a crucial marital situation and set an agenda of issues that must be dealt with if a rupture of relationship is to be averted) I will attempt to narrate the case as the various elements revealed themselves to me and began to shape the direction of the counseling process.

John and Nadine Hunt, a couple in their middle forties, were referred for marriage counseling by their pastor to whom they had turned following an episode in which Nadine had bolted from a quarrel, gone to a motel in another city for three days without communicating with the family, and then returned, saying that if there were any more fights she would leave permanently. The quarrel had started over disagreement concerning the way Nadine had disciplined the Hunts' teen-age son while John was away on one of his frequent business trips. John felt Nadine had been too strict and punitive with the boy for skipping school; Nadine felt John was much too lenient and easily manipulated by his son.

In the first interview I noted that the Hunts rarely spoke directly to each other. Rather each talked to me about the other. Nadine was obviously still angry with her husband, though she verbally insisted that the incident was over and that she was sorry she had "caused all the fuss." She acknowledged that she had been unhappy since John had accepted a new job two years before which required not only that they move away from her home and friends in a nearby state, but that John travel frequently for several days at a time. I later learned that in John's previous work as a manufacturer's representative Nadine had assisted him with the business, keeping records and making contacts with customers by telephone. She felt left out of his present work and, though she was proud of his success in it as evidenced by a recent major promotion, felt he was wedded to the job and had little time or energy for her or their two children. From John I learned that he had come to dread telling his wife about an upcoming trip and often postponed informing her until the last minute "because it always means a row." He had in fact begun to avoid any talk with Nadine about his work and felt they no longer had very much to talk about "except the kids and we can't ever agree about what to do with them. It has got to where I just try to keep quiet and let her run the house and I bring home the bacon."

The Hunts' sexual relationship had always been an active and satisfying part of their relationship until recently when John had begun to have frequent incidents of impotence. He was quite apparently ashamed over his inability to perform sexually, though he had some vague idea that it might be related to the other difficulties they were having. Nadine acknowledged that the impotence was frustrating to her but denied being angry with John about it. "I just wish that when we get all ready he could go ahead and get on with it."

That expression somehow seemed to capture my early impression of the conflict between the Hunts. Nadine, a short, stocky woman, made me think of frustrated aggression barely held in check. She spoke quickly and directly, seemed to want more action and interchange in the relationship and exuded impatience with her husband. John, on the other hand, seemed more passive, even fearful of his wife's rage. He spoke more tentatively, as if checking himself to make sure he did not precipitate a disagreement.

But there was another, somewhat opposite side to this picture of the aggressive, angry wife and the hesitant, equivocating husband. Nadine spoke of being frightened to be by herself when John was away and in subtle ways expressed her need of and dependency on John. She seemed genuinely to dislike having to cope with the children alone and particularly seemed to be soliciting her husband's help with managing the son now growing up and becoming more headstrong. John was obviously a successful person in a field that demanded aggressive salesmanship. He seemed with his wife to be holding his strength in check as if fearful not only of her rage but of his own impulses as well. The tension between the two seemed thick and potentially explosive. I began to wonder if Nadine's runaway had not been to avoid a more destructive confrontation.

In the first few interviews I learned something of the Hunts' early histories. Nadine was the youngest in a family of three and the only girl. She described her upbringing as very strict under the iron rule of her father. She also described him as a man with a violent temper who, when he became angry, could be very punitive with the children. I gathered that Nadine had from the beginning of her life learned to live by rigid rules while competing and not infrequently fighting with her older siblings. It was a close but intense and tightly managed family. Her relationship with her mother had been a good one in which she had learned well a model of being a woman that included seeing that everyone was well fed, well clothed, and well behaved.

John's background was somewhat different from Nadine's, though he, too, had been reared in a home where obedience and good behavior had been emphasized. My impression was, however, of a much more gentle, relaxed atmosphere with less competitiveness, less management by rules, and more incentive for good behavior in order to please loving parents. His background seemed somehow softer, less harsh and demanding: one in which parental leadership had been more by inspiration and giving and withholding of affection rather than the strictness of Nadine's family.

My exploration of the Hunts' individual and marital history left me with two primary impressions and a number of questions. (The first impression was of the similarity yet marked difference in the styles of their families of origin. The values and behavioral expectations of the two families had, it seemed, been quite similar. Right behavior as defined by middle-class respectability, hard work, honesty, religious commitment, and obedience to parents had been valued highly in both homes as they now were in the Hunts' household. But the styles of teaching and enforcing those values in the two homes were in sharp contrast.)Nadine's family was a tight, closed system with strict rules and harsh punishments. This had created a home with considerable conflict over behavior of family members: a home with competition and disagreement, accusation and blame placing. John's home had been quieter, with conflicts held more in check and expressed more subtly, even avoided wherever possible.

My second major impression was that this had been a good marriage that had functioned quite well until recently. Nadine's spunky disposition and John's more phlegmatic style had been more complementary than conflicting. Their good sexual relationship, common value commitments, and interactional contract had sustained their marriage. But recently things had changed.(They were no longer communicating well. Old differences between them seemed now to separate them. They disagreed about the children and how to manage them as well as about John's work and its demands on his time and energy. His travel had become a sore point they could scarcely talk about. Their sexual difficulties seemed clearly to spill over from their other conflicts. Why the change? What had brought it about? Where could we best take hold to reestablish communication?

Gradually over the next several sessions my attention became focused on two events which, when taken together with the fact that the Hunts' children were now into the adolescent period, began to make sense to me as the precipitating factors for the break in the Hunts' relationship that had brought them to their present crisis state.

In recounting the history of the marriage Nadine made reference to a health problem that had kept her "slowed down" until a successful operation three years ago. Further inquiry about that revealed that a heart condition had kept Nadine on a limited activity schedule for a number of years until open heart surgery was finally undertaken. The operation had been successful, and since that time she had been much more active, in fact "so full of energy I hardly know what to do with myself." Not long after the operation the family had moved so John could take his new job. I began to wonder if these two events had not, coming as close together as they had, brought about a significant change in both the structure and the quality of interaction in the marriage. Just at the time when, as a result of her surgery, Nadine could become more active in the life she had obviously enjoyed and valued, the move had taken from her not only the friends and community activities that had nurtured her life, but, equally as important to her, her involvement in her husband's work. Since the move she had invested much more of her energy in the children and their activities until she had become overinvested in them.

John, on the other hand, was finding success and an outlet for his considerable leadership abilities in his new job. Home and marriage had become less significant to him as primary sources of nurturance. Add the complicating factor of the new discipline problems encountered by the entrance of the children into adolescence, and the ingredients for marriage crisis began to become apparent. This latter new developmental stage in the family's life had stirred old background differences relative to the management of behavior in families and the expression of family conflict. Nadine seemed angry at John for not being as strict as had been her father; John was baffled that his wife could not seem to keep things as tranquil at home as had his parents. Transferred expectations were cluttering up the interactions in the marriage.

Counseling with the Hunts, based on the above formulation of the marriage crisis dynamics, began to take shape on several levels. Work at all these levels took place simultaneously, with one or the other being in the forefront of consideration from time to time depending upon what came to the fore in our week by week conversations.

Primary, of course, was the restoration of direct and open communication along with an effort to enlarge the area of subject matter and feeling in which communication could safely and productively take place. An active effort had to be made to get them to talk directly to each other rather than each taking turns talking to me about the other and about what each was feeling and thinking. This at first was difficult because of Nadine's pent-up anger and John's reticence about saying anything that might evoke Nadine's wrath. Only as I began to value Nadine's "spunk" and confront John with his holding back did both begin to risk more in speaking directly with each other about the perceptions and feelings about what was going on. Gradually John became less fearful and guilty over Nadine's anger and tears; she became less angry. The Hunts slowly became more able to speak to and hear each other on a wider range of topics including each other's feelings, sex, differences about the children, John's work, and plans for their life together.

A second area of counseling work concerned coming to

301

terms with and accepting their differences in style of personhood and background. Conversation about the differences in their upbringing opened to their awareness their different ways of perceiving situations and responding to them. The complementarity of their differences began to be recognized, as well as the two sidedness of each partner's expectations of the marriage. Nadine's dependency needs were affirmed as was John's pride in the aggressive accomplishments of his work.

By far the most difficult work in counseling had to be done with relation to the changing parenting task in the home. Differences over rules, discipline, and approaches to conflict resolution in the family ran deep and contained the dynamic struggle for dominance of the marriage. The teen-age son on many occasions managed to get between his parents, playing one off against the other or taking advantage of their differences with regard to strict limits on behavior. I encouraged John to take a more active role in these matters and supported Nadine in her expectation that he would take charge of discipline. Nadine's ambivalence about that became evident and had to be dealt with so that she could support rather than undermine his decisions. (For a time Nadine became somewhat depressed while trying to check her angry struggle for control with the children, but as communication improved her depression seemed to lift except for brief episodes usually triggered by some problem with her son.) Gradually and only partially were the Hunts able to get together on how decisions would be made and family policy established and enforced. John's constant travel proved a difficult barrier in these negotiations.

The fourth area of work in the counseling that only gradually emerged as much or more as a by-product of work at other levels as by direct effort concerned opening some new avenues of shared activity in the marriage which provided outlets for expression of the strengths of both partners. The Hunts were congruent in that both were activity oriented rather than being reflective and intellectual in their pursuits. (They needed to do something together.) Nadine genuinely missed the sharing of her husband's work that she had once enjoyed. Her children were needing her less and less, and that double vacuum in a naturally active and aggressive woman's life had played no small part in the onset of the crisis. The Hunts were active in their church, and that helped. A rather impulsive decision to accept a joint money-raising responsibility for the Parent-Teachers Association became, however, the major vehicle for moving back toward sharing in a time-consuming and mutually satisfying cooperative activity. The result was that the P.T.A. budget began to prosper as well as the marriage!

As other areas of communication and shared activity in the Hunts' marriage improved, the problem of John's impotence in their sexual relationship gradually began to disappear. With some helpful conversation about other kinds of exchanges of intimacy and affection, the importance of timing and feeling together in the rest of their life, and changes in sexuality with aging, the pressure on their sexual relationship to carry the burden of their commitment to each other gradually diminished.

I have meant this somewhat detailed summary of the marriage counseling relationship with Nadine and John Hunt to communicate the manner in which a multi-faceted analysis of the dynamic factors involved in the formation of a marriage crisis can, when carefully and not hastily formulated, provide an agenda of levels of work to be done in the counseling. The issues are not always as clear as they were with the Hunts, nor are the precipitating events always as readily apparent. But without a sense of the pilgrimage of the marriage and formative elements that have come together to create the crisis such as we have formulated in this case, marriage counseling is apt to be haphazard and fraught with many pitfalls and frustration for both the couple and the pastor. Marriage crisis counseling needs to be both open ended and purposeful, both analytic and intentional in its effort to come to grips with the several levels at which relationships become broken.>

The Importance of a Theological Perspective for Marriage Crisis Counseling

Nowhere in his or her crisis ministry will the pastor find more difficult and fundamentally theological choices to be made than in the ministry to persons whose marital relationship has become broken.⟨The pressures either to bless and facilitate the final separation of estranged marital partners, on the one hand, or to exercise pastoral authority to preserve a marriage in its broken state, on the other, can be tremendous⟩The pastor who enters into marriage crisis ministry without a well-conceived theology of marriage will soon find that decisions are being made by both parishioners and pastor on the basis of intense feelings of the moment, contemporary cultural images of what a healthy marriage should be, popular notions about the right to individual happiness, guilty feelings about "what is best for the children," or what have you. The sturdy ability to grasp the crisis in its wholeness and within its largest context that is provided by a carefully considered theological frame of reference is needed if the pastor is not to be caught up either in the crisis atmosphere of the marriage rupture or the temporariness and value confusion of societal pressures on the marriage.)

It is beyond our purpose in this writing to attempt a full and definitive statement of what a Christian theology of marriage and/or marriage counseling should be. However, a brief statement of the general direction such a theological stance might take and some reflection concerning the theological implications of our exploration of marriage crisis phenomena seems in order.

The radical rise in the incidence of marriage crisis and

the divorce rate has brought our culture to the point of crisis in marriage as a social institution. The traditional understanding of marriage as a lifelong monogamous commitment has by the sheer numbers of broken marriages been called sharply into question. Social change seems increasingly to legitimate a quality of temporariness or "for so long as we both shall love" rather than "for so long as we both shall live" quality in marriage commitments that threatens to set a standard of limited commitment over against the traditional Christian standard of lifelong obligation. What is the church's stance in relation to this phenomenon of social disorganization and change? More specifically, what is to be the pastor's stance when presented with a broken marriage relationship?

Traditional theological views of Christian monogamous commitments have been based upon divine law as interpreted from the seventh commandment,[8] divine commandment based upon a larger christological interpretation of divine calling,[9] or biblical interpretation of human sexuality.[10] All of these views present, each on a somewhat different basis, the norm of the single marital relationship lasting throughout the lifetime of both marital partners. Barth, interestingly, states that this norm is only applicable for those marriages that have been formed by divine command.[11] Barth goes on to recognize that it is not humanly possible to distinguish those marriages that have or have not been concluded by God and that human judgments in this regard are always acts of faith and response to the word of God.

The stance of the theologies of hope and expectation upon which we have been formulating much of our theological reflection up to this point would suggest a further modification of Barth's theology of the marriage commitment as calling. Oriented to the future fulfillment of God's promise for all human relationships, this perspective would suggest that all marriage commitments contain as their fundamental ingredient a promise or commitment to a promise not yet fully realized. It is not that some marriages are made by God and others by erroneous human choice as Barth's position suggests. Rather the beginning of a marriage commitment structures a possibility, the fulfillment of which must be left to an open-ended future toward which the partners to the commitment are called to work and respond. This calling to the future fulfillment of a commitment corresponds closely to our earlier definition of the marriage relationship as a developing covenant of mutual care and concern. In the beginning this covenant may be weak and fragile, easily broken apart by the conflicts of the partners' separate expectations and desires for the marriage. Nevertheless the structuring of a commitment to marriage, for whatever complex and often immature purposes, needs to be both respected and opened to fulfillment of its larger, more fully human possibilities. By the appropriation of gifts of grace and the mutual nurture of self-giving love in the relationship, the covenant may grow and be confirmed. Yet it always remains a partial and in that sense unfulfilled promise. It is therefore always vulnerable to the onset of contingencies and pressures from outside as well as the possibility of violation and failure from within. The marriage covenant commitment thus develops, yet remains more or less fragile, more or less able to fulfill the promise it contains.

It is to this developing covenant, this response to the promise for the future of the marriage that the pastor is called upon to minister. He or she will seek to respond to the crisis in the marriage so as to give all possible hope for the opening of the marriage toward fulfillment of its promise. Barriers that stand in the way of that fulfillment must be exposed, examined, and, if possible, broken through. Differences in expectations and desires that hinder and undermine the formation of a covenant of mutual care and concern must likewise be confronted, worked through, and gradually brought more closely into harmony with the emerging covenant and promise of the marriage.

Sometimes the barriers to fulfillment and the conflict in expectation and desire will be so great as to render the promise of a given marriage impossible to sustain. In those cases the partners to the attempted marriage should be helped to come to terms with that reality and to accept the failure of the marriage to fulfill its promise. In this case the partners need to be reminded that the final fulfillment of God's promises for their separate lives is not finally dependent upon the fulfillment of the promise of the marriage. There is forgiveness and the continuing activity of God in their behalf, though they now separate.

Sometimes in the course of a marriage the external contingencies and pressures on the marriage or the internal failure to fulfill its promise in the midst of contingent forces and personal failure will be so great as to render it broken beyond repair. That conclusion should never be allowed to be drawn hastily and most often should be drawn only after, in the context of a counseling relationship, the broken covenant of mutual care and concern has been given a chance to reconstitute itself. In these circumstances the pastor will again stand with the partners in their irreparably broken marriage, helping them to assess what has happened, the possibilities for restoration of the promise of the marriage, and, if it is judged in the end impossible, the dissolving of the marriage covenant with as little destructiveness to the partners as possible. Here again there is hope in that the final fulfillment of God's promise for human life, the final human hope for continuity and security, is not dependent upon any single human relationship.

But in many if not most cases of marriage crisis, careful ministry and honest confrontation of the dynamic forces creating the crisis on the part of the marriage partners will over time open the marriage to new possibilities for fulfillment of its promise and an enlargement of its covenant of mutual care and concern. Differences will be accepted, some of them resolved by changes brought about in both partners. Some complementarities will be accepted as necessary to the life of the marriage in its present state; others will be transcended by new congruities discovered in intentions for the marriage by both partners. Thus the crisis of broken relationship in the marriage will itself provide the opening to nurture of the marriage covenant and the placement of the marriage commitment within the context of God's future-oriented providence and promise.

CHAPTER X

Toward a Theology of Crisis Ministry

We have attempted in the preceding chapters to explore several paradigms of the most common ways in which crisis is experienced in modern life. Our list, while broadly varied, has not been exhaustive. Other paradigms could be explored. Loneliness, often of crisis proportions, is a form of the alienation that many persons endure in our time. The crisis of indecision and irresolution results in a kind of perpetual suspense of unsettled bondage for some. Readers who may approach the question of crisis in modern life from angles of observation and reflection different from mine will undoubtedly have other paradigms to propose. Nevertheless, we will end our exploration of the variety of contemporary forms of crisis here and turn in this last chapter to reflection on some of the fundamental human questions that have reappeared in various forms throughout our exploration. As has been the case at a number of points along the way, it will be my contention that these questions are at their core religious and therefore require theological reflection that moves beyond mere description. They are questions of faith.

We began with a general statement of the religious problem of modern life that becomes most visible when persons are in crisis. We said that those persons who consciously or unconsciously have felt the impact of the modern secular consciousness on their way of comprehending and making intelligible what life brings to them have experienced a loss of any profound sense of divine providence. Even those who may intellectually affirm faith in a God who cares for people may, when the experiential evidence is examined, be found to live their lives and cope with the crises that occur as if they were without resources beyond their own psychological capacity to cope. They may be sustained by a more or less tight network of close human relationships that provides continuity and security to their lives, but threats to those human sources of security which may render them impotent are frequently inherent in the crises that occur.

We further proposed that the modern consciousness has so seductively enticed persons to value human potential that many people now find themselves caught in what is felt to be an impossible bind between infinite aspirations on the one hand, and very finite, limited possibilities, on the other. Lacking a potent faith in God's providential activity on their behalf, these persons experience the psychological crisis of frustrated hopes. Transcendence of the human structures that both provide them with tenuous security and limit the realization of their potential becomes impossible. The crises of identity, despair, and broken relationships often are the result, as are the exaggerated crises of destructive bereavement when significant centered relationships are lost.

The task then presents itself to pastoral theology as to how a potent sense of divine participation in human life can be restored. The final security in which individual and corporate life is grounded must come from an ultimate source. All human sources are themselves finally vulnerable, though they may participate in ultimacy in the sense that they are transparent to ultimacy. This means theologically that ultimate security comes from a hopeful faith rooted in God's promise to fulfill his purposes for all creation. But for moderns that faith must be expressed in ways that do not violate the modern sensibility. How is that to be accomplished?

Does Providence Mean Protection?

In our preliminary analysis of the contemporary problem relative to faith in God's providential activity, we proposed that in the mind-set of popular religious culture in America the providence of God as concerned with human life has become fused with an image of protection and the guarantee of the continuity of human hopes. To understand just how that fusion took place in the flow of religious cultural development from the nineteenth into the twentieth century is a task for the historian beyond our purpose or competence in this writing. It is difficult, however, to resist some tentative speculation on the matter.

My own notions in this regard have been fed by impressionistic reflection on two rather remotely separated events. The first dates from my ministry in the 1950s in an institution for adolescent delinquent youth formerly administered as a typical "reform school" of the post–World War I period. The so-called "chapel" in the institution, a small auditorium with a stage used for various activities including compulsory twice-weekly religious services, had a curtain across the front of the stage that could be rolled up to the ceiling or dropped down to form a backdrop for the portable pulpit that during divine services became the central fixture of the otherwise rather shabby room. The curtain, made of canvas, had been painted by an obscure local artist who at some time had done volunteer religious work in the institution. One corner depicted the Christmas manger scene complete with shepherds, wise men, and rather frightening looking cows and sheep. The center of the canvas, however, depicted a scene with children in the attire to be found in children's story books of the period—cherubic, scrubbed, and innocent appearing. There were two of them, a boy and a girl, as I remember. They were pictured on a bridge over a roaring stream. The bridge had several boards missing in its center. The children were about to fall to disaster. But above and behind them hovered an angel of God whose intent was no doubt to protect the innocents from harm, though the sternness of his countenance left that somewhat in doubt! It took several months, but I finally managed to get the curtain replaced by a portable communion table and three-arched plywood reredos. Meanwhile, I wondered just what that crude symbol of divine providence could mean to the worldly wise delinquents who gathered there. But to the artist, God's providence and the protection of the innocent from harm were quite obviously synonymous.

The second event was an encounter at the National Gallery with four paintings by the American artist Thomas Cole done in 1842. I saw the paintings at about the time that the theological problem for this writing was taking shape in my mind. The four paintings are titled "Voyage of Life" and depict in succession Childhood, Youth, Manhood, and Old Age.

For Cole, life begins in the garden of childhood innocence with the austere and rocky crags of fallen reality dimly appearing in the distant background. The boat in which the masculine child figure is launched into the stream of life has an angelic figurehead on its prow holding aloft an hourglass through which the sand is beginning to run. Another angel emitting heavenly light stands in the boat behind the infant as if to protect and guide the progress of the life voyage.

In Cole's visual image of Youth the boat has been launched toward a distant vision of the heavenly city. The jagged and mysterious peaks of life's future stand remotely between the quiet stream on which the boat is beginning its journey, the youthful figure now at the helm, and the heavenly temple of the City of God. The guardian angel stands separately in the garden pointing the way to the heavenly city. The figurehead with the hourglass leads the boat forth into the stream of adult responsibility and decision beyond the garden.

Manhood is for Thomas Cole a time of fall from

The Voyage of Life: Childhood—Thomas Cole—National Gallery of Art, Washington—Ailsa Mellon Bruce Fund

The Voyage of Life: Youth—Thomas Cole—National Gallery of Art, Washington—Ailsa Mellon Bruce Fund

The Voyage of Life: Old Age—Thomas Cole—National Gallery of Art, Washington—Ailsa Mellon Bruce Fund

innocence and of testing. No longer is there a guardian angel hovering to protect or to point the way. The dark and ominous cliffs of harsh reality have replaced the garden. Ahead lie dangerous rapids filled with gnarled, broken trees. The angelic figurehead with the hourglass remains at the bow of the boat. The adult male, no longer with his hand at the helm, kneels in supplication. Furthermore, in the fallen state of adulthood the man in the boat seems to have lost the direction of the heavenly city; the bright city of light is behind him above the dark cliffs that shape present reality. The dim outline of a Christ figure with arms outstretched stands in the light as if to beckon and welcome the pilgrim if he will but turn toward the light. But ominously in the dark clouds just overhead can be seen the bearded images of the forces of darkness.

Cole's envisagement of Old Age shows signs both of the ravages of passing time and the mysterious peace of emergence into the more tranquil waters of the later years of life. The boat is damaged by what it has been through; its figurehead with the hourglass is broken away. The dark hair of the figure of adulthood has now turned white, his posture of supplication now transformed into the upturned face and open hands of gratitude. Both the hovering guardian angel protectively pointing the way and the bright light ahead have returned. The darkness and the rocks have receded as if overpowered by the streams of light from above.

If we thrust Thomas Cole's artistic vision of the voyage of human life into our consideration of the loss in the twentieth century of a potent sense of God's providence, some potentially useful motifs begin to emerge. Reflection on these motifs may help us in drawing together the theological themes of our exploration of contemporary forms of crisis. Into what at first glance appears as a unified vision of divine protection through all vicissitudes of the course of human life and the certainty of final human participation in the heavenly kingdom is thrust an ambivalence and uncertainty. The ambivalence concerns both Cole's image of human potential and responsibility and his understanding of divine protection from the dangers and trials of stark reality. In the innocence of childhood and youth, to which in some degree Cole's old age returns, the protective angelic symbol is present. But in his pictorial image of man come of age not only is the protective symbol absent, but the direction of movement toward the heavenly city of God has been lost. The boat is rudderless as it enters the rapids of life's adult crises. Adult man is left with his prayers and his ability to survive. The powers of darkness surround adult reality.

Here it is possible to see the beginnings of what by the 1970s has become a more wholehearted visualization of adult life for many people, some of whom have even lost track of the power of the image of prayer and supplication. One wonders if it is not true for many persons today as it was for Cole that only in the battered retrospect of old age does the sense of divine protection and the lure of the heavenly city return. For many today both the present reality of God's protective, guiding participation in the navigation of life's exigencies and a clear apocalyptic vision of the final outcome of things are absent. Thus in a more radical sense than Cole's adult, many modern persons are thrown back upon the raw stuff of their own abilities to cope with the contingent events of life that, like Cole's dark rapids, carry people along in a rudderless boat.

The realization that this is indeed a fallen state in which humanity may have lost its way so that we are being carried along by forces over which we have little control is only recently beginning to dawn upon some of us. The vision of human progress that seemed clearly to have replaced the vision of the heavenly city for many is increasingly threatened by the frightening awareness of both human potential for violence and destruction and the "principalities and powers" of modern corporate structures that define so much of present reality.

The two images that sustained Cole's sense of divine providence were both otherworldly images, one present with the voyaging pilgrim in his immediate situation and the other above and beyond present reality in the distant future. Both the guardian angel and the angelic figurehead holding time in his hands signify protective, guiding presence, though both are themselves otherworldly figures. The vision of the heavenly city toward which the voyage of life carries the individual is likewise otherworldly, above the stream of earthly, historical existence. Cole's Christ figure is highly spiritualized; the risen Christ beckons from that other world to which he has gone to prepare a place. The adult, fallen from Cole's highly sentimentalized vision of the innocence of childhood and youth, is left without the protection of the guardian angel. He must navigate the hazards of life on his own powers, sustained by whatever guidance he can obtain from his supplications directed to that other world. Faith in a highly spiritualized Christ is matched against the more immediately present forces of darkness and evil.

Assuming that Thomas Cole's work is an authentic expression of what was already happening in American popular religious culture in the 1840s, we can begin to see how the separation between highly spiritualized religious faith and the crises of present experience took place. The providence of God was linked to an otherworldly faith and to a sentimentalized desire for a return to human innocence. Thus a profound ambivalence was introduced in vernacular religious experience concerning the possibility and power of God's providential intervention in human affairs in this world. The way was opened for what we referred to in chapter 1 as the image of heroic humanism in coping with crisis—the image that we increasingly see in our time. God's providence, having been pushed out into the remoteness of otherworldly faith, becomes problematic. A spiritualized, otherworldly

Christ loses the potency of his incarnation in the midst of human affairs.

The theological reflections that have emerged in our exploration of present-day crisis experience reveal something of the same ambivalence. There is a tension in the theological work we have done. On the one hand, we have sought to place our confidence in the image of God's eschatological promise to consummate his kingdom at the end of history before which all present reality is provisional. The otherworldliness of Cole's apocalyptic has been replaced by the theology of hope with its historical eschatology, its "hope against hope" for the final fulfillment of God's promise within history. This has been helpful to us in recovering a sense of the authority of the future toward which we must look in resolving the tensions and ambiguities—the imperfections—of present existence.

But the God of the theologies of hope is one who seeks to transform present reality and shape it into conformity with his coming kingdom. This entails not only a recovery of the authority of God in the future, but also a certain approach to the present. If God is at work seeking to transform present existence, our openness to the in-breaking of the new reality in our present life becomes crucial as a potential source of recovery of a sense of God's participation with us here and now. Having given up Cole's desire for human innocence and divine protection against the ever-present danger of life's threats, we have turned instead to a reappropriation of the incarnational faith in God's presence with us in our trials and suffering. Here we have moved toward what we earlier in our work with the crisis of despair called "the engendering of an incarnational style of tending to present life experience."

The concept of tending to present life experience in the style of incarnation needs further elaboration, which may open the possibility of a linkage between tending to life experience in an altered way and the transformation of life in greater conformity to the power of the future. The term "tend" is here used with several shades of meaning, each providing an important ingredient in the incarnational life-style. To tend to one's experience is, first, to *attend* to what occurs and to apprehend its meaning and significance. It means to perceive accurately and openly what is happening without the need to defend against it or deny what is taking place. To attend means to allow one's experience to speak in the fullest sense. To tend likewise means literally to *care for*, be responsible for, what occurs—in the sense that one tends a garden or a flock of sheep. To tend one's experience is to cultivate what is perceived, reflect upon it, and integrate it into one's sense of self and world. Finally, tending means to *intend* in the sense of forming tendencies for future experience, directions for future life and relationship. To tend is to form intentions.

Human experience is here seen as requiring a hermeneutic, a means whereby it may be symbolized, given significance and direction now. To tend one's experience in an incarnational style is to tend what occurs in all three meanings of the word within the hermeneutic of openness to signs and symbols of the epiphany of God's disclosure in the events of everyday life. It is this quality of openness to God's present disclosure that can transform life, bringing it into fuller conformity with what has been disclosed about what life in relation to God is intended to be.

Transformation implies the alteration of that which is being transformed while yet accepting and respecting the integrity of what has been in the past. To be transformed is not to throw away as if of no account whatever has been before. Rather transformation means to take the elements of what has been and put them together with the new that has been revealed or uncovered so that a new being or a new reality comes about which is itself subject to transformation. In all the varied situations of human crisis we have encountered, what is most needed in order to cope with what has happened or is happening is a transformation in the sense of self and world, self and God.

The work we have done with the crisis of human despair brought us most closely to a renewed understanding of the power of an altered hermeneutic of interpretation to transform life. In the case of Mrs. Reed, experience that had been tended through the eyes of despair gradually was transformed into experience open to the awareness of the presence and function of grace incarnate in ordinary events and relationships. The result was observed to be a transformed sense of both self and world so that new, less constricted intentions for future life could be entertained and tended. In the process Mrs. Reed's vision of her life became grounded transparently in God so that her faith in God's providential care was renewed continuously by new experience.

The question of God's presence or absence in human suffering became most compelling in our study of ministry to the dying. In what sense does God participate with us in that final crisis of life, the paradigm of all human suffering? Our trinitarian explication of the problem, following Moltmann's interpretation of "the crucified God," took us to the center of the paradox of God's presence *and* his absence in the suffering of death. The God who, as Jesus on the cross, suffers with us, is also the God who, as the Father, suffers the necessity of leaving us to experience what life brings to us even as he left Jesus to the cross. This God both suffers with us and suffers in abandoning us. Here the ambiguity of our sense of God's presence and his absence from our suffering is caught up in the symbol of God's act in the cross.

Time and the Human Condition

One connecting theme that runs through all our study of contemporary crisis experience is that of human life as set in the flow of time. Human crisis is shaped by the changes of both life cycle time and socio-historical time. Continuity and change provide the dialectic that holds life for humans in tension. Given that condition, our study has revealed a stubborn human resistance to change and a profound human need for continuity. Without continuity, identity becomes fluid and facile, relationships become temporary and lack commitment. But the human need for continuity makes for a concomitant resistance to life's transformation. The human need for and expectation of continuity tends to become linked tightly to the human need for security. Both individually and socially, human beings tend to structure time so as to make the past continuous with the present and future in order to feel safe.

Coping with crisis, however, requires transformation. It requires the capacity to transcend the past, move through the change of the present, and embrace the open-ended, unknown quality of the future. As such, coping with crisis experience is rooted in eschatological trust—the implicit or explicit trust of the future. Our study of separation and bereavement in families perhaps most clearly revealed this necessity. To the degree that individuals and families lack this level of trust they are at war with time and prone to suffer existential crisis complicated by the need to resist and control time-related changes. Bereavement by death likewise reveals the necessity of a trust in those possibilities and relationships that lie in the future if identity is not to be arrested and stunted by the need to cling to the lost relationships of the past. So it is that the transformation of life and eschatological trust are joined in an interdependent relationship.

But our study also reveals that eschatological trust, the trust of the future, is closely linked to what Erikson calls basic trust, that confidence that begins with earliest experience that the world into which we have been thrust is trustworthy and friendly to our deepest needs and strivings. Erikson is correct in his understanding of the linkage between basic trust and capacity for hope. Basic trust, the trust made possible by past experiences of trustworthiness, and eschatological trust, the trust that enables hopeful embracing of change, are joined. Each is made possible by gifts of grace.

So we come again to the necessity of conjoining an existential, incarnational theology and a theology of hope and futurity. A theology of hope cannot stand alone, even if rooted, as is the case with both Pannenberg and Moltmann, in the earnest of the promissory event found in Jesus. God's grace is more than a promise; it is a reality present in human experience to be recognized and appropriated as it appears in myriad forms incarnate in the events and relationships of life. Its appearance is a mystery to be grasped only through the eyes of faith. Its grasping is, as our study of the emergence from the pit of despair demonstrated, dependent upon an altered interpretation of experience, a new way of seeing and giving significance to what occurs. Certain events can become parabolic, as if capturing in their significance the power and meaning of grace. Grace becomes transparent through these events.

Thus it is grace incarnate, appearing now and again in crisis experience itself, that opens a fresh perspective on the self in relation to all three dimensions of time—past, present, and future—transforming all three. From our study not only of despair, but of bereavement and identity crisis as well, we have seen that grace and judgment often appear together in the same event. The sometimes catastrophically new, when interpreted in ultimate terms, breaks through old hermeneutic styles of interpretation and presses for a new self-world under-standing. A judgment is experienced in the fractured images of self and world. Through grace, however, the possibility is opened of seeing the self as primarily identified as a child of God and heir to his promise. A fresh vision is opened on the self in relation to the events and relationships of the past, the crisis of the present and the hope for the future.

So the tension remains between the search for God's providential activity in events of grace incarnate in present experience, and the hope for God's final fulfillment of his promise in that future he is bringing about. We have by no means resolved all the ambiguities in that tension. But our study has in at least tentative and suggestive ways opened these two possible avenues for a viable restoration of confidence in God's providence as a powerful dynamic in human coping with crisis.

Theological Models for Crisis Ministry

At the outset of our study we acknowledged three major streams of tradition in pastoral theology with regard to theological structuring of pastoral care methodology: pastoral proclamation, the imaging of pastoral ministry as analogous to the incarnation in Jesus, and the engendering of an incarnational style of tending to life experience in order that openness to signs and symbols of God's disclosure may be nurtured. We declared our intention to carry through and perhaps refine particularly the latter two models in relation to contemporary forms of crisis experience. Our search was to be for a coherent model of pastoral method that draws upon some of the significant themes of contemporary theology and relates them to the pastoral problem shaped by modern forms of crisis experience.

Having carried through with that intention in an informal but relatively consistent fashion, we come now to the task of drawing together some of the rather scattered threads of pastoral methodology that have appeared in earlier chapters and relating them to the theological themes that were discussed in the previous section. How has our work contributed to the specifics of pastoral care methodology?

CRISIS EXPERIENCE IN MODERN LIFE

Refining the Incarnational Model for the Pastoral Relationship.

It is readily apparent that most of what has been said concerning the pastoral relationship itself falls well within the tradition of the pastoral relationship as analogous to the incarnation in Jesus. The theme of pastoral presence with persons undergoing crisis seeking to represent acceptance and grace appears again and again in the suggestions we have made concerning the pastoral relationship. We have however, sought to refine that image of the pastoral relationship at a number of points.

First, our trinitarian analysis of the theological sources for the authority, endurance, and limits on ministry in relation to the dying led to the proposal that the pastoral relationship images itself not only after the second person of the Trinity, who suffers with the dying, but also after the first person, who suffers the pain of abandoning the Son to the death of the cross. Here we encountered the theological limits placed upon pastoral care as intervention with, and on behalf of, the person in the crisis of death. To a greater or lesser degree this theme of pastoral acceptance of, and representation of, limits appears in direct or more subtle forms throughout our study. That this theme comes forth as a major one can perhaps be attributed in part to the judgment we have made that persons in our culture in the present time are having profound difficulty with the acceptance of the limits of finitude. In an age of human potential and technological achievement, the limits of time, death, and finite perspective are increasingly difficult to accept for many people. To model pastoral ministry on the incarnation in such a time is to take seriously the representation of that aspect of God which sets the boundaries of our life and in that sense stands over against human aspirations that ignore or deny those limits. Ministry must, within its own finite limits, embody grace and acceptance of the other as an aspiring, hoping, suffering child of God; ministry must also embody the acceptance of both the limits of finitude and the limits God has placed upon his intervention on human behalf. At the same time, God's own entering into those limits in the person of Christ the crucified Son, is brought near to the sufferer by the pastor's presence and sharing.

A second subtle but definite refinement of the incarnational model for pastoral relationships that has emerged in our exploration is that of an active as opposed to a passive mode of pastoral presence. In a subtle way pastoral presence with persons in crisis has in recent years come to mean a certain passivity, as if suffering with another implies the emptying of oneself of the power to change the situation and simply to suffer alongside the other person. In the sense in which we have pointed in the previous paragraphs to the limits on all caring, that is a true image. And yet there has emerged in our work all through this writing a stronger, more actively engaging model for pastoral care ministry that seeks in its presence to confront the existential, ethical, and life-style issues that are hidden in the crises of life. In that sense the appropriation of an incarnational model for the pastoral relationship shapes up as more prophetic, more active, stronger than the image that became popular among clergy trained in the arts of listening, reflecting, and accepting, so characteristic of the period of modern renewal of pastoral care. Here our model is undoubtedly influenced by a number of factors in our present situation. There are, in the first place, those developments that have occurred in recent years in therapeutic methodology generally that have modeled a more active therapeutic stance. More important from the perspective of Christian ministry, however, has been our encounter with the pervasive value and life-style issues of our time. These issues become most crucially apparent in the crises of identity, generation gap, and marriage in particular. In an age of moral value and life-style confusion, normative questions become more urgent and must be actively engaged. Grace embodied as acceptance remains fundamental to the art of caring. But grace translated as the firm effort to help persons order their lives so as to give a Christian structure to their existence becomes necessary.

Hope and the Expectation of God's Disclosure

It is at this point that the effort we have made to shift the stance of pastoral care from one of assurance toward one of anticipation and expectation becomes significant as a normative model for pastoral methodology. The pastor does not simply seek to embody an analogy to the incarnation in terms of his or her relationship vis-à-vis the other person. The pastor also seeks to model a style of living in relation to the experience of the present and the future. By modeling an expectation of God's disclosure in the ordinary events and relationships of life, the pastor seeks to engender what we have earlier called an incarnational style of tending to life experience in the parishioner. Theologically we have rooted this stance in both the future-oriented anticipation of God's movement toward us, drawing us toward the fulfillment of his kingdom, and in the more immediate interpretative task of symbolization of experience.

Much work remains to be done before the model of hopeful, incarnational tending for pastoral care methodology will be fully matured. The tentative directions set in our exploration of ministry to the despairing need further testing with a wider range of experiential data. The synthesis of Kierkegaardian thought relative to the identification of the self as child of God and the openness of the self to the contingent life of the future implied by the theologies of hope, as attempted in our study of despair, brings together theological themes that are not in the systematic sense fully consistent. Ministry seen as the establishment of a hermeneutic of hope, interpreting present experience as containing signs and symbols of God's gracious disclosure, contains the risk that symbolic interpretations may simply impose themselves on experiential events by either pastor or parishioner. Openness to God's disclosure can easily become a reading of divine signs in very humanly determined occurrences. Hope in God's future can become idle fancy that ignores or seeks to escape the necessity of confrontation with present hard reality and choice. Events and nuances of relationship must be allowed to speak for themselves without easy, casual theological labeling. Nevertheless, our study of the emergence from the pit of despair in the case of Mrs. Reed, for example, offers some potentially fruitful possibilities for restoring to pastoral relationships a more genuinely religious intention.

Pastoral Care and the Shepherding of Life's Transformation

Earlier in this chapter we said that coping with crisis requires transformation. Crisis experience is instigated by the existential necessity of change. Change not only is built into the human experience of ongoing time, it is inherent in the activity of God in the world. For humans either to change or to integrate the changes that have occurred around them requires transformation. Most particularly, for humans to change in response to God's disclosure requires transformation. Old ways of structuring individual and corporate existence must be transformed into new ways that more nearly fit the altered situation. Old self-understanding must undergo transformation if new possibilities for selfhood are to be realized. The altered meanings of things that come with the inbreaking of fresh insights and new symbolization of experience must be integrated into a transformed hermeneutic of interpretation. This is true for persons now under the threat of death as it is for persons experiencing the shame of fractured identity or broken relationships.

The image of transformation as a requirement demanded by crisis experience carries with it the image of the pastoral relationship as the relationship that shepherds or facilitates the transformation of life. This does not mean that the pastor is in himself or herself the power that transforms life. That power is located in the mysterious confluence of persons, events, meanings, and altered circumstances that by the grace of God can flow together to make possible a new reality. Rather the pastor is the one who seeks to be present with persons in situations where the need for life's transformation is presented, but present in particular ways that invite and facilitate the transformation of life in the direction of the new reality God is bringing about. The constraint placed upon the activity of pastoral presence in these situations is the constraint of respect for the integrity of the persons involved and their right to respond to the necessity of transformation within the boundaries of that integrity. Persons undergoing the necessity of life's transformation must find their way into the transformed life on the terms of their own response to God's invitation and disclosure. The new reality will become real for them only as it becomes ingredient within their own way of symbolizing and interpreting their experience. It is the pastor's task to shepherd and facilitate that process.

The pastoral methods to be utilized in the shepherding of life's transformation will vary considerably, as has been evident in our earlier explorations. Methodological choices must be made to fit the requirements of the situation and the need of the persons involved. The fundamental normative criterion to be applied to all methodologies will be whether or not they assist in making possible the transformation of life. The direction that the transformative process is to take is set by the norm of the coming Kingdom. That means that only those methods will be utilized that keep open the possibility of life transformed in greater conformity to the emergence of the Kingdom for all concerned—pastor, parishioner, and those to whom they are related.

One final difficult word needs to be said. The transformation of life is a mystery not always open to the proof of empirical evidence. The outward appearance of a transformed life may remain to the casual observer very much the same as it was before. The widow remains bereaved. The traveling salesman who has undergone an identity crisis goes on about his traveling business. The marriage relationship that has been in crisis continues to have its times of conflict. The dying still die. Finite life is still finite life. But by the mystery of transformed meanings, by a fresh hermeneutic of hopeful interpretation, by altered relationships and a new awareness of God's gracious disclosure, life is transformed and new reality is present in and among persons.

A Concluding Postscript

Pastors who have persevered to the end of this writing will perhaps feel that, rather than simplifying and clarifying the task of ministry to persons in crisis, we have greatly complicated it. When the wide-angle lenses we have attempted to use are applied to the variety of crises experienced by contemporary persons, such a rich and complex range of data and perspectives emerge that the pastor can feel overwhelmed, if fascinated, by what he or she sees. One may be tempted to turn back and look for an easier, more simplified approach.

The conviction behind this book has been, however, that what the pastor does in response to a human situation of need will depend primarily on what the pastor perceives and how what is perceived is interpreted. Sensitive, perceptive ministry most often depends first upon richness and depth of perception. In a sense, what we have attempted is, at a level of pastoral skill and reflection, to engender in pastors a style of presence and ministry parallel to what we have called the incarnational style of tending to life experience. The competent pastor is one who tends to the experience of his or her people in that style that is open to the richness of life, most particularly to the often subtle and varied ways in which the need for life's transformation is presented. Responding to that need is a worldly ministry that utilizes whatever the world provides to enhance the understanding of what is taking place and what is to be done about it. But the pastor's perceptive sensitivity moves beneath and within all that is to be seen in outward appearance, from whatever perspective, to that other level of faith and interpretation. Here the pastor will find the primary rootage and the hope for his or her ministry. That rootage and hope will be through participation in the disclosure of God's activity on human behalf and the transformation of life by the power of his incarnation.

Notes

INTRODUCTION

1. Cf. David Switzer, *The Minister as Crisis Counselor* (Nashville: Abingdon, 1974), and Howard W. Stone, *Crisis Counseling* (Philadelphia: Fortress Press, 1976).

2. Here I am in agreement with people like John B. Cobb, Jr., who says in the preface of his book, *A Christian Natural Theology* (Philadelphia: Westminster Press, 1965), p. 13: "For much of the culture that is growing up about us and within us, 'God' has an empty sound. It is no longer a problem only for those Christians trying to communicate with a special segment of the intelligentsia estranged from the church. It has become the problem of the suburban pastor in his dealing with his most sensitive church leaders and youths. Most of all it has become the problem of the perceptive minister in dealing with himself and his own understanding of the ministry." Despite the fact that one can cite what appears to be the reversal of this trend in the apparent growth of the conservative and evangelical churches, the process of secularization in American culture appears to be continuing at a rapid pace.

CHAPTER I

1. For a brief but highly suggestive explication of the notion of images, see Kenneth E. Boulding, *The Image: Knowledge in Life and Society* (Ann Arbor: University of Michigan Press, 1956).

2. Erik Erikson, *Childhood and Society,* 2nd ed. (New York: W. W. Norton, 1963).

3. Lael Tucker Wertenbaker, *Death of a Man* (Boston: Beacon Press, 1959).

4. Reference is made here most particularly to the writings of Wolfhart Pannenberg and Jürgen Moltmann. Specific titles can be found in the bibliography.

5. Wolfhart Pannenberg, *Theology and the Kingdom of God* (Philadelphia: Westminster Press, 1969), p. 56.

6. "The perverse (in the literal sense of the word) apperception of the divine reality in religious experience is only one more form assumed by the perversion of sin's relation to the future. The perversion, of course, is the conventional perspective of experience in which the future is understood as a prolongation of what is already existing, rather than

being understood as the creative origin of reality. This perverse attitude occurs because the divine love creates autonomous forms of existence. These forms of existence in turn strive to prolong their existence. Present actualities are marked by an arrogance which blinds them to the preliminary character of their form of being. . . . But only in man does this enmity against the future become sin. When man asserts himself against the future, he misses his authentic existence, betrays his destiny to exist in full openness toward what is to be, and abdicates his participation in God's creative love." *Ibid.*, pp. 68, 69.

7. For a helpful discussion of the distinction between security and trust and the human tendency to develop security relationships that can be controlled, see Wolfhart Pannenberg, *What Is Man,* trans. Duane A. Priebe (Philadelphia: Fortress Press, 1970), chapter 3, "Security Instead of Trust?"

8. *Ibid.*, p. 38.

9. Edward Thurneyson, *A Theology of Pastoral Care* (Richmond: John Knox Press, 1962).

10. For a more extended and helpful critique of Thurneyson's methodology of pastoral proclamation see Edward E. Thornton, *Theology and Pastoral Counseling* (Englewood Cliffs, N.J.: Prentice-Hall, 1964), pp. 48-55. Another useful discussion of the use and abuse of biblical language in pastoral ministry may be found in Wayne Oates, *The Bible in Pastoral Care* (Philadelphia: Westminster Press, 1953).

11. Paul Johnson, *The Psychology of Pastoral Care* (Nashville: Abingdon, 1953) and *Person and Counselor* (Nashville: Abingdon, 1967) or Carrol A. Wise, *The Meaning of Pastoral Care* (New York: Harper, 1966) are good examples of pastoral care methodologies built primarily on the understanding of pastoral care as analogous to the Incarnation. Thomas Oden in his *Kerygma and Counseling* (Philadelphia: Westminster Press, 1966) elaborates on the notion of the implicit "gospel" in all therapeutic relationships.

12. The psychologist Paul Pruyser has recently pointed pastors in this direction with his suggestive and helpful little book, *The Minister as Diagnostician* (Philadelphia: Westminster Press, 1976). Pruyser outlines a set of variables to be assessed by the pastor in gaining an understanding of the quality of religious awareness of his people. Harville Hendrix in a recent keynote address to the American Association of Pastoral Counselors (*Pastoral Psychology,* Vol. 25, No. 3, pp. 157-72) likewise points in this direction: "I suggest . . . that behind all forms of alienation in personal existence is a fundamental alienation from the transcendent dimension of reality and that the fundamental human search behind all forms of search for health and wholeness is the search for transcendence. Transcendence is in this sense *the* fundamental human need" (p. 167).

CHAPTER II

1. Here the work of the sociologists of knowledge is particularly helpful in elucidating the way in which patterns of perceiving and ordering experience tend to become fixed and communicated to the

ordinary citizen as natural or ontological reality. Cf. Peter L. Berger and
Thomas Luckman, *The Social Construction of Reality* (Garden City, N.Y.:
Doubleday, 1966).

2. Alvin Toffler, *Future Shock* (New York: Random House, 1970).

3. Seward Hiltner, *Self Understanding* (New York: Scribner's, 1951),
chapter 3.

4. It would be both beyond our purpose and needless duplication to
spell out fully Erikson's epigenetic theory here. Readers interested in
pursuing this study are directed to Erikson's writings, most particularly
Childhood and Society, 2nd ed. (New York: W. W. Norton, 1963), and
Insight and Responsibility (W. W. Norton, 1964).

5. Thomas C. Oden, *The Structure of Awareness* (Nashville: Abingdon,
1969).

6. John B. Cobb, Jr., *The Structure of Christian Existence* (Philadelphia:
Westminster Press, 1967), chapter 9.

7. Berger and Luckman, *The Social Construction of Reality,* p. 27.

8. For an engaging and enjoyable exercise in mystical reflection
about the fecund cycle of nature's story, the reader is encouraged to try
Annie Dillard's warm account of her observation of nature in *Pilgrim at
Tinker Creek* (New York: Harper, 1974).

9. Eric Bermann, *Scapegoat* (Ann Arbor: University of Michigan
Press, 1973).

10. Erich Fromm, *Escape from Freedom* (New York: Holt, Rinehart
and Winston, 1941) and *The Sane Society* (Holt, Rinehart and Winston,
1955) and Karen Horney, *The Neurotic Personality of Our Time* (New
York: W. W. Norton, 1937). Fromm's more recent book, *To Have or to
Be?* (New York: Harper, 1976) carries forward essentially the same
themes as in his earlier works with a new emphasis on acquisitive vs.
being-oriented styles of personhood.

11. B. F. Skinner, *Beyond Freedom and Dignity* (New York: Knopf,
1971).

12. Cf. Richard Rabkin, *Inner and Outer Space* (New York: W. W.
Norton, 1970).

13. For a discussion of this ambiguity of freedom and destiny see
Paul Tillich, *Systematic Theology,* III (Chicago: University of Chicago
Press, 1963), 75.

14. Karl A. Menninger with Martin Mayman and Paul W. Pruyser,
The Vital Balance (New York: Viking Press, 1963).

15. *Ibid.,* p. 106.

16. George W. Baker and Dwight W. Chapman, eds., *Man and Society
in Disaster* (New York: Basic Books, 1962), p. 222.

17. "Because the future has not yet been decided upon, we attach to it
the basic anxiety of existence. Human beings will never overcome this
anxiety completely. Nor should we wish to be rid of this anxiety, for it is
related intimately to something else which we attach to the future—
hope for a more exuberant fulfillment of our existence. Anxiety and
hope transcend the anticipation of single imminent events. Yet when
events which we anticipated in anxiety and/or hope do occur, the
ambiguity of the impending future congeals into finite and definite fact.
In every event the infinite future separates itself from the finite events

which until then had been hidden in this future but are now released into existence. The future lets go of itself to bring into being our present. And every present is again confronted by a dark and mysterious future out of which certain relevant events will be released. Thus does the future determine the present. If we, in our anxiety and hope, contemplate this power of the future, we recognize both its breathtaking excitement and its invitation to trust. For those who accept the invitation, the world is widened with new possibilities for joy. In every present we confront the infinite future, and in welcoming the particular finite events which spring from that future, we anticipate the coming of God." Wolfhart Pannenberg, *Theology and the Kingdom of God* (Philadelphia: Westminster Press, 1969), p. 59.

CHAPTER III

1. Robert Jay Lifton, "On Death and Death Symbolism: The Hiroshima Disaster," *The American Scholar,* Spring 1965, p. 266.
2. See Kastenbaum's *New Thoughts on Old Age* (New York: Springer Publishing Company, 1964).
3. Robert Kastenbaum, ed., *Contributions to the Psychology of Aging* (New York: Springer Publishing Company, 1965), p. 7.
4. *Ibid.,* p. 17.
5. Elisabeth Kübler-Ross, *On Death and Dying* (New York: Macmillan, 1969).
6. Jürgen Moltmann, *The Crucified God* (New York: Harper, 1974), pp. 252-53.

CHAPTER IV

1. John Bowlby, *Attachment* (New York: Basic Books, 1969); *Separation: Anxiety and Anger* (Basic Books, 1973).
2. For an excellent discussion of intergenerational patterns of family relationships, norms, and intergenerational communication, see Ivan Boszormenyi-Nagi and Geraldine Spark, *Invisible Loyalties* (New York: Harper, 1973).
3. R. J. Neuhaus, "Profile of a Theologian" in Wolfhart Pannenberg, *Theology and the Kingdom of God* (Philadelphia: Westminster Press, 1969), p. 46.
4. My own understanding of the distinction between implicit and explicit faith and pastoral care as a developing hermeneutical dialogue has been helped greatly by a short article titled "Hermeneutics and Personhood" by Heinrich Ott in Stanley R. Hopper and David L. Miller, eds., *Interpretation: The Poetry of Meaning* (New York: Harcourt, Brace and World, 1967), chapter 2. Ott proposes that "the model and basic structure of every hermeneutical event is the dialogue" and spells out a suggestive phenomenology of dialogical encounter. The thrust of Ott's thesis is that the dialogue moves from what is implicit in the relationship between the two dialogical partners and their consideration of a given subject matter toward the implicit becoming more and more explicit and in the course of that process more open to creative change so that

finally something new results which nonetheless was already there when the dialogue began.

CHAPTER V

1. Paul Tillich, *Systematic Theology* (Chicago: The University of Chicago Press, 1951), I, 13.
2. *Ibid.*
3. We will not repeat here much of the information readily available in one or another of the texts that deal with bereavement phenomena. The seminal study of acute grief by the psychiatrist, Erich Lindemann, is probably most pertinent and comprehensive. Parts of that study are reprinted in Edgar Jackson, *Understanding Grief* (Nashville: Abingdon, 1957), pp. 146-47.
4. Beverley Bowie, *Know All Men by These Presents* (New York: Bookman Associates, 1958), pp. 22-23. Reprinted with the permission of Twayne Publishers, a division of G. K. Hall & Co., Boston.

CHAPTER VI

1. Emile Durkheim, *Suicide,* trans. John A. Spaulding and George Simpson (Glencoe: The Free Press, 1951).
2. *Ibid.,* p. 209.
3. *Ibid.,* p. 221.
4. *Ibid.,* p. 258.
5. Maurice L. Farber, *Theory of Suicide* (New York: Funk and Wagnalls, 1968).
6. *Ibid.,* p. 14.
7. *Ibid.,* p. 15.
8. *Ibid.,* p. 75.
9. Oden, *The Structure of Awareness* (Nashville: Abingdon, 1969), p. 243.
10. *Ibid.,* p. 246.
11. *Ibid.,* pp. 247-48.
12. Kierkegaard, *Fear and Trembling; and, The Sickness Unto Death,* trans. Walter Lowrie (Garden City, N.Y.: Doubleday Anchor Books, 1955). Originally published in two volumes by Princeton University Press in 1941, 1954.
13. *Ibid.,* p. 163.
14. Karl A. Menninger, *The Vital Balance* (New York: Viking Press, 1963).
15. Kierkegaard, *Fear and Trembling,* pp. 211-12.
16. Thomas W. Klink, *Depth Perspectives in Pastoral Work* (Englewood Cliffs, N.J.: Prentice-Hall, 1965), p. 108.
17. Langdon Gilkey, *Naming the Whirlwind: The Renewal of God-Language* (Indianapolis: Bobbs-Merrill, 1969), p. 425.

CHAPTER VII

1. See the bibliography for a list of Erikson's more important readings concerning identity theory.

2. Peter Marris, *Loss and Change* (New York: Random House, Pantheon Books, 1974), chapter 1.

3. *Ibid.,* p. 10.

4. Jürgen Moltmann, *The Passion for Life,* trans. M. Douglas Meeks (Philadelphia: Fortress Press, 1978), pp. 39-40.

5. Erik Erikson, *Insight and Responsibility* (New York: W. W. Norton, 1964), pp. 125-26.

6. Gerhart Piers and Milton B. Singer, *Shame and Guilt* (New York: W. W. Norton, 1971), p. 29.

7. Helen Merrell Lynd, *On Shame and the Search for Identity* (New York: Harcourt, Brace and World, 1958), pp. 204-10.

8. *Ibid.,* p. 208.

9. *Ibid.,* p. 185.

10. Don S. Browning, *The Moral Context of Pastoral Care* (Philadelphia: Westminster Press, 1976).

11. *Ibid.,* pp. 48-52.

CHAPTER VIII

1. Erik Erikson, *Toys and Reasons: Stages in the Ritualization of Experience* (New York: W. W. Norton, 1977), chapter 1.

2. Louis S. Feuer, *The Conflict of Generations* (New York: Basic Books, 1969), p. 25.

3. Kenneth Keniston, *Young Radicals: Notes on Committed Youth* (New York: Harcourt, Brace and World, 1968). *The Uncommitted: Alienated Youth in American Society* (Harcourt, Brace and World, 1965).

4. Erik Erikson, *Identity and the Life Cycle* (New York: International Universities Press, 1959), chapter 3.

5. Erik Erikson, *Life History and the Historical Moment* (New York: W. W. Norton, 1975), Part Three, I, "Reflections on the Revolt of Humanist You:h."

6. Alice E. Moriarty and Povl Toussieng, *Adolescent Coping* (New York: Grune and Stratton, 1976).

7. *Ibid.,* pp. 140-41.

8. *Ibid.* "Coping involves emphasis on internal balance and lacks the aspect of concession implied by the term 'adjustment.' Furthermore, coping implies realistic perception and awareness with a minimum of ideological interpretation and hence, distortion. Depending on the limitations inner realities place on persons, their coping efforts allow them to deal appropriately with reality without making concessions. This comes about because reality is no longer seen as an enemy, but as a given, a part of the total picture, the border pieces of the picture puzzle. Perceiving the overall picture depends more on realistic awareness than on intelligence."

9. *Ibid.,* p. 2.

10. *Ibid.,* p. 3.

11. *Ibid.,* p. 135.

12. *Ibid.,* pp. 141-42.

13. *Ibid.,* p. 142.

14. Jürgen Moltmann, *The Church in the Power of the Spirit* (New York: Harper, 1977), p. 278.

15. *Ibid.*, pp. 275-88.

16. Several of these strategies are taken from the now extensive literature on family therapy, some of which has been included in the bibliography.

17. Salvador Minuchin, *Families and Family Therapy* (Cambridge: Harvard University Press, 1974), pp. 58-59.

18. For a useful discussion of siding strategies (though it is somewhat limited in value for our purpose by its secular, power orientation), see Gerald Zuk, *Family Therapy: A Triadic Approach* (New York: Behavioral Publications, 1971).

19. For a more detailed discussion of the elements of pastoral counseling oriented toward the future than space permits here, see my article, "On the Renewal of Ministry as Pastoral Guidance," *The Candler Review*, January, 1974, pp. 9-17.

20. Moltmann, *The Church in the Power of the Spirit,* pp. 287-88.

CHAPTER IX

1. "What keeps love from altering? What makes it possible to bear it out 'even to the edge of doom'? Feelings, warmth, closeness? Hardly. We have to go back to Kierkegaard's understanding of love as a choice—a choice, moreover, that is permanent, for as de Rougemont observed, 'the irrevocable alone is serious.' Serious love . . . has to be based on an unalterable decision." William Kilpatrick, *Identity and Intimacy* (New York: Dell, 1975), p. 236.

2. Clifford J. Sager, *Marriage Contracts and Couple Therapy* (New York: Brunner/Mazel Publishers, 1976).

3. *Ibid.*, p. 4.

4. *Ibid.*, p. 28.

5. *Ibid.*, p. 56.

6. Lynda Lytle Holmstrom, *The Two-career Family* (Cambridge, Mass.: Schenkman Publishing Co., 1972).

7. Sager, *Marriage Contracts and Couple Therapy,* p. 127.

8. Larry Christenson, *The Christian Family* (Minneapolis: Bethany Fellowship, 1972).

9. Karl Barth, *On Marriage,* ed. Franklin Sherman (Philadelphia: Fortress Press, 1968).

10. Otto Piper, *The Biblical View of Sex and Marriage* (New York: Scribner's, 1960).

11. "We have no right to expect and require from every such human couple that under no circumstances can it be separated. The calling and gift of God on which this indissolubility depends flow from the mercy which he does not owe to anyone in this particular form. It may be that he has not called a specific couple to marriage, that the divine basis and constitution are lacking from the very outset, that in the judgment of God and according to his will and command, it has never become a married couple and lived as such. In this case the partnership is radically dissolvable because there has been no real union in the judgment of God." Barth, *On Marriage,* p. 35.

Bibliography

Social Scientific Theory
Pertinent to Understanding Crisis Experience

Baker, George W., and Chapman, Dwight W., eds. *Man and Society in Disaster.* New York: Basic Books, 1962.

Bellah, Robert. *The Broken Covenant.* New York: Seabury Press, 1975.

Berger, Peter L., and Luckman, Thomas. *The Social Construction of Reality.* Garden City, N.Y.: Doubleday, 1966.

Boulding, Kenneth E. *The Image.* Ann Arbor: University of Michigan Press, 1956.

Douglas, Ann. *The Feminization of American Culture.* New York: Knopf, 1977.

Erikson, Erik H. *Childhood and Society,* 2nd ed. New York: W. W. Norton, 1963.

———. *Insight and Responsibility.* New York: W. W. Norton, 1964.

Freud, Sigmund. *Collected Papers.* Authorized translation under the supervision of Joan Riviere. New York: Basic Books, 1960.

Horney, Karen. *Collected Works.* New York: W. W. Norton, 1963, 1937, 1939, 1942, 1945, 1950.

Luckman, Thomas. *The Invisible Religion: The Problem of Religion in Modern Society.* New York: Macmillan, 1967.

Mannheim, Karl. *Essays on the Sociology of Knowledge,* ed. Paul Kecskemeti. New York: Oxford University Press, 1952.

Menninger, Karl, with Mayman, Martin, and Pruyser, Paul W. *The Vital Balance.* New York: Viking Press, 1963.

Rabkin, Richard. *Inner and Outer Space.* New York: W. W. Norton, 1970.

Skinner, B. F. *About Behaviorism.* New York: Knopf, 1971.

———. *Beyond Freedom and Dignity.* New York: Knopf, 1971.

Toffler, Alvin. *Future Shock.* New York: Random House, 1970.

Pastoral Care Theory

Browning, Don S. *The Moral Context of Pastoral Care.* Philadelphia: Westminster Press, 1976.

Clinebell, Howard. *Basic Types of Pastoral Counseling.* Nashville: Abingdon, 1966.

———, ed. *Community Mental Health: The Role of Church and Temple.* Nashville: Abingdon, 1971.

Cobb, John B., Jr. *Theology and Pastoral Care.* Philadelphia: Fortress Press, 1977.

BIBLIOGRAPHY

Hiltner, Seward. *Preface to Pastoral Theology.* Nashville: Abingdon, 1958.
———. *Self Understanding.* New York: Scribner's, 1951.
Johnson, Paul E. *The Psychology of Pastoral Care.* Nashville: Abingdon, 1953.
———. *Person and Counselor.* Nashville: Abingdon, 1967.
Klink, Thomas W. *Depth Perspectives in Pastoral Work.* Englewood Cliffs, N.J.: Prentice-Hall, 1965.
Oates, Wayne E. *The Christian Pastor.* Philadelphia: Westminster Press, 1951.
———. *The Bible in Pastoral Care.* Philadelphia: Westminster Press, 1953.
Pattison, E. Mansell. *Pastor and Parish—a Systems Approach.* Philadelphia: Fortress Press, 1977.
Stone, Howard W. *Crisis Counseling.* Philadelphia: Fortress Press, 1976.
Switzer, David. *The Minister as Crisis Counselor.* Nashville: Abingdon, 1974.
Thornton, Edward E. *Theology and Pastoral Counseling.* Englewood Cliffs, N.J.: Prentice-Hall, 1964.
Thurneyson, Edward. *A Theology of Pastoral Care.* Atlanta: John Knox Press, 1962.
Wise, Carroll A. *The Meaning of Pastoral Care.* New York: Harper, 1965.

Theology and Crisis Experience
Bellah, Robert N. *Beyond Belief: Essays on Religion in a Post-traditional World.* New York: Harper, 1970.
Browning, Don S. *Atonement and Psychotherapy.* Philadelphia: Westminster Press, 1966.
Cobb, John B., Jr. *A Christian Natural Theology.* Philadelphia: Westminster Press, 1965.
———. *Christ in a Pluralistic Age.* Philadelphia: Westminster Press, 1975.
———. *God and the World.* Philadelphia: Westminster Press, 1969.
———. *The Structure of Christian Existence.* Philadelphia: Westminster Press, 1967.
Gilkey, Langdon. *Naming the Whirlwind: The Renewal of God Language.* Indianapolis: Bobbs-Merrill, 1969.
Hiltner, Seward. *Theological Dynamics.* Nashville: Abingdon, 1972.
———, ed. *Toward a Theology of Aging.* New York: Human Science Press, 1975.
Hopper, Stanley R. and Miller, David L., eds. *Interpretation: The Poetry of Meaning.* New York: Harcourt, Brace and World, 1967.
McClendon, James Wm., Jr. *Biography as Theology: How Life Stories Can Remake Today's Theology.* Nashville: Abingdon, 1974.
Michalson, Carl. *Faith for Personal Crises.* Nashville: Abingdon, 1958.
Moltmann, Jürgen. *The Church in the Power of the Spirit.* New York: Harper, 1977.
———. *The Crucified God.* New York: Harper, 1974.
———. *The Experiment Hope.* Philadelphia: Fortress Press, 1975.
———. *Man: Christian Anthropology in the Conflicts of the Present.* Philadelphia: Fortress Press, 1974.

————. *The Passion for Life—a Messianic Lifestyle*. Philadelphia: Fortress Press, 1977.

————. *Theology of Hope*. New York: Harper, 1967.

Oden, Thomas C. *Kerygma and Counseling*. Philadelphia: Westminster Press, 1966.

————. *The Structure of Awareness*. Nashville: Abingdon, 1969.

Pannenberg, Wolfhart. *Basic Questions in Theology*, Vol. I, trans. George H. Kehm. Philadelphia: Fortress Press, 1970.

————. *Basic Questions in Theology*, Vol. II, trans. George H. Kehm. Philadelphia: Fortress Press, 1971.

————. *Faith and Reality*. Philadelphia: Westminster Press, 1977.

————. *The Idea of God and Human Freedom*. Philadelphia: Westminster Press, 1973.

————. *Jesus, God and Man*, trans. Lewin L. Wilkins and Duane A. Priebe. Philadelphia: Westminster Press, 1968.

————, ed. *Revelation as History*, trans. from German by David Branskon. New York: Macmillan, 1968.

————. *Theology and the Kingdom of God*. Philadelphia: Westminster Press, 1969.

————. *What Is Man? Contemporary Anthropology in Theological Perspective*, trans. Duane A. Priebe. Philadelphia: Fortress Press, 1970.

Pruyser, Paul. *The Minister as Diagnostician*. Philadelphia: Westminster Press, 1976.

Soulle, Dorothee. *Suffering*. Philadelphia: Fortress Press, 1975.

Tillich, Paul. *The Courage to Be*. New Haven: Yale University Press, 1952.

————. *Systematic Theology*, Vol. I. Chicago: University of Chicago Press, 1951.

————. *Systematic Theology*, Vol. II. Chicago: University of Chicago Press, 1957.

————. *Systematic Theology*, Vol. III. Chicago: University of Chicago Press, 1963.

Aging and Death

Aries, Philippe. *Western Attitudes Toward Death from the Middle Ages to the Present*. Baltimore: Johns Hopkins University Press, 1974.

Bane, J. Donald; Kutcher, Austin H.; Neale, Robert E.; and Reeves, Robert B., Jr., eds. *Death and Ministry: Pastoral Care of the Dying and the Bereaved*. New York: Seabury, 1975.

Becker, Ernest. *The Denial of Death*. New York: The Free Press, 1973.

Cumming, Elaine, and Henry, William. *Growing Old: The Process of Disengagement*. New York: Basic Books, 1961.

Fulton, Robert L., ed. *Death and Identity*. New York: John Wiley, 1965.

Glaser, Barney G., and Strauss, Anselm L. *Awareness of Dying*. Chicago: Aldine Publishing Co., 1965.

————. *Time for Dying*. Chicago: Aldine Publishing Co., 1968.

Kastenbaum, Robert, ed. *Contributions to the Psychology of Aging*. New York: Springer Publisher Co., 1965.

————. *New Thoughts on Old Age*. New York: Springer Publishing Co., 1964.

BIBLIOGRAPHY

————, and Aisenberg, Ruth. *The Psychology of Death*. New York: Springer Publishing Co., 1972.

Kübler-Ross, Elisabeth, ed. *Death: The Final Stage of Growth*. Englewood Cliffs, N.J.: Prentice-Hall, 1975.

————. *On Death and Dying*. New York: Macmillan, 1969.

Lifton, Robert Jay. "On Death and Death Symbolism: The Hiroshima Disaster," *The American Scholar*. Spring, 1965.

Mills, Liston O., ed. *Perspectives on Death*. Nashville: Abingdon, 1969.

Ruitenbeek, H. M., ed. *The Interpretation of Death*. New York: Jason Aronson, 1973.

Soulen, Richard N., ed. *Care for the Dying*. Atlanta: John Knox Press, 1975.

Spiegel, Yorick. *The Grief Process: Analysis and Counseling*. Nashville: Abingdon, 1978.

Stannard, David, ed. *Death in America*. Philadelphia: University of Pennsylvania Press, 1975.

Weisman, Avery D. *On Dying and Denying*. New York: Behavioral Publications, 1972.

Wertenbaker, Laal Tucker. *Death of a Man*. Boston: Beacon Press, 1959.

Wyschogrod, Edith, ed. *The Phenomenon of Death: Faces of Mortality*. New York: Harper, 1973.

Bereavement, Separation, and Loss

Bermann, Eric. *Scapegoat: The Impact of Death-fear on an American Family*. Ann Arbor: The University of Michigan Press, 1973.

Bowie, Beverley. *Know All Men by These Presents*. New York: Bookman Associates, 1958.

Bowlby, John. *Attachment*. New York: Basic Books, 1969.

————. *Separation: Anxiety and Anger*. New York: Basic Books, 1973.

Caine, Lynn. *Widow*. New York: Morrow, 1974.

Glick, Ira O.; Weiss, Robert S.; and Parkes, C. Murray. *The First Year of Bereavement*. New York: Wiley, 1974.

Jackson, Edgar. *Understanding Grief*. Nashville: Abingdon, 1957.

————. *When Someone Dies*. Philadelphia: Fortress Press, 1971.

Marris, Peter. *Loss and Change*. New York: Random House, Pantheon Books, 1974.

Parkes, Colin M. *Bereavement: Studies of Grief in Adult Life*. New York: International Universities Press, 1972.

Phipps, Joyce. *Death's Single Privacy*. New York: Seabury Press, 1974.

Pincus, Lily. *Death and the Family: The Importance of Mourning*. New York: Random House, 1974.

Sudnow, David. *Passing On: The Social Organization of Dying*. Englewood Cliffs, N.J.: Prentice-Hall, 1967.

Switzer, David K. *The Dynamics of Grief. Nashville: Abingdon,* 1970.

Suicide and Despair

Alvarez, Alfred. *The Savage God: A Study of Suicide*. London: Weidenfeld and Nicolson, 1971.

Bakan, David. *Disease, Pain and Sacrifice: Toward a Psychology of Suffering*. Chicago: University of Chicago Press, 1968.

CRISIS EXPERIENCE IN MODERN LIFE

Durkheim, Emile. *Suicide,* trans. John A. Spaulding and George Simpson. Glencoe: The Free Press, 1951.

Farber, Maurice L. *Theory of Suicide.* New York: Funk and Wagnalls, 1968.

Farberow, Norman L., and Schneidman, Edwin S., eds. *The Cry for Help.* New York: McGraw-Hill, 1961.

Kierkegaard, Søren. *Fear and Trembling; and The Sickness Unto Death,* trans. Walter Lowrie. Garden City, N.Y.: Doubleday Anchor Books, 1955.

Pretzel, Paul. *Understanding and Counseling the Suicidal Person.* Nashville: Abingdon, 1972.

Reynolds, David K, and Farberow, Norman L. *Suicide: Inside and Out.* Berkeley: University of California Press, 1976.

Shneidman, Edwin S., ed. *Essays in Self Destruction.* New York: Science House, 1967.

———, ed. *On the Nature of Suicide.* San Francisco: Jossey-Bass, 1969.

———; Farberow, Norman L.; and Litman, Robert. *The Psychology of Suicide.* New York: Science House, 1970.

Stein, E. V. *Guilt: Theory and Therapy.* Philadelphia: Westminster Press, 1968.

Identity Crisis and Change

Bednarik, Karl. *The Male in Crisis.* New York: Knopf, 1970.

Bugental, James F. *The Search for Existential Identity.* San Francisco: Jossey-Bass, 1976.

Curle, Adam. *Mystics and Militants: A Study of Awareness, Identity and Social Action.* London: Tairstock Publications, 1972.

Erickson, Erik H., ed. *Adulthood.* New York: W. W. Norton, 1978.

———. *Dimensions of a New Identity.* New York: W. W. Norton, 1974.

———. *Identity and the Life Cycle.* New York: International Universities Press, 1959.

———. *Identity: Youth and Crisis.* New York: W. W. Norton, 1968.

———. *Insight and Responsibility.* New York: W. W. Norton, 1964.

———. *Life History and the Historical Moment.* New York: W. W. Norton, 1975.

———. *Toys and Reasons: Stages in the Ritualization of Experience.* New York: W. W. Norton, 1977.

———. *Young Man Luther.* New York: W. W. Norton, 1958.

Fromm, Erich. *Escape from Freedom.* New York: Holt, Rinehart and Winston, 1941.

———. *To Have or to Be?* New York: Harper, 1976.

———. *The Sane Society.* New York: Holt, Rinehart and Winston, 1955.

Fingarette, Herbert. *The Self in Transformation.* New York: Basic Books, 1963.

Kilpatrick, William. *Identity and Intimacy.* New York: Dell, 1975.

Levinson, Daniel J. *The Seasons of a Man's Life.* New York: Knopf, 1978.

Lynd, Helen Merrill. *Shame and the Search for Identity.* New York: Harcourt, Brace and World, 1958.

Piers, Gerhart, and Singer, Milton B. *Shame and Guilt.* New York: W. W. Norton, 1971.

BIBLIOGRAPHY

Slater, Philip. *The Pursuit of Loneliness.* Boston: Beacon Press, 1970.
Wheelis, Allen. *The Quest for Identity.* New York: W. W. Norton, 1958.

Generation Gap and Alienation

Ackerman, Nathan W., ed. *Family Process.* New York: Basic Books, 1970.
————. *The Psychodynamics of Family Life.* New York: Basic Books, 1958.
Bell, John E. *Family Therapy.* New York: Jason Aronson, 1975.
Boszormenyi-Nagy, Ivan, and Spark, Geraldine. *Invisible Loyalties.* New York: Harper, 1973.
Brody, Warren M. *Changing the Family.* New York: C. N. Potter, 1968.
Erickson, Gerald, and Hogan, Terrence P., eds. *Family Therapy: An Introduction to Theory and Technique.* Monterey, California: Brooks/Cole Publishing Co., 1972.
Feuer, Louis S. *The Conflict of Generations.* New York: Basic Books, 1969.
Foley, Vincent D. *An Introduction to Family Therapy.* New York: Grune and Stratton, 1974.
Haley, Jay. *Changing Families: A Family Therapy Reader.* New York: Grune and Stratton, 1971.
————. *Problem-solving Therapy: New Strategies for Effective Family Therapy.* San Francisco: Jossey-Bass, 1977.
Kantor, David, and Lehr, William. *Inside the Family.* San Francisco: Jossey-Bass, 1975.
Keniston, Kenneth. *The Uncommitted: Alienated Youth in American Society.* New York: Harcourt, Brace and World, 1965.
————. *Young Radicals: Notes on Committed Youth.* New York: Harcourt, Brace and World, 1968.
Minuchin, Salvador. *Families and Family Therapy.* Cambridge: Harvard University Press, 1974.
Mitscherlich, Alexander. *Society Without the Father.* New York: Jason Aronson, 1973.
Moriarty, Alice E., and Toussieng, Povl. *Adolescent Coping.* New York: Grune and Stratton, 1976.
Niemi, Richard G. *How Family Members Perceive Each Other: Political and Social Attitudes in Two Generations.* New Haven: Yale University Press, 1970.
Papajohn, John, and Spiegel, John. *Transactions in Families.* San Francisco: Jossey-Bass, 1975.
Satir, Virginia. *Conjoint Family Therapy,* rev. ed. Palo Alto: Science and Behavior Books, 1967.
Weinstein, Fred, and Platt, Gerald M. *The Wish to Be Free: Society, Psyche and Value Change.* Berkeley: The University of California Press, 1969.
Winter, William D., and Ferreira, Antonio J., eds. *Research in Family Interaction: Readings and Commentary.* Palo Alto: Science and Behavior Books, 1969.
Young, Leontine R. *The Fractured Family.* New York: McGraw-Hill, 1973.
Zuk, Gerald. *Family Therapy: A Triadic Approach.* New York: Behavioral Publications, 1971.

————, and Boszormenyi-Nagy, Ivan, eds. *Family Therapy and Disturbed Families*. Palo Alto: Science and Behavior Books, 1967.

Marriage Crisis and Broken Relationships

Barth, Karl. *On Marriage,* ed. Franklin Sherman. Philadelphia: Fortress Press, 1968.

Christenson, Larry. *The Christian Family*. Minneapolis: Bethany Fellowship, 1972.

Duberman, Lucille. *Marriage and Its Alternatives*. New York: Praeger, 1974.

————. *The Reconstituted Family, A Study of Remarried Couples and Their Children*. Chicago: Nelson-Hall Publishers, 1975.

Greene, Bernard L., ed. *The Psychotherapies of Marital Disharmony*. New York: The Free Press, 1965.

Holmstrom, Lynda Lytle. *The Two-Career Family*. Cambridge, Mass.: Schenkman Publishing Co., 1972.

Johnson, Dean. *Marriage Counseling Theory and Practice*. Englewood Cliffs, N.J.: Prentice-Hall, 1961.

Lederer, William, and Jackson, Don D. *The Mirages of Marriage*. New York: W. W. Norton, 1968.

Mace, David R., and Mace, Vera. *We Can Have Better Marriages If We Want Them*. Nashville: Abingdon, 1974.

Martin, Peter A. *A Marital Therapy Manual*. New York: Brunner/Mazel Publishers, 1976.

O'Niell, Nena, and O'Neill, George. *Open Marriage*. New York: Avon Books, 1972.

Piper, Otto. *The Biblical View of Sex and Marriage*. New York: Scribner's, 1960.

Sager, Clifford J. *Marriage Contracts and Couple Therapy*. New York: Brunner/Mazel Publishers, 1976.

Seidenberg, Robert. *Marriage Between Equals*. Garden City, N.Y.: Doubleday, 1973.

Sheehy, Gail. *Passages: Predictable Crises of Adult Life*. New York: E. P. Dutton, 1974.

Skynner, A. C. Robin. *Systems of Family and Marital Psychotherapy*. New York: Brunner/Mazel, 1976.

Stewart, Charles William. *The Minister as Marriage Counselor,* rev. ed. Nashville: Abingdon, 1970.

Woody, Robert Henley, and Woody, Jane Divita. *Sexual, Marital and Familial Relations. Therapeutic Interventions for Professional Helping*. Springfield, Ill.: Charles C. Thomas, 1973.

Wynn, John Charles, ed. *Sex, Family and Society in Theological Focus*. New York: Association Press, 1966.

Index